Salesforce®
Marketing Cloud

by Chester Bullock
and
Mark Pollard

D1127045

for
dummies®
A Wiley Brand

Salesforce® Marketing Cloud For Dummies®

Published by: **John Wiley & Sons, Inc.**, 111 River Street, Hoboken, NJ 07030-5774, www.wiley.com

Contents at a Glance

Table of Contents

Introduction

Ever since that first corporate website found its way onto the Internet, the marketing universe has been expanding and changing. One after another, things such as text-message marketing campaigns, social media marketing, and mobile apps have come on the scene. Suddenly, even email marketing — which was in its infancy only a generation ago — is now just the tip of the iceberg of what today's marketers need to know how to do.

Fortunately, sophisticated tools, such as Salesforce Marketing Cloud, have evolved at the same time to help you manage all these marketing channels. Marketing Cloud makes an online marketer into a superhero. But, of course, it has its own learning curve. That's where this book comes in: We want to show you around a product that we adore, help you get started, and sprinkle in a few insider tips that we've picked up over time.

About This Book

This book is born of love. We both had the pleasure to be actively involved in the early development of the software that is now known as Salesforce Marketing Cloud, and the experience led to career opportunities and new friendships. Rarely do you have the opportunity to work with such talented people, all of whom are dedicated to their clients' success.

Now we're thrilled to have the chance to share our knowledge — and dare we say wisdom — about Salesforce Marketing Cloud and online marketing in general. We've been accumulating experience for close to a decade. With the help of *Salesforce Marketing Cloud For Dummies*, we can transfer what you need to know so you can hit the ground running on your own Marketing Cloud adventure.

Like all the titles in the *Dummies* series, this book provides tools for people who are confident enough to say, "I don't know what I'm doing (yet)." We give you no-nonsense answers to how to think about your audiences and data, as well as practical step-by-step procedures to get your marketing messages out the door.

You can read this book from cover to cover, or jump directly to an individual chapter about the functionality you're currently working on. Marketing Cloud contains many apps, so keep this book nearby for a quick refresher when you need to get back into a part of the tool that you haven't used in a while.

Foolish Assumptions

You can tell from the title that we wrote this book for people who are new to using Salesforce Marketing Cloud, including Basic, Pro, Corporate, and Enterprise Editions. However, almost anyone interested in learning more about online marketing can find useful information within. Any time you write instructions, though, you have to make a few assumptions. In your case, we assume the following:

>> You're familiar with how to operate a computer, a keyboard, and a mouse.

>> You've used enough software to recognize conventions such as opening menus, clicking buttons, and pausing your mouse pointer on something to make a tooltip appear.

>> You know the definitions of words such as *email, URL,* and *social media.*

If any of these assumptions leave you scratching your head, we recommend visiting your local library, where a librarian can point you in the right direction.

Icons Used in This Book

You'll see the following icons as you read the chapters of this book. This section describes what they mean.

The Tip icon indicates a tidbit of information that may not be necessary to the procedure you're working on but may make things easier.

Remember icons refer to information that we talked about before but that's especially important to recall at this point in the chapter.

Technical Stuff gives you a peek at how the Marketing Cloud application works behind the scenes. You can skip over this information and still use the product just fine, but reading and understanding it will help you know what to expect from Marketing Cloud.

WARNING

The Warning icon means watch out! It tells you when doing something wrong could damage your data or put your sensitive information at risk.

Beyond the Book

Salesforce Marketing Cloud has a large online documentation site. You can click a link right inside Marketing Cloud to get to the documentation. (An Internet search will probably get you there as well.) You'll find a lot of the same information in the documentation that you see in this book, but there are definite benefits to reading the book. We have the freedom, for example, to point out things that don't work as you might expect them to and suggest shortcuts.

We've provided a few handy cheat sheets: a glossary of terms, a sample pre-sending checklist, and a diagram to help you when you're mapping out your customer journeys — it'll make more sense when you get there! To get to the cheat sheet, go to www.dummies.com, and then type *Salesforce Marketing Cloud For Dummies cheat sheet* in the Search box. This is also where you'll find any significant updates or changes that occur between editions of this book.

Where to Go from Here

Salesforce Marketing Cloud is more like a platform than an application. That is to say, Marketing Cloud has a few bits of its own functionality, but the real power of your account is in the apps you can open in the Marketing Cloud platform.

The first part of this book is about getting around the Marketing Cloud platform itself and using the tools available there. If this is the first time you've used Marketing Cloud, you'll definitely want to start here.

The second part of this book is about subscriber data: understanding what you already know about your customers, figuring out what you need to learn about your customers to execute the best campaigns, and setting up Marketing Cloud to hold and use that data. Don't miss this part if you're an admin or in charge of designing the over-arching journey your customers take while interacting with your brand. Having said that, we'll also say that anyone at any level of the organization can get a better foundation in where your data comes from and how you use it by reading the chapters in this part.

Most of the rest of the chapters dive deep in to the day-to-day operation of each of the apps. If you're just getting started using one of the apps, your next stop is the table of contents to find the chapter about the app you're learning about.

Whichever page you turn to next, we hope that it is the first page in an epic story of you and Salesforce Marketing Cloud. May your story find your customer delighted, your company thriving, and you enjoying accolades for your sophisticated and well-managed online marketing campaigns.

1

Getting Started

Take a walk through the history of online marketing to get to the technology we have today.

Understand how the power of data lets online marketers create specific messages tailored to each customer.

Envision how you can automate repetitive tasks to free yourself for creative problem solving.

Meet Salesforce Marketing Cloud: online marketing platform and home to at least a dozen useful apps.

Tour Marketing Cloud's administrative screens.

Chapter **1**

Introducing the One-to-One Customer Journey

E mail marketing has grown into a direct marketing powerhouse. Because you have access to so much data about the people you're sending emails to, you can create automation that tailors your messages to each customer's unique needs and circumstances. Email marketing not only delivers marketers unparalleled value but also ensures that customers actually want to read the messages they receive from you.

No other marketing channel is so customizable at such an affordable price. You can personalize the content of your email even more than the content in a direct mailer, plus your email doesn't require printing or postage, isn't subject to the mail delivery schedule, and doesn't use paper. At the same time, your email marketing campaigns can be as broad reaching as a television commercial because, after you've set up your marketing campaigns, each additional email might add only a fraction of a second to send.

Add to this the capability to get feedback on your campaigns through testing and then to use that feedback to optimize the campaigns going forward, and there is no question why email marketing continues to drive so much business.

Over time, Salesforce Marketing Cloud has added communication channels to supplement your email marketing campaigns. Now you can use Marketing Cloud as the central place to manage all the components of your online marketing campaigns, including web pages, text messages, and your Facebook page.

The Dawn of the Customer Journey

We're at a tipping point in digital marketing, where data, tools, and predictive analytics are coming together to drive a concept known as the *customer journey*. Before we can dive into the depths of modern-day customer journeys, however, we need to take you on a journey of our own. We're going to go back to where it began — email marketing — to understand email marketing as a channel and how we got from there to where we are today.

Early email marketing

The technology to send email messages emerged in the early 1970s, but only government and educational institutions really had access to it. In the mid-1980s, commercial networks began opening up the potential of this messaging channel to private citizens — mostly early adopters who loved technology for its own sake. Email as a common messaging medium, with practical applications for average citizens, didn't really take off until the 1990s.

At that time, major commercial networks, such as CompuServe and AOL, started connecting to the Internet and allowing messages to pass among competing systems. These messages were mostly text based and basic, as shown in Figure 1-1.

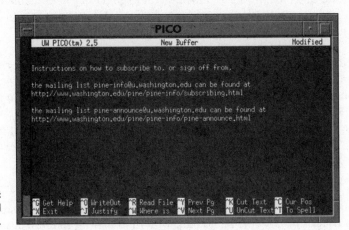

FIGURE 1-1:
Early email
was basic.

It's impossible to say who sent the first email that contained a marketing message or when they sent it, but it was probably pretty early. Even when the technology is unsophisticated and certainly not built with marketing purposes in mind, innovative marketers always find a way to use new tools to get an edge! Early email marketers borrowed strategies from direct mail to send electronic versions of what they would have sent to your mailbox.

Today, companies develop tools specifically for designing, automating, and delivering your email marketing, and marketing strategies and best practices exist that are specific to this channel. The tools that deliver these messages are available from companies called *email service providers* (ESPs). Salesforce Marketing Cloud is one such tool.

Email marketing is a highly effective method of delivering *one-to-one marketing messages* (messages to just one customer at a time, such as a thank-you message after an order) or *one-to-many marketing messages* (messages to an entire list of customers, such as a monthly newsletter). However, some marketers have misused email and given it a bad reputation. The term *spam* refers to unwanted marketing messages. Spam is the digital equivalent of all the junk mail you receive in your physical mailbox, but it causes even more irritation: In the early days of email, consumers oftentimes had to pay by the minute for their online time, and having to waste that time to read and delete unwanted messages made them angry.

The backlash grew further when mobile devices became popular for reading email. Again, consumers were paying a price for precious online time and sifting through unwanted messages felt expensive.

The great irony is that email marketing offers the power to provide highly customized messages that customers want to receive. The fact that email marketing developed a bad reputation for creating too many unwanted messages says more about the techniques used by marketers than the technology itself.

To combat this reputation — and to get more value out of email marketing efforts — online marketers began to develop best practices to ensure that subscribers could control their own email marketing experience and not develop so much resentment. For example, it's a best practice to offer a link in every email that a customer can click to unsubscribe from your email list.

As evidence of how important this particular best practice is, unsubscribe links are now required in marketing messages by law. Among other things, the Controlling the Assault of Non-Solicited Pornography and Marketing (CAN-SPAM) Act of 2003 requires that subscribers can opt-out of your email lists. Brands that ignore the wishes of their subscribers may find themselves in court.

From batch and blast to the highly personalized message

Email marketing's early bad reputation wasn't built by scammers — or at least not *only* by scammers. Since email marketing was a new medium, guidelines on how or what to send didn't exist, nor were there any experts or thought leaders to consult with. It was the Wild West, and online marketers just tried whatever idea occurred to them to see if it worked.

Because there were no email-marketing experts, companies commonly called on their direct-mail marketing experts to design their email-marketing campaigns. The result was a campaign methodology called *batch and blast.*

The concept is simple — you get as many email addresses as you can, however you can, and send them all the same message at the same time. The message you send is generic so that it will apply to everyone. If you put too much specialized information in a message, you risk damaging your relationship with message recipients who don't care about your specialized information.

Fortunately, for us modern-day online marketers, data has become more plentiful and tools can take advantage of that data to create personalized messages. For example, an early improvement was to add a subscriber's first name to a message. Figure 1-2 shows how this kind of personalization appears in an email in Salesforce Marketing Cloud.

Personalization is a relatively simple feature to implement in emails, but it's not remotely the limit of what you can do. By using the data you have about your subscribers, you can build different, personalized email content for each subscriber. This can include specialized content for the subscriber's particular interests, local weather conditions based on ZIP code, or a list of items the subscriber has ordered recently past, as shown in Figure 1-3.

Delivering this kind of highly customized email is no longer optional for most businesses: Customers have come to expect the brands that they engage with to understand and act on their preferences. Keep this in mind for your messaging efforts, so you can delight your customers.

From two channels to too many to count

For the longest time, online marketers had only two digital channels from which to choose: websites and email. The explosion of mobile devices and social media apps, however, has resulted in more channels than you can count — and the number keeps growing. Today's online marketer has many choices about how to communicate with subscribers.

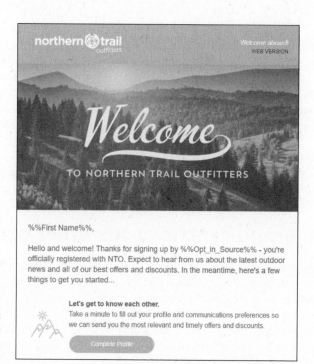

FIGURE 1-2:
An example of email personalization.

FIGURE 1-3:
A highly customized email example, based on an online order.

With each channel comes a different approach to marketing. After you decide that you're interested in promoting your brand through a particular channel, you may need to rethink your goal. For example, a normal goal is to lift sales, but on Instagram (a social networking app for sharing videos and photos), a better goal may be to reinforce your branding or to introduce a new product. Building awareness about your offering can be just as important as grabbing an immediate lift to sales.

Even with so many channels and all they can offer, email is still the core of your online marketing efforts. Email is the number-one channel for reaching your customers, educating them about your products, and developing a relationship with them.

From brand-centric to customer-centric

A major shift has been occurring in the marketing landscape over the last ten years. Although it has happened faster for some companies than others, everyone is waking up to this reality: Customers are now in control of your message.

You put a brand message out into the world, but you no longer have control over how it's consumed, what happens to it, and ultimately where it appears. The days of dictating one-way proclamations from on high are over.

Case studies abound of online marketing campaigns getting out of the brand's control:

>> Companies asking Twitter users to add a *hashtag* (a series of characters starting with # that makes it easier to search for related tweets) to the posts they share, only to find the hashtag appended to complaints about the brand

>> Companies encouraging customers to share photos of themselves using their products on Instagram, only to see countless photos of broken products

>> Customers creating parody Facebook pages dedicated to chronicling a company's poor customer service

This sea change can be terrifying to traditional marketers who learned to keep control of the message at all costs, but there is a bright side. The fact that customers want to tell you what they think means that they're engaged, and you can improve your offering to meet their changing demands. Embrace your customers, value their feedback, and demonstrate that you're listening, and they will reward you beyond your dreams.

The customer journey revolution

As online marketers understood the great level of control that customers have, they began to develop a new concept: the customer journey. A customer journey is a tool to craft a total customer experience with your brand.

For a long time, marketers treated the customer experience as a simple linear progression. Customers

>> Realize they need something

>> Possibly research what products are available to meet that need

>> Make a purchase, and the experience is over

Obviously, this was an oversimplification even then, but marketers truly did not care nearly as much about customers as they did about *prospective* customers.

In the digital age, though, marketers understand that a customer has an ongoing relationship with your brand that may not be linear. For example, some customer might need to engage with your customer support or warranty teams, and those interactions affect their perception of your brand.

Today's consumers have countless online platforms that they can use to influence others' opinion of your brand. You can't afford to neglect your customers, even after the purchase is complete. You need to craft customer journeys to keep your customers delighted throughout your entire relationship with them.

The Importance of the Customer Journey

Without customers, you have no business, but you can do better than just selling to faceless customers. The marketer's job is to design the interactions that keep customers delighted with your brand. As we discuss in this section, delighted customers lead to business success.

Marketers in today's businesses

Excepting executive administration, marketing is the one discipline that can touch every part of a business. Various kinds of marketers in your company might do any of the following things, and more:

>> Identify profitable markets to pursue with product offerings.

>> Interview prospects to understand what the market needs from products.

>> Set standards for the user experience of the product.

>> Craft the promotional messages that create the market's perception of the brand.

>> Create guidelines for how customer-facing teams, such as sales and customer support, talk about the product.

>> Identify opportunities to sell current clients additional products.

Being steeped in the market, the market's needs, and how the product fulfills those needs gives marketers a unique perspective on how to talk to prospects and customers. Marketers have a good understanding of how to target messages to particular populations to get them to take action.

In the modern business world, marketers have vast amounts of data available. Advances in technology have made it so that you can electronically store data about even very, very large groups of clients. You can pull data together from disparate sources, as well. You might already have a list of email addresses from your email newsletter sign-up sheet, for example, but you can cross-reference that list against the information in your point-of-sale (POS) system to bring other details about the customers together with those email addresses.

The downside of having so much information about customers is that customers now have an expectation that you will use that information to provide higher quality service. As a marketer, you need to be able to pivot quickly, and you might find yourself overwhelmed by all the options you have.

Decisive moments for customers

Marketing wisdom says that customers will make a purchase during specific points in time. The trick for you is to figure out those points in time and make sure that your brand is top-of-mind when they arrive.

Early in the prospects' research process is a great time to collect their contact information. For example, you can set up a form on your website where prospects enter their email address and other information to receive a white paper or discount offer. Sending that white paper or discount is the perfect opportunity to invite the prospect to begin receiving your free newsletter. Ongoing communications, such as newsletters or happy birthday messages, help you keep your brand fresh in the prospect's mind.

After the prospect makes a purchase and becomes a customer, your post-purchase offers can provide an opportunity to upsell. You can suggest purchasing an add-on product, a warranty, or an enhanced service plan. Even if you have nothing else to sell, you can get valuable information by soliciting feedback from your purchasers that you can use as customer testimonials or to improve your internal processes.

Grow the top line

Whereas the *bottom line* is the profit (or loss) that your business experiences after you account for all expenses, the *top line* is the total revenue. A business can become more profitable by growing the top line or by reducing the expenses that you have to subtract from it. Generally, marketers focus on the top line.

To grow the top line, you need customers making purchases. Getting new customers is expensive because you're starting from square one with people who might never have even heard of your brand. Before you can hope for new customers to make a purchase, you need to educate them about the following:

>> The problem your product solves

>> Why your product solves that problem better than the competition

>> What your company stands for

Your existing customers, however, already know most of these things, which is why it's much cheaper to retain existing customers than to get new ones.

One way that you can retain existing customers is to show that you know them and care about their preferences by tailoring products or offers to them. You need to leverage data to deliver tailored messages, and make the customer experience seamless across all channels and throughout the sales process.

Another way to retain existing customers is to get them talking. You want to create content that encourages them to engage with you. Engagement can take many forms, including things such as the following:

>> Clicking links in emails

>> Responding to surveys

>> Downloading information from your website

>> Making purchases

>> Reviewing products

>> Sharing your information on social networks

Data-based insights

The data you collect as you engage your customers and prospective customers can be as valuable as strictly making a sale. You can leverage the data that you collect from your digital campaigns to do the following:

>> **Understand your audience.** As you communicate different kinds of messages over different channels, you'll see what gets the best response from your audience and results in the best top-line growth.

>> **Create personas.** *Personas* are composite characters that marketers create based on information about the actual client base. A persona is a profile of a typical client, complete with demographic information, hobbies, and even a stock photo. Marketers share the personas with other teams in the company to help everyone empathize with the client base as they make decisions.

>> **Test content.** You may have heard of the *wisdom of the crowd,* or the idea that the aggregate opinion of a large group of people is better than the opinion of any individual member of the group. By engaging your customer base, you can compare the performance of, say, two photographs, and see which one drives more engagement. The wisdom-of-the-crowd idea says that you'll get a more accurate idea of which photo is better this way than by asking individuals in a focus group.

>> **Test product or service mixes and offerings.** Similarly, engaging a wide variety of customers and prospective customers opens up the opportunity to see what mix of products gets the best response, while at the same time making your customer base feel recognized.

Operating in real-time

Real-time operations means different things to different people. In general, we expect *real time* to mean actions that occur as soon as the required data becomes available. Even that simple definition can encompass a broad range of activities.

For example, on the simple end, using API code to trigger sending a welcoming email message as soon as a new subscriber joins your list is a kind of real-time activity. Alternately, an example of a complex real-time operation might be to use a feed of data from your online shopping cart to send a series of targeted emails to subscribers who put items in the cart but never finished the purchase.

To operate in true real-time mode, the data that triggers the activities is critical. You have to plan for it to be reliable, secure, and tightly integrated with your marketing system so that the activities begin immediately after you receive the data.

Depending on the nature of your real-time messaging, you may also need to consider business rules to control the totality of your messaging to each subscriber.

You don't want disparate automated processes sending any one subscriber emails that are incorrect, inconsistent, or just too numerous. The last thing you want is for a glitch to result in you being labeled as a spammer.

Mastering the metrics that matter

One of the big challenges you'll face in getting your online marketing efforts off the ground is understanding your goals and the metrics you can collect to see if you are meeting those goals.

The goals that you will pursue depend on your particular business, but they should be more thoughtful than just "get a lot of people to open the email." Good, business-oriented metrics include things such as the following:

>> Increasing sales (back to growing the top line)

>> Convincing people to download your white papers because this increases engagement more than simply opening an email

>> Getting people to share your content on social media because the customers who share amplify your brand message

>> Receiving survey responses with information that you can use to improve your offering

The journey is the reward

When we say that the journey is the reward, we mean this metaphorically because it is the process of engaging your customer base that creates brand advocates, improves your product offering, and grows your top line.

We also mean it literally, because all this work leads you to understand and define your customer journeys. The process of defining your journey ensures that you're delivering the right content to the right people at the right time.

Mapping out your customer journey can tie all of this together.

Defining the Customer Journey

The very process of understanding the importance of the customer journey and the customer journey itself gives you a mental picture of who your clients are that is useful in doing your job. However, to get the most technical use out of this understanding, you need to write it down.

After you've defined the parts of your customer journey, you're on your way to representing it in Salesforce Marketing Cloud and taking advantage of the powerful automation and personalization tools available there.

Start with the basics

If you're new to online marketing, this process might seem overwhelming. Just remember that you have to walk before you can run. It's all right to start with the simple components of your customer journey and add sophistication later.

A good first step is to establish a basic set of emails. Start sending them to your customer and prospective customer and see how people respond. Simple engagement metrics are enough to start fine-tuning the text and pictures in your emails and get a sense for how the process works.

The sticky note exercise

When you're ready to dive in to defining your journey, you can start with a sticky note exercise.

In this exercise, you brainstorm all the possible potential touch points between your company and your customers or prospective customers. As you think of touch points, you write each one on a sticky note and stick it to the wall or whiteboard.

You may think of even more touch points as you begin putting your sticky notes in order on the wall, and that's fine. An iterative process helps you flush out what your customer journey looks like.

Dividing your overarching customer journey into smaller journeys can provide bite-size pieces to ponder. This section discusses possible types of smaller journeys and the kinds of marketing campaigns you might run for customers currently on that part of the journey.

Onboarding/welcome campaigns

The onboarding campaign, also called a welcome campaign, is a series of communications that you have with new clients right after they make a purchase or sign up for a communication from you. The following example illustrates the steps that might be in an onboarding campaign:

- » Start with a simple welcome to your brand.

- » Lead in to how to get the most out of the product the customer just purchased.

- » Remind the customers why they purchased the product and make sure they are using it to its potential.

- » Suggest upgrades or complimentary products.

Engagement campaigns

After you have welcomed new clients and get past the honeymoon phase, you want to keep them engaged. Engaging with existing customers makes them feel cared about and helps keep them as customers in the future. The following example steps might appear in an engagement campaign:

- » Remind the customers of the breadth of your product offering.

- » Suggest other ways to use items that the customer purchased.

- » Encourage social engagement; for example, suggest that customers share photos of using your product on Instagram, if that channel is important to your brand.

- » Run a contest that offers prizes for engagement.

Reengagement campaigns

If you have been lax in engaging your existing customers, or if those customers have just fallen off the radar, a reengagement campaign brings them back into the fold. Example steps include the following:

- » Include a "Click here if you want to keep hearing from us" link. Even if the customer does not click, you will have gained important information about the customer's preferences.

- » Send a coupon code and track the usage of that code to see whether the customer engages again.

Ad hoc campaigns

Marketing does not own every single communication between your company and your customer. Different departments of your business communicate with your customer base for various reasons, such as customer support.

The campaigns for these kinds of journeys are not as clear to define or as easy to automate. Nevertheless, you should still make sure that all departments are using your brand appropriately in their communications and that they are honoring the customers' expectations in both service and communication.

Mapping it out

Your customer touch-point sticky notes and campaigns map out what your customer journeys look like. After you transfer this knowledge to Marketing Cloud, customers will be able to move through and between the customer journeys you've defined.

Fulfilling the Customer Journey with Marketing Cloud

In the spirit of beginning with the end in mind, we discussed how to understand and envision customer journeys extensively here, but we won't get to the technical instructions on how to create them until Chapters 16 and 17. (We do discuss Journey Builder in Chapter 10 and how it's different from Automation Studio, which is another tool you can use to create less sophisticated portions of your customer journeys.)

You can implement various bits and pieces of your campaigns individually with all the apps available in Marketing Cloud, as discussed in the remaining chapters in this book. However, to bring the components together into seamless customer journeys, you need to use the Journey Builder app.

In the meantime, you also need to prepare some other components, as described in the following sections.

Data

We dedicate all of Chapter 5 to identifying the data that you need for your journeys. Then we dedicate all of Chapter 6 to creating structures in Marketing Cloud to contain your data.

As you will understand when you get there, you have choices about how to structure the customer data you store. You can use the more simplistic list model, or you can implement relational database tables called *data extensions*. Journey Builder requires that you use the data extension model, so keep that in mind when you get to that point in your process.

Channels

Your customer journey can include messages through only email or through additional channels as well. You have to decide how you want to reach your customers.

Marketing Cloud supports messaging through the following channels:

>> Email (see Chapter 11)

>> SMS messages (see Chapter 12)

>> Social networks (see Chapter 13)

>> Advertisements (see Chapter 14)

>> Web pages (see Chapter 15)

Using the Marketing Cloud API, you could also use additional channels not listed here. The Marketing Cloud API is a set of tools that developers can use to access Marketing Cloud functionality using code. The API is outside the scope of this book.

Automation

Using Journey Builder to manage your customer journeys automates them. Automation is critical for setting a program that runs in perpetuity or for a short duration at a scheduled time.

Automation frees you to do other things and keeps data flowing, but it's a drastic mental shift for marketers accustomed to controlling the sending of messages by hand. Prepare yourself psychologically to automating your processes!

Preparing to use Marketing Cloud

You're just about ready to open Salesforce Marketing Cloud and begin using its powerful tools. In addition to this book, you should take advantage of the excellent training resources that Marketing Cloud offers as well as the online help system, which is available via a link in the Marketing Cloud interface.

Getting access to Marketing Cloud

All that's left is to get your user credentials, log in to Marketing Cloud, and get started. If you don't already have your user credentials, contact your Salesforce representative for help. When you're ready, log in and let's take a tour.

Chapter **2**

Navigating Salesforce Marketing Cloud

S alesforce Marketing Cloud starts with the dashboard. The dashboard contains its own overarching tools — such as a calendar of your planned marketing activities and a real-time snapshot of your campaign performance — and is also how to access your apps. Apps are the meat of Marketing Cloud's functionality. Marketing Cloud contains a variety of powerful apps you can use for your online marketing campaigns.

You can license all or just a few of the Marketing Cloud apps, depending on your online marketing tool needs. Regardless of whether you have licensed a particular app, though, you can see all Marketing Cloud apps in the dashboard. (If you try to open an app that you haven't licensed, a message appears to explain that the app is not available.) Salesforce wants you to know that the tool you need could be just a click away!

In this chapter, you take a whirlwind tour of all the dashboard tools and the apps. This journey sets the stage for later chapters, where you dig into the specifics of how to use the tools and apps.

Exploring Marketing Cloud

The Salesforce Marketing Cloud dashboard, shown in Figure 2-1, is the first thing you see when you log in to your Marketing Cloud account. From the dashboard you can access the following:

» The dashboard tools, which are available to every Marketing Cloud account. Links to the dashboard tools appear in the toolbar.

» The apps, which are available in your Marketing Cloud account if you licensed them. Links to the apps appear in the app switcher. The app switcher is visible when you first log in to your Marketing Cloud account. It disappears when you choose a tool or an app. You can get back to it at any time by hovering your mouse pointer over the Salesforce Marketing Cloud icon on the left side of the toolbar.

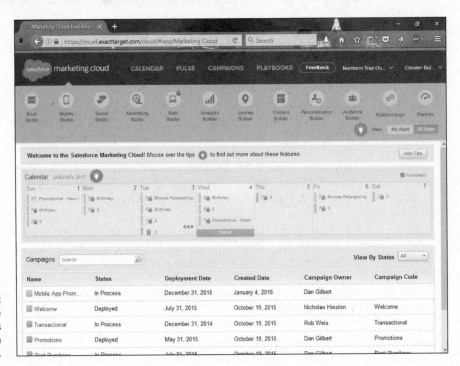

FIGURE 2-1:
On the dashboard, tools and apps are a click away.

Dashboard components

The Salesforce Marketing Cloud dashboard comprises the following two elements:

>> The toolbar, which remains at the top of the screen no matter where you go within Marketing Cloud

>> The canvas (the large area below the toolbar), which changes as you move through Marketing Cloud to show you the app or tool you select from the toolbar

Toolbar

The toolbar, shown in Figure 2-2, is a dark gray bar near the top of the screen.

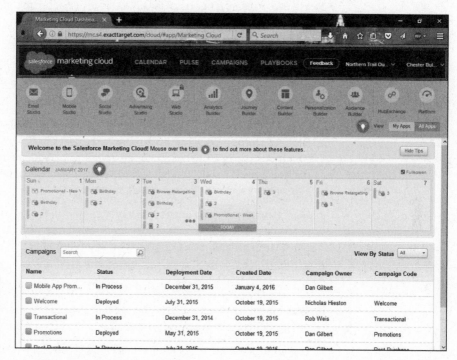

FIGURE 2-2:
The toolbar is the lighthouse you use to orient yourself in Marketing Cloud.

It contains the following elements:

>> **Salesforce Marketing Cloud logo:** Use the logo to return to the dashboard and also to access the app switcher. Click to return to the dashboard; pause your mouse pointer on this logo to see the app switcher.

TIP

The app switcher is too powerful and important to squeeze everything about it into a single bullet. See the "Accessing Your Apps" section, later in this chapter, for details about this essential tool.

>> **Dashboard tools:** The dashboard tools are Calendar, Pulse, Campaigns, and Playbooks. For a detailed description of the dashboard tools, see Chapter 4.

>> **Feedback button:** Use this button to display a form for sending feedback about Salesforce Marketing Cloud, such as ideas for new features, to the product team.

REMEMBER

This form is not the place to report support issues. Because the form goes to the product team instead of the support team, submitting a support request here just creates delays. Instead, use the Salesforce Help & Training link.

>> **Account menu:** After the Feedback button you see the account menu, which is the name of your account or business unit followed by a down arrow. Clicking this menu displays a list of all the business units to which you have access. See "Accessing business units," later in this chapter, for information about business units.

>> **User menu:** At the far right of the toolbar is the user menu, which is your username with a down arrow. Clicking your name shows the following options:

• **Cloud Preferences** takes you to a screen where you can edit information about your own user. See Chapter 3 for detailed information about user settings.

• **Hide Tips** turns off the light bulb icons that appear on the screen. Pause your mouse pointer on the icon to see a helpful tip about the feature that the icon is near. If you click Hide Tips, this menu option changes to Show Tips, which you can click to turn the tips back on.

• **Marketing Cloud Help** opens a new browser tab and takes you to the online help for Marketing Cloud. See the "Getting help with Marketing Cloud" section, later in this chapter, for more information.

• **Salesforce Help & Training** opens a new browser tab with the online help for all of Salesforce, not just Marketing Cloud.

• **Trust** opens a new tab with a web page that shows real-time data about any incidents that have caused the application to become unavailable.

• **Logout** logs you out of your Marketing Cloud account and returns you to the login screen.

Canvas

By default, the *canvas* contains a view of the activities you've scheduled for the week in the calendar tool. It also displays an overview of the status of your campaigns. Once you select a dashboard tool or app, the canvas changes to display what you chose.

Getting help with Marketing Cloud

Salesforce Marketing Cloud offers at least four different paths you can follow to get help:

>> **Check out the online help.** The online help is available from the user menu on the toolbar, as described in the previous "Toolbar" section.

>> **Read the contextual tips.** A light bulb icon appears on the screen when helpful information is available about a particular feature. Hover your mouse pointer over the icon to see the tip. You can turn these tips on and off from the user menu on the toolbar.

>> **Submit a case to support.** You can call or fill out an online form to contact Marketing Cloud support. You might have received special instructions about how to contact support, but general instructions are available in several places, such as on the Marketing Cloud website, in the Marketing Cloud online documentation, and from the online community.

>> **Visit the online community.** Marketing Cloud has a well-established user community with both in-person user groups and online forums. The user community is a great resource for learning insider tips, getting fresh ideas, and benchmarking your own online marketing successes. Like the support form, links to the online community are available in multiple places, such as on the Marketing Cloud website.

The user menu on the dashboard is a good place to start when you need help, as shown in Figure 2-3.

Accessing business units

Depending on how your company and your Salesforce Marketing Cloud account are set up, your account might have multiple business units. A *business unit* is like a sub-account of your main parent account. For example, you might have multiple business units when

>> Multiple departments in your company each use Marketing Cloud

>> Sister companies owned by the same parent company each use Marketing Cloud

>> Different locations of a retail corporation each use Marketing Cloud

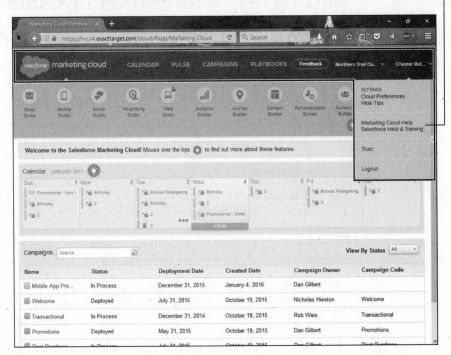

FIGURE 2-3:
Help options are
available from
the user menu.

When you log in to a particular business unit, you see only the content that is relevant for that business unit. By having a sub-account, users don't have to wade through the material for the entire account. Meanwhile, the parent account can still make shared content available to all business units and aggregate statistics.

The permissions assigned to your user account determine which business units you can access while you are logged in to Marketing Cloud. See Chapter 3 for more information about user permissions. If your user account has permission to access more than one business unit, you change business units using the account menu on the toolbar, as described in the "Toolbar" section, presented earlier in the chapter. Figure 2-4 shows a list of business units available from the account menu.

Use the following steps to change business units:

1. From the toolbar, hover your mouse pointer over your account name.

The account name is to the right of the Feedback button. A list of business units you can access appears.

2. Click the business unit you want to access.

The system logs you in and displays the dashboard for that business unit.

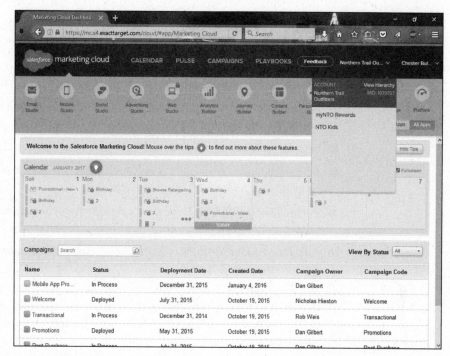

FIGURE 2-4:
All your business
units appear
in your
account menu.

Accessing Your Apps

The most important tool for navigating into, out of, and around apps hides itself as soon as you leave the dashboard.

While you're in the dashboard, the app switcher appears immediately below the toolbar, as shown in Figure 2-5. Once you leave the dashboard, you can find the app switcher by hovering your mouse pointer over the Salesforce Marketing Cloud logo. This light-gray bar provides links to all the apps that are enabled in your account.

Marketing Cloud puts apps into groups called *channels*. The channels are as follows:

>> **Email Studio:** Send email marketing messages to your subscribers. See Chapter 11 for full details.

>> **Mobile Studio:** Send SMS/text campaigns. See Chapter 12.

>> **Social Studio:** Use tools for social listening, engagement, and page management. See Chapter 13.

- >> **Advertising Studio:** Manage social advertising through Social.com. See Chapter 14.

- >> **Web Studio:** Leverage CloudPage tools to deliver personalized content on landing pages, Facebook tabs, mobile apps, and more. See Chapter 15.

- >> **Analytics Builder:** Keep track of your progress with reports and analytics. See Chapter 9.

- >> **Journey Builder:** Automate your online marketing efforts. See Chapter 10.

- >> **Content Builder:** Create and manage images, documents, and other kinds of content to be used in other apps. See Chapter 7.

- >> **Personalization Builder:** Serve personalized content to each subscriber. See Chapter 9.

- >> **Audience Builder:** Segment your subscribers based on behavior and other kinds of data. See Chapter 8.

- >> **HubExchange:** Acquire (sometimes free, sometimes at a cost) applications that plug into Salesforce Marketing Cloud so you can tie in to other systems and tools. We particularly like the Litmus, Persado, and Audience Point apps in HubExchange.

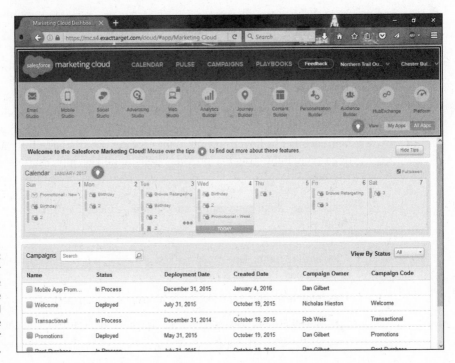

FIGURE 2-5: Hover your pointer over the Salesforce Marketing Cloud logo to expose the app switcher from any screen.

TIP

Is your app switcher crowded with apps you haven't licensed? You can remove them by using the My Apps/All Apps switch, shown in Figure 2-6.

Switch

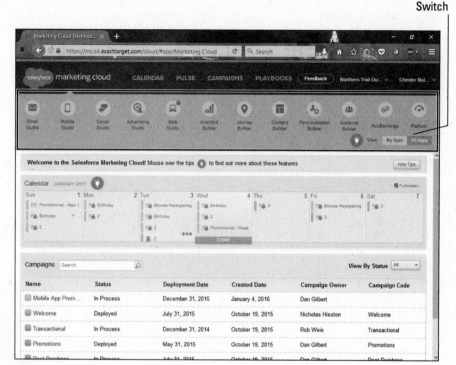

FIGURE 2-6:
Choose My Apps
to declutter your
app switcher.

Chapter **3**

Administering Marketing Cloud

I f you have the responsibility of acting as an administrator for your Salesforce Marketing Cloud account, the decisions you make ensure that your account is secure, your users can do their work, and your marketing campaigns get delivered without issue. No pressure!

Thankfully, many of the administrative tasks don't require a lot of ongoing time or effort to maintain. This chapter is not intended to be a comprehensive view of every administrative function, just the necessities to set up your account for success.

This chapter assumes that your Marketing Cloud user account has administrator permissions. If your user doesn't have administrator permissions, you won't be able to see many of the features described here.

Every person who uses your Marketing Cloud account should have his or her own user account. That means each person will have a username and password that he or she doesn't share with anyone.

Having a separate user account for each person makes your Marketing Cloud account more secure. You can track when and from where each user accesses Marketing Cloud. And if a person leaves the company, you can disable his user account without disrupting the other users' workflow.

Marketing Cloud uses permissions and roles to determine which features in Marketing Cloud a particular user can access. So having separate user accounts for each person has the added benefit of giving you granular control over who accesses what in Marketing Cloud.

You maintain Marketing Cloud user accounts on the Users page. You can get to this page, shown in Figure 3-1, from the Marketing Cloud toolbar or the Email app.

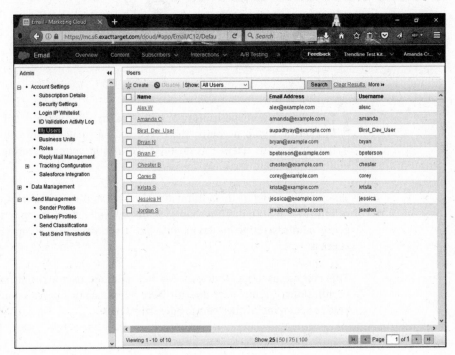

FIGURE 3-1:
The Users page is where you create, view, and edit user accounts.

From the Users page, you can perform the following actions:

>> See a list of user accounts and when each user last logged in.

>> Enable or disable each user's access.

>> Reset each user's password.

>> Assign roles and permissions to the user.

>> Indicate which business units the user has access to. For more information on business units, see Chapter 2.

>> Create, edit, and disable user accounts.

Accessing the Users page

To get to the Users page from the Marketing Cloud toolbar, follow these steps:

1. **Pause your mouse pointer on your username and select Administration from the drop-down menu that appears.**

   The administration page appears.

2. **Pause your mouse pointer on the Account menu and select Users from the drop-down menu that appears.**

To get to the Users page from the Email app (which is part of Email Studio), do the following:

1. **Select Admin from the Email toolbar.**

   The administration page appears.

2. **In the navigation tree on the left, click the + next to Account Settings and then click My Users.**

Creating a user account

Use the following steps to create a user account:

1. **From the Users screen, click the Create button.**

2. **Complete the following fields:**

   • **Name:** The user's name as you want it to appear in Marketing Cloud. This is not the same as the username to log in.

- **Reply Email Address:** In most cases, this is the user's email address. Marketing Cloud uses this email address when the user clicks Forgot Password on the login screen.

- **Notification Email Address:** The user's email address. Marketing Cloud uses this email address when a user chooses to have results of a process, such as a tracking report, emailed to him or her.

- **Username:** The username to log into Marketing Cloud. Usernames must be unique, so people often use the user's email address.

- **External Key:** A value the API uses to identify the user. If you leave this field blank, Marketing Cloud will assign a value when you save the user account.

- **Time Zone:** The user's time zone. Marketing Cloud uses this value to display dates and times.

  TIP

  Experience says you might want to set all your users to the same time zone, even if they're working from different time zones, to prevent confusion.

- **Culture Code:** Basically the user's language. Marketing Cloud uses this value to tweak the user interface, such as the display of dates and times.

- **API User check box:** Indicates that the user account is used by programming code. You can set up your account security to prevent API user passwords from expiring.

- **Temporary Password:** The password for the user's first login. The user must change this password and answer a security question when he or she logs in for the first time.

- **Verify Password:** The temporary password again. Marketing Cloud uses this field to make sure you typed the password you meant to type.

3. **Do one of the following:**

   - *If your contract is for an Enterprise 2.0 account, click Save and see the following Warning. Most contracts are for Enterprise 2.0 accounts.*

   - *If your contract is not for an Enterprise 2.0 account, select the check boxes to set the permissions for the user, and then click Save.*

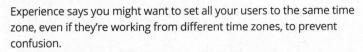
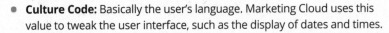
WARNING

If you're using an Enterprise 2.0 account, you must assign user roles to the user account and grant it access to business units after you create it. Otherwise, the user will be able to log in to the account but will not be able to access any of the apps or tools. See the upcoming "Providing Access for Users" section for detailed information about roles.

Giving an Enterprise 2.0 user access to business units

The following procedure is required only if you're using an Enterprise 2.0 Marketing Cloud account and have multiple business units. Use the following steps to give a user access to the business units:

1. **From the Users screen, select the check box next to the user's name and then click Manage Business Units.**

   The Manage Roles screen appears. The default business unit area to which the user is assigned appears shaded in the box at the top of the page. You can select a different business unit area if necessary.

2. **In the lower section of the page, select the check boxes next to the business units to which you want to give the user access.**

3. **Click Save.**

TIP

If you need to create or update many user accounts at once, you can save time by performing a bulk import of user account data. Select Import from the toolbar on the Users page and then follow the on-screen instructions for configuring and importing a .csv data file containing your user information.

Providing Access for Users

As Marketing Cloud evolved from a simple email application to a sophisticated online marketing platform, the scope of user permissions grew. For the purpose of this section, we mostly focus on configuring access to Email Studio and its related tools. However, you can configure your user accounts to control whether the user has access to almost every individual feature in the Marketing Cloud app.

REMEMBER

For a user in an Enterprise 2.0 account to access Email Studio, you must assign a role that has permission to do so. Users in non-Enterprise 2.0 accounts automatically have access to Email Studio.

The role of roles in Enterprise 2.0

Roles make it easier to deal with so many permissions. When you *create* a role, you define the permissions associated with that role. When you *assign* one or more roles to a user, you grant all the associated permissions at once.

Marketing Cloud delivers some predefined roles that you can customize or use as-is instead of creating your own. An example of a predefined role is shown in Figure 3-2.

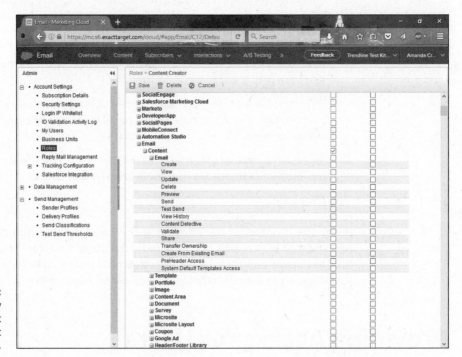

The predefined roles follow:

>> **Administrator:** Manages all functions in the account and has permission to create, edit, delete, or share anything in your account structure.

>> **Content Creator:** Sets up content but does not access subscriber information or tracking. This role can't send emails.

>> **Data Manager:** Maintains subscriber records and account data structure through lists and data extensions. Can also use the data import and export features.

>> **Analyst:** Views and interacts with tracking and results from email sends.

>> **Marketing Cloud Administrator:** Assigns Marketing Cloud roles to other users and manages the Mobile, Social, and Web Studios, Marketing Cloud Apps, and Marketing Cloud tools.

>> **Marketing Cloud Viewer:** Views activity and results in Marketing Cloud.

>> **Marketing Cloud Channel Manager:** Creates and executes campaigns and administers Social and Mobile Studios.

>> **Marketing Cloud Security Administrator:** Manages security settings and monitors user activity and alerts.

>> **Marketing Cloud Content Editor/Publisher:** Creates and delivers content through Mobile and Web Studios.

Assigning roles

You must assign roles to all Enterprise 2.0 Marketing Cloud user accounts. Simply follow these steps:

1. **From the Users screen, select the check box next to the user's name and click Manage Roles.**

   The Manage Roles screen appears.

2. **Select Edit Roles, and then select the check boxes next to the applicable Email Studio permissions and Marketing Cloud roles.**

   See the preceding section for a description of the predefined roles that you can select here. See the procedure in the upcoming "Creating or editing a role" section to create a new role that you can then select here.

3. **Click Save.**

Overriding role permissions

This section is relevant for Enterprise 2.0 Marketing Cloud accounts. Once you assign a role to a user, you can edit the permissions for that specific user without changing the entire role, as shown in Figure 3-3.

To override the role permissions for a single user, follow these steps:

1. **From the Users screen, select the check box next to the user's name and click the Manage Roles button in the toolbar.**

   The Manage Roles screen appears.

2. **Select Edit Permissions.**

   A list of all apps appears, with a + next to each one to expand the numerous permissions.

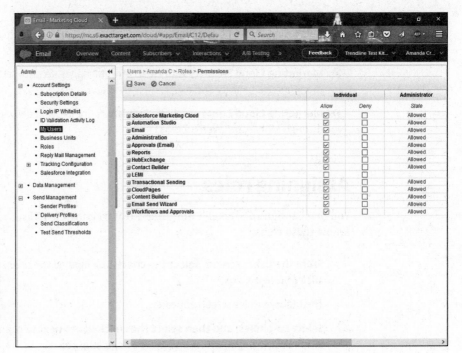

Defining
permissions
for an individual
user is the
utmost in access
customization.

3. **Click the + next to the app whose permissions you want to override, and then select the area of the app related to the permissions you want to override.**

   For example, to give a user access to view emails in the Email app, click + next to Email, then + next to Content, then + next to Email. Then select the Allow check box next to View.

4. **Click the Allow or Deny check box for each permission you want to override.**

   If you leave the check boxes blank, the permission from the role decides whether the user has access. Deny will trump any other choices made, in the case of overlaps.

5. **Click Save.**

TIP

Finding the permissions you want to override is a bit like peeling an onion, but it does provide you with an extraordinary level of access control. The downside of hundreds of permission choices is that this screen is overwhelming. Fortunately, you can select the check boxes at the section level to enable or disable all the permissions in a particular section.

Creating or editing a role

This section is relevant to Enterprise 2.0 Marketing Cloud accounts. If the predefined roles delivered with your Marketing Cloud account just aren't working for you, you can edit them or create your own using the following steps:

1. **From the administration screen, select Roles from the navigation tree on the left.**

   The Roles screen appears.

2. **To create a role, click Create and enter a name for the role. To edit a role, click the role you want to edit.**

   The role appears.

3. **Select the Allow or Deny check boxes next to each Marketing Cloud app you want to assign.**

   You can also drill down to specific areas within the apps by clicking the + next to the heading. Use the Expand All link to quickly see all possible permissions.

4. **Click Save.**

Securing Marketing Cloud

The Security Settings page, shown in Figure 3-4, is where you control login policies, password requirements, and permissions for exporting data from your account. The settings are set to a default value when you receive your account, but you can edit them to suit the needs of your business.

Marketing Cloud includes many security settings that we almost always leave set to the default. In the interest of space, the following procedure mentions the security settings that you're most likely to want to configure according to your specific needs. Use the following steps to get to your Security Settings page and specify the settings and policies that you need:

1. **On the toolbar, pause your mouse pointer on your username and select Administration from the drop-down menu that appears.**

   The Administration screen appears.

2. **Pause your mouse pointer on the Security menu and select Security Settings from the drop-down menu that appears.**

   The Security Settings page appears.

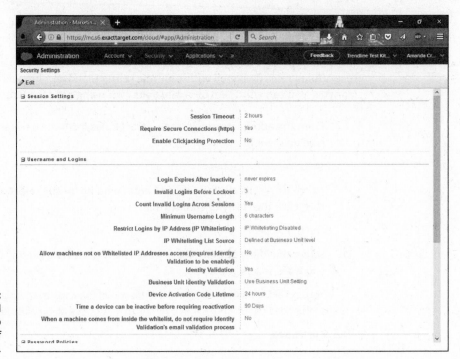

FIGURE 3-4:
Marketing Cloud options to keep bad guys out of your data.

3. **Click Edit and complete this field in the Session Settings section:**

   - **Session Timeout:** Determines how long a user can be inactive before being logged out. You can choose 20 minutes, 1, 2, 4, or 8 hours from the drop-down menu.

4. **Complete the following fields in the Username and Logins section:**

   - **Login Expires After Inactivity:** Sets how long a user can go without logging in before his or her password expires. Options include 30, 60, or 90 days, one year, or never expire.

   - **Invalid Logins Before Lockout:** Determines how many failed login attempts before locking the user's account. You can choose 3, 5, or 10.

   - **Minimum Username Length:** Specifies the minimum number of characters that can appear in a username. Options are 4, 6, 8, or 10 characters.

   - **Restrict Logins by IP Address (IP Whitelisting):** Decides whether to require users to log in from an approved IP address.

     This restriction is disabled by default, but you can use the drop-down to choose to record logins made by non-whitelisted IP addresses or deny login access to non-whitelisted IP addresses.

If you choose to enable this restriction, you must provide the range of whitelisted IP addresses on the Login IP Whitelist page, which is available under the Account Settings menu.

This setting is highly secure but also highly restrictive and may require ongoing maintenance to keep your whitelist up-to-date. If you enable this restriction, you don't have to require identity validation codes.

- **Device Activation Code Lifetime:** Sets how long an identity validation code is good after being sent by the system.

5. **Complete the information in the Password Policies section:**

- **Minimum Password Length:** Requires a certain number of characters in a password. Options are 6, 8, 10, or 15 characters.

- **Password Complexity:** Defines a combination of alpha, numeric, and special characters requirement for passwords. Select how many of each type of characters you want to require.

- **Enforce Password History:** Sets how far back in the list of previous passwords the user has to go before reusing an old password. You can select a number from 1 to 15.

- **User Passwords Expire In:** Determines the length of time that a user password is valid before requiring a change. Options are 30, 60, or 90 days, one year, or never expires.

- **Exclude API Users from Password Expiration:** Allows the password on a designated API user account to never expire, even if your other passwords do. Unless you have a very strict security policy, you should leave this option set to Yes to avoid headaches in the future.

- **Send Password Change Confirmation Email:** Indicates whether to send an email notification to a user after a password change. Sending the confirmation email is a good idea because it can alert users of their account being compromised before they otherwise would have noticed.

6. **Complete the information in the Single Sign-On Settings section.**

These settings set up your account so that users can log in with credentials from another system. This requires additional configuration in Marketing Cloud as well as with the other system that provides the authentication service. Single sign-on is outside the scope of this book. Contact Salesforce Marketing Cloud support or see the Marketing Cloud online help for more information.

7. **Complete the information in the Data Export Settings section.**

This section determines whether the email address that receives data exports must come from an approved list. If you choose to enable this restriction, you must provide the list of whitelisted email addresses on the Export Email Whitelist page, shown in Figure 3-5.

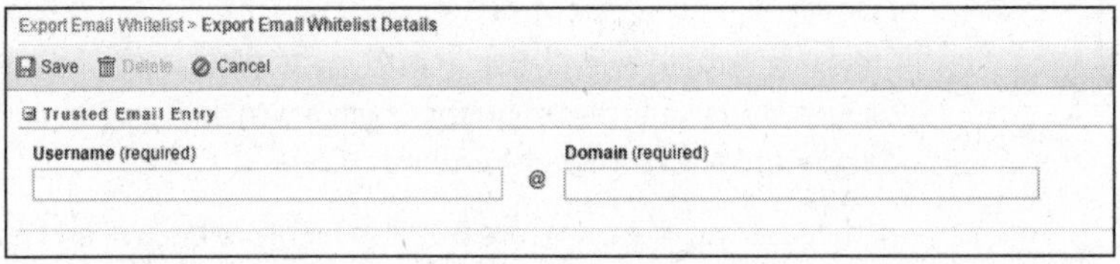

FIGURE 3-5:
The Export Email
Whitelist page is
available from
the Account
Settings menu.

Export Email Whitelist > **Export Email Whitelist Details**

💾 Save   🗑 Delete   ⊘ Cancel

📧 **Trusted Email Entry**

Username (required)   **Domain** (required)

[_____] @ [_____]

Sender and Delivery Profiles and Send Classifications

Before you ever write your first bit of email content, your account configurations are already contributing to the success of your email campaigns. Your sender and delivery profiles and your send classifications are simple, but they play an important role in helping your emails make it to your subscribers' inboxes and convincing your subscribers to open them.

Following is a brief definition of these features:

» **Sender profile:** Where you set up the From name and email address that appears in your subscriber's inbox.

Using a recognizable From name is one of the most important factors in establishing brand awareness and trust with your audience. Studies have found that the From name is as important as — or even more important than — the subject line in determining whether a subscriber opens an email.

» **Delivery profile:** Where you indicate the IP address from which the email is sent, as well as the header and footer.

The header that we're talking about here is the text at the very beginning that includes code to generate a link to the web page version of the email. This is not the header graphic or other content you design to appear at the beginning of a particular email.

The footer is the text at the very end of the email. It includes, among other things, the legally required elements of your email, such as a physical mailing address and an unsubscribe link.

» **Send classification:** Where you categorize the email content as Commercial or Transactional. Commercial messages are more tightly regulated under the CAN-SPAM (Controlling the Assault of Non-Solicited Pornography and Marketing) act.

You can use a send classification to set the priority level of the email. The platform uses the priority to determine which sends to process first when there is a lot of sending activity.

The send classification is also where you specify the sender and delivery profiles. When it comes time to send the email, the send classification is the only thing you need to choose because the correct sender and delivery profiles are also included.

By setting up these three tools before you send emails, you save time and reduce the chance for human error. You're not limited to just one of each, either: You can create as many sender and delivery profiles and send classifications as you need to achieve your email goals.

Creating a sender profile

Use the following steps to create a sender profile:

1. **From the toolbar in the Email Studio app, select Admin.**

   The Admin screen appears, including a navigation tree on the left side of the screen.

2. **From the left navigation menu, click the + next to Send Management to expand the menu. Click Sender Profiles and then click Create from the toolbar.**

   A new sender profile appears.

3. **Enter the name for the profile.**

4. **In the Sender Information section, choose the option to Use Specified Information and enter your From name and From email address.**

WARNING

   Make sure that the domain of your From email address matches a domain that is set up with authentication using SPF (Sender Policy Framework) or domain keys, or both. Usually this is the same domain that has been configured in your account for sending. Using a different, non-authenticated domain can seriously harm your message's chance of being delivered.

5. **If applicable, use the options under Custom Reply Mail Management to indicate how to process any replies you receive to your messages.**

6. **Click Save.**

TIP

You can use substitution strings in the From name and From email fields to cause a different value to appear depending on which subscriber the email is addressed to. For example, if your subscribers have a personal relationship with your agents, you could use substitution strings to populate the From name and email address with the contact information of the subscriber's agent.

To do this, you must create a subscriber attribute or a data extension field with the agent's name and email address and reference that attribute or field with a substitution string. For example, if the subscriber attribute or data extension field were called *agentname* you would enter *%%agentname%%* in the From name field. See Chapter 6 for in-depth information about subscriber attributes and data extensions.

Creating a delivery profile

Usually the default delivery profile created for your account is the only one you need. Unless you have a specific reason to create an additional delivery profile, you can skip this procedure and simply specify the default delivery profile when you create your send classification.

If you decide to create a delivery profile, follow these steps:

1. **From the toolbar in the Email Studio app, select Admin.**

   The Admin screen appears, including a navigation tree on the left side of the screen.

2. **From the left navigation menu, click the + next to Send Management to expand the menu. Click Delivery Profiles and then click Create from the toolbar.**

   A new delivery profile appears.

3. **Enter the name for the profile.**

4. **If applicable, in the Delivery Information section, select an IP address from the Private drop-down menu.**

5. **Select a header and a footer to use with this delivery profile.**

6. **Click Save.**

Creating a send classification

Use the following steps to create a send classification:

1. **From the toolbar in the Email Studio app, select Admin.**

   The Admin screen appears, including a navigation tree on the left side of the screen.

2. **From the left navigation menu, click the + next to Send Management to expand the menu. Click Send Classification and then click Create from the toolbar.**

   A new send classification appears.

3. **Enter the name for the profile.**

4. **In the About CAN-SPAM Classification section, choose either Commercial or Transactional from the drop-down menu.**

5. **If you choose Transactional, decide whether to select the Honor Source and Publication List Level Opt Outs check box.**

   Selecting this check box prevents messages with this send classification from sending to subscribers with an Unsubscribed status.

WARNING

   If you select a Transactional send classification for your email send, Marketing Cloud doesn't check for the email elements that the CAN-SPAM act requires in marketing emails. Additionally, if you do not select the Honor Source and Publication List Level Opt Outs check box, people who previously unsubscribed will receive the email message.

6. **In the Sender Information section, choose the sender profile and delivery profile you want to use for this classification of send.**

7. **In the Send Priority section, choose the priority of the message.**

   Usually you leave this field set to Normal. Higher priority sends may cost more to send.

8. **Click Save.**

For a truly transactional message, such an email receipt from an online purchase, these behaviors are exactly what you want. However, there are legal ramifications for these behaviors if the message is truly commercial in nature.

Please proceed with caution! If you're not sure whether your message meets the legal definition of "transactional" or if you're not fully aware of the policies around CAN–SPAM compliance, please discuss this with your legal counsel before proceeding.

IP Warm

When you start a new Marketing Cloud account, you have a new, unused IP address for sending messages. You might think that a fresh, new IP address would give you a clean slate with Internet Service Providers (ISPs). But ISPs are almost as suspicious of an IP address with no history as they are of one with a bad history.

It is vitally important to establish a good reputation with ISPs as you begin to send from your account. How do you establish your good reputation? You do it over a period of methodically controlled sending, which is known as an *IP warm*.

Establishing your reputation

ISPs use a variety of techniques, including evaluating the IP address from which the email message was sent, to decide which emails are trustworthy enough to deliver to their users. Since the IP addresses that spammers use are quickly black-listed, spammers must frequently change IP addresses. This puts ISPs in the mindset that an IP must prove itself before it can be trusted.

If you establish a good sending reputation with ISPs, your messages will be delivered more promptly and will more often show up in your subscriber's inboxes rather than in their junk folders.

Although the specifics of how you implement your IP warm may vary depending on the size and activity of your subscriber database, the overall process is the same: You build your reputation with ISPs by sending email messages on a slow, consistent basis. By sending only a few emails at a time, you can identify and correct any deliverability issues that arise before they occur on a larger scale and harm your reputation.

Warming your IP

Warming an IP address usually takes at least 30 days. It might take slightly more or less, depending on how many problems you run in to. You address deliverability issues as you encounter them, so the more issues you have, the longer it takes to reach optimal deliverability levels.

If you're migrating to Marketing Cloud from another provider and can access subscriber engagement information, you can start your IP warm sending to your most active subscribers first. Choosing subscribers who are already highly engaged increases the chances that you'll get a lot of activity during your early sends on the new IP address. A high level of engagement from your email message recipients is one of the factors an ISP looks at to determine your reputation.

Most ISPs set a limit on how many email messages they accept from a new IP address. In general, the daily volume limits during the first week range between 5,000 messages for the most restrictive (AOL) to 20,000 for most others. To ensure that you don't exceed the limits, segment your recipients by ISP. Sending to each ISP separately also makes it easier to keep a close eye on deliverability rates.

Chapter **4**

Dashboard Tools

Although apps are powerful, flexible, and customizable components of functionality in Salesforce Marketing Cloud, they rely on the foundation of the Marketing Cloud platform. For users of Marketing Cloud, the dashboard tools make up the core functionality of the platform.

Calendar, Campaigns, and Playbooks are the dashboard tools. They are available in every Marketing Cloud account, regardless of which apps you've licensed. You access any one of these tools from any screen in Marketing Cloud by choosing its name from the toolbar.

In this chapter, we focus on the Calendar and Campaigns tools. Salesforce Marketing Cloud has added features to the Journey Builder app that make some of the functionality of Playbooks redundant. You can find more details about Journey Builder in Chapter 10.

Using the Calendar

The Calendar tool provides a view of your scheduled marketing activities. A calendar ribbon, including just the current week, appears on the dashboard, as shown in Figure 4-1.

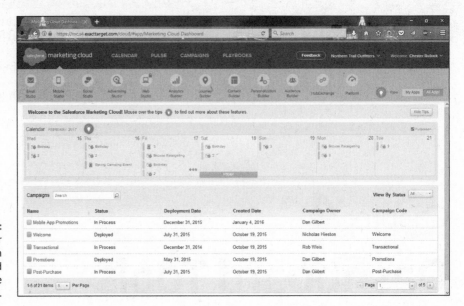

FIGURE 4-1:
The calendar ribbon on the dashboard shows just the current week.

When you pause your mouse pointer on the calendar ribbon, arrows appear on the left and right ends of the ribbon so you can change which week is displayed. You can also click the Fullscreen link in the upper right of the ribbon or click Calendar from the toolbar to open the Calendar tool and see the entire month, as shown in Figure 4-2.

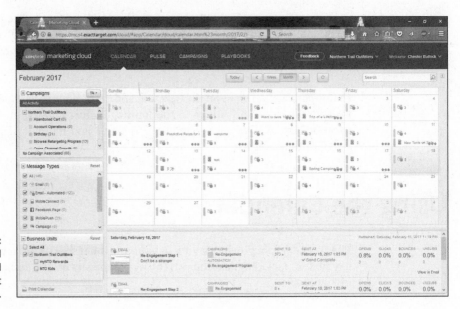

FIGURE 4-2:
The Calendar tool shows the full month, plus it includes filters.

Pause your mouse cursor over an event on the calendar, as shown in Figure 4-3, to see more information about that event, including the event type and its scheduled time. For past email-sending events, you also see whether the event ran successfully and you can click the event name to go to tracking details. For future email-sending events, you can click the event to edit the parameters.

FIGURE 4-3:
Drill down to
event details
through the
calendar.

Calendar event sources

The events you see on the calendar come from two sources:

>> **Other apps in Marketing Cloud:** For example, if you use the Email Studio app to schedule an email to be sent on a specific date, that email send appears automatically on the calendar. The following types of events from other apps appear on the calendar:

• User-initiated sends through the Email app (see Chapter 11 for full details).

• Guided user sends through the Email app (see Chapter 11).

• Sends through Content Builder (see Chapter 7).

• Programs (see Chapter 16).

• Automation Studio programs (see Chapter 10).

- Sends scheduled through the API. A developer can use the API to initiate a send that you create in Marketing Cloud. API sending is outside of the scope of this book.

- Scheduled MobileConnect events (see Chapter 12).

>> **You:** You can create an event in your calendar so that you see it in the schedule alongside your automated activities. For example, you might add a trade show to the calendar, even though you attend trade shows in person rather than online.

Creating a calendar event

Many events on the calendar appear automatically when you create and schedule a marketing activity from a Marketing Cloud app. However, you can also create events directly on the calendar.

Events that you schedule in the calendar don't cause anything to occur in Marketing Cloud. Instead, they serve as reminders to your team that an event is happening — or needs to happen — on a certain date. For example, you might add an event to the calendar to represent the date you're sending a brochure in the mail. You include this event on the calendar, even though it's done entirely outside Marketing Cloud, so that everyone on you team knows about the brochure.

REMEMBER

You must have the Create and Edit permission for the Calendar to schedule an event.

To schedule an event in the calendar, follow these steps:

1. **Move your cursor to the day for which you want to schedule an event.**

The window in Figure 4-4 appears, prompting you to add a campaign or an event.

2. **Select Add Event.**

A new window appears, asking for details about the event.

3. **Add the details and then click Save.**

The event is saved on your calendar.

Managing Campaigns

A key to a successful marketing campaign is keeping track of the components that make up your campaign. Salesforce Marketing Cloud includes a dashboard tool intuitively called Campaigns, where you can group the email, mobile, social, and other marketing efforts related to the same campaign.

By grouping the campaign components in the Campaigns tool, it's easier to plan, execute, and measure the various kinds of efforts all in one place. For example, by associating multiple email sends with a campaign, you can easily review the performance of all the emails, as shown in Figure 4-5.

Campaign associations

The process for creating a campaign has two distinct phases. First you must define the campaign itself, and then you must select the *associations* (email, mobile, social, and other marketing efforts) that belong to the campaign.

You have to create the associations in the appropriate Marketing Cloud apps before you can add them to the campaign. You can add the following association types to your campaigns:

>> **From Email Studio** (see Chapter 11):

- *Email:* A regular email that you create and send to a list of subscribers

FIGURE 4-5:
Separate email sends brought together in a campaign.

- *Triggered send:* An email that Marketing Cloud sends automatically in response to a subscriber action, such as completing a support form

» **From Mobile Studio** (see Chapter 12):

- *Mobile message:* An SMS (text) message
- *Push message:* A message sent to subscribers through a mobile app

» **From Social Studio** (see Chapter 13):

- *Twitter update:* A tweet sent from your corporate Twitter account
- *Facebook update:* A status update added to your Facebook page
- *Facebook tab:* Facebook fan pages managed through the SocialPages app

» **From Web Studio** (see Chapter 15):

- *Sites:* Collections of website pages hosted through your Marketing Cloud account
- *Landing page (email):* A single website hosted through Marketing Cloud

» **Audiences** (see Chapter 6):

- *Subscriber list:* A collection of email subscribers
- *Subscriber group:* A filtered subset of a subscriber list
- *Data extension:* A collection of email records stored in a configurable data table

» **Other content:**

- *Automation:* A series of tasks performed in sequence (see Chapter 10)
- *Event:* A calendar event that you created using the steps in the "Creating a calendar event" section, earlier in this chapter

TIP

You can add associations to a campaign from the Campaigns tool (described later in this chapter) or from the app where the association was initially created. For example, you can add an email as an association to a campaign from the Email app. See the chapter on the relevant app for details.

Touring the campaign screen

Like the calendar, the Campaigns tool has a ribbon view that appears on the Marketing Cloud dashboard. To open the full Campaigns tool, shown in Figure 4-6, select a campaign name from the ribbon or choose Campaigns from the toolbar and then click a campaign.

FIGURE 4-6:
The details of a campaign.

The Campaigns tool is divided into three horizontal sections:

» **The top section** shows the information you entered when you created the campaign: The name, description, campaign code, tags, deployment date, campaign owner, and campaign status. To edit any of these details, select the pencil icon on the right side of the screen. (You need the Create and Edit permission for Campaigns to see the pencil icon.) You can delete the campaign by selecting the trash can icon, which appears next to the pencil. (You need the Delete permission for Campaigns to see the trash can icon.)

» **The center section** consists of the storyboard, which displays the number of each type of association added to this campaign.

» **The bottom section** displays a summary of each association in the campaign. You can filter the associations by type by using the category list on the left side of the section. Three columns appear for each association:

- *Summary:* Displays the association name, the group it belongs to (such as Mobile), and the type (for example, Mobile Messages). Additional association-specific information, such as the subject line of an email, may also appear.

- *Details:* Contains viewable or actionable information, such as counts of sent messages for an email or the number of subscribers in a list, along with links to view more information or quickly access an action (such as set up an email send) in the appropriate app.

- *Actions:* Enables you to jump directly to the association's details in its app by selecting Go To. For example, if you select Go To for an email association, you'll go directly to the message edit view in the Email app. (Unfortunately, when you're finished, you must navigate back to the Campaigns tool through the toolbar.) To remove an association from a campaign, select the chain link icon next to Go To.

Creating the campaign

Before you can associate marketing activities to a campaign, you have to define the campaign itself. You provide just a small amount of information in the Create Campaign dialog box, shown in Figure 4-7, so that Marketing Cloud has something to add associations to.

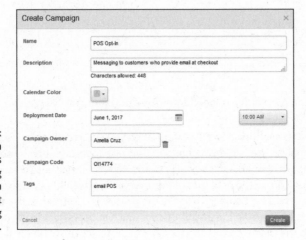

FIGURE 4-7: Defining a campaign gives Marketing Cloud an umbrella to put your marketing efforts under.

You need the Create and Edit permission for Campaigns to perform this procedure.

To define a campaign, follow these steps:

1. **On the toolbar, select Campaigns.**

    The Campaigns tool appears.

2. **In the upper-right corner of the Campaigns tool, select Create Campaign.**

    The Create Campaign dialog box opens (refer to Figure 4-7).

3. **Complete the following fields:**

    - *Name:* Enter the name of your campaign. Choose a name that is unique and lets a user know right away what the campaign is about.

    - *Description:* (Optional) Describe your campaign, including its intent.

    - *Calendar Color:* Use the color picker to assign a color to the campaign. Items in this campaign appear in this color on the calendar. Colors are a good way to create a visual link between similar types of campaigns.

    - *Deployment Date:* Assign a campaign start date and time. These dates determine where the campaign appears on the Calendar tool but do not affect the actual campaign deployment.

4. **(Optional) Complete any of the following fields:**

    - *Campaign Owner:* Assign a Marketing Cloud user as the owner. The owner is the only person who can make modifications to the campaign settings.

    - *Campaign Code:* Assign a campaign code. Marketing Cloud does not assign campaign codes, but it provides this field so you can store a campaign code generated by another system you use, such as Aprimo.

    - *Tags:* Assign applicable tags. You also can add tags to a campaign later if you need to.

5. **Click Create.**

Adding associations to a campaign

After you've defined the campaign, it's time to add the associations.

You need the Associate permission for Campaigns to perform this procedure.

To add associations to a campaign, follow these steps:

1. **In the Campaigns tool, open the campaign to which you want to add associations.**

2. **In the storyboard section, click the down arrow next to the Add to Campaign button.**

   A drop-down list of associations appears, as shown in Figure 4-8.

3. **Select the association you want to add, and then click Add to Campaign.**

   The system adds the association to your campaign. Repeat these steps for each association you want to add.

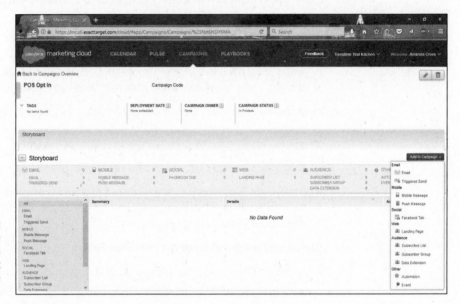

Tagging a campaign

Tags are descriptive keywords that you add to your campaign to help categorize it. You can use tags on a campaign to filter the list of campaigns that appears in the Campaigns tool and the events that appear on the calendar. You can use the tags on a campaign also in the Reports app to retrieve analytics on multiple campaigns with the same tag.

For example, you might add tags to the campaign to identify the following:

>> The marketing channels you use in the campaign, such as email, mobile, or web

>> The campaign type, say, monthly newsletter

>> The type of offer or content that the campaign promotes, such as one-day sales

Figure 4-9 shows a sample of tags that you might use in your campaign.

FIGURE 4-9:
Tags on a
campaign give
you information
at a glance.

To create a new tag to use in your campaigns, follow these steps:

1. **Pause the mouse pointer on your username in the upper-right corner of the Marketing Cloud toolbar, and select Administration from the drop-down list.**

   A new window appears, listing several administrative options.

2. **In the top navigation bar, select the Account drop-down menu and choose Tags.**

   The Tags overview screen appears, displaying any existing tags and the number of campaigns with those tags. There's also an option to delete each tag.

3. **Select Create Tag.**

4. **Type the tag's name and an optional description.**

   Tag names must be unique.

2

Utilizing Data

Chapter **5**

Identifying and Preparing Your Data

Without question, the biggest hurdle we've encountered in our marketing careers is data. Early on, the challenge was getting access to meaningful information. Everything seemed to stand in our way — from systems that weren't designed for sharing to corporate fiefdoms that were threatened by the incorrect assumption that we were trying to compete with their sales team.

These days, however, the situation is reversed. Rather than struggling to find any useful data, we are now overwhelmed with data from all over the organization. It seems like everyone wants a finger in the pie because he thinks his own data is the most important to incorporate into the online marketing efforts. In this type of situation, it's easy to lose sight of what is essential.

Defining Your Data Set

Your *data set* is the list of the pieces of information you maintain about each subscriber. Sadly, we can't define your data set for you. Although some kinds of data are useful for almost everyone, the combination of your marketing plan, target demographics, and business objectives make your data needs unique.

What we can do, though, is help guide your thinking about what data components you need as we walk you through the process of designing your data set for use in Salesforce Marketing Cloud. In Chapter 6, we discuss how to implement the plan you define here.

What data do you have?

A good first task is to take inventory of the customer data you already have. Even the smallest business has data, but it might be residing in a surprisingly wide variety of business systems. Customer contact information is essential, of course, but you might be able to make use of other kinds of data, such as purchase history.

Cast a wide net when listing your possible data sources. Don't limit yourself at this point; you pare the scope of the data later. Don't forget to consider the following locations:

>> **Customer relationship management (CRM) system:** For example, an automotive service shop probably has contact information, information about the vehicle, and a history of services.

>> **Point-of-sale or billing system:** If you collect information from your customers as part of the sale, your point-of-sale or billing system can be a rich resource of customer data.

>> **Existing communications methods:** For example, if you've ever set up a form for customers to sign up for a newsletter or request more information, that form has been collecting valuable data you can use.

>> **Loyalty program:** If you offer rewards to your customers for their continued business, don't forget to mine the system you use to administer it.

>> **Customer preference center:** Your existing content publishing processes might have already inspired you to set up a website where customers can indicate preferences, such as what topics they're interested in and how often they want to receive messages from you.

>> **Website analytics:** The analytics tools you install on your corporate website can provide an amazing amount of information about the people who visit your site, even if they don't make a purchase. Be especially careful with how you use this data, though, because it's easy to jump to the wrong conclusions about what your visitors want and end up upsetting prospective clients before they even have a chance to buy.

>> **Spreadsheets, file cabinets, and stacks of business cards:** Think about the life cycle of a customer interacting with your business and check out all the locations where the interactions might be stored.

Figure 5-1 illustrates the information you might have about clients and how you could store that information in Marketing Cloud.

FIGURE 5-1:
A data-driven view into a particular customer.

TIP

You must have explicit permission from your customers before you send them marketing messages. If you've already gathered that permission through any of these channels, be sure to make a note of it. If you haven't, you'll have the opportunity to ask for that permission when you begin your campaign.

What data do you wish you had?

As a marketer and a businessperson, of course you would like to know everything about your customers. But the question of "What data do you wish you had?" isn't about curiosity. It's about the specific data you need to power the marketing campaigns you plan to execute.

"What data do you wish you had?" sounds like a straightforward question, but it can quickly turn in to a chicken-and-egg situation. You need to predict what data your future online marketing will rely upon, but the needs of your future campaigns will depend in part on the data you have.

Regardless of what other data you need, you're definitely going to need data to segment your subscriber lists into groups to which you send your different messages. After you have that, you can use more data to choose the content in the message on a subscriber-by-subscriber basis.

Data for list segmentation

You use some of the data that you collect specifically to choose which subscribers to send messages to. Figure 5-2 shows a sample data set of subscribers you might send to.

first_name	last_name	email	timezone	loyaltyid	activity
Kenneth	Simmons	ksimmons0@merriam-webste	Europe/Vienna	13734-032	Seldom
Raymond	Lawrence	rlawrence1@tumblr.com	America/Guatemala	58411-135	Seldom
Kelly	Burke	kburke2@networksolutions.co	Asia/Rangoon	49738-289	Often
Joan	Stevens	jstevens3@biglobe.ne.jp	Pacific/Apia	62584-988	Seldom
Ann	Sanchez	asanchez4@ft.com	Australia/Hobart	10702-014	Once
Gregory	Wright	gwright5@psu.edu	Australia/Hobart	52261-2501	Monthly
Eugene	Hill	ehill6@jimdo.com	Africa/Johannesburg	53746-204	Seldom
Bobby	Willis	bwillis7@bizjournals.com	Asia/Vladivostok	54868-6254	Once
Paul	Harvey	pharvey8@reverbnation.com	Asia/Novosibirsk	0135-0429	Daily
David	Daniels	ddaniels9@admin.ch	Asia/Irkutsk	52959-747	Never
Ernest	Matthews	ematthewsa@foxnews.com	Asia/Kolkata	43353-706	Seldom
Todd	Williams	twilliamsb@dedecms.com	Asia/Tashkent	60432-131	Seldom
Fred	Martinez	fmartinezc@jigsy.com	Europe/Moscow	65841-706	Once
Thomas	Hart	thartd@t-online.de	Europe/Bucharest	66658-234	Never
Amy	George	ageorgee@moonfruit.com	Pacific/Honolulu	0067-6274	Never
Alice	Garcia	agarciaf@myspace.com	Europe/Madrid	54473-220	Once
Stephanie	Robinson	srobinsong@prnewswire.com	Asia/Magadan	52125-619	Seldom
Eric	Carpenter	ecarpenterh@dropbox.com	America/Argentina/Buenos_Aires	34645-8030	Never

FIGURE 5-2: A list of subscribers to target based on data.

Logical groupings depend on your business (we know we say "it depends" a lot, but it's just the reality of online marketing). Natural ones we've used in the past include the following:

>> **Geography:** This can be by ZIP code, state, or country, or even hemisphere! You'll need the data to support your audience groupings, whatever they are.

>> **Class of customer:** You might have a loyalty program that has different tiers, like an airline has gold and platinum members. You might want to send a

specific email to people who are basic members, so you would use your membership-level data to send to just this audience.

>> **Active subscribers:** You can leverage the click and open data within Marketing Cloud to target your most active subscribers, such as those who have opened or clicked in the last 60 days.

>> **Specific interest:** If your preference center has interests that people can select, and you have content specific to that interest, you can use that information to target the audience.

>> **Recent purchases:** You can leverage your sales data to follow up with your customers, encouraging them to complete website feedback about the items they purchased or write a review about your business. Customers are more likely to give positive feedback if you remind them.

REMEMBER

One phrase we hear too often in email marketing is "email blast." Compared to most other types of marketing, email marketing is precise. It gives you enough customer data to target both the subscriber and the content. If you're taking advantage of your tools and data, your email marketing could never be described as a randomly scattered blast.

Data to choose message content

One of the most underutilized features of Marketing Cloud is the capability to change what content you include in an email based on data about the specific subscriber.

Simple personalization, such as including the subscriber's first name, takes little effort. With more elbow grease and the right data, though, you can create a single email send that selects content tailored for each individual subscriber. One example appears in Figure 5-3.

For example, you could use this capability for the following sample cases:

>> **Geography:** Let's say you have an offer that is going to become available at the same time across the country. You can use the subscriber's time zone to include the local time when the offer will go live.

>> **Class of customer:** You might want to show subscribers how many more points they need to get to the next tier in your loyalty program.

>> **Upsell:** If your products have a natural progression, you could use the subscriber's purchase history to suggest the next item to buy. For example, if a subscriber just bought your printer, you could send an email with a link to buy toner.

> >> **Weather:** Imagine there's a big snowstorm in the Atlantic Northeast. You could send an email that advertises snowshoes to subscribers in that area but other kinds of shoes to the rest of the country.

em	firstnam	latitu	longitu	avg_ord
ahansen0@indiegogo.com	Anthony	28.26311	89.38187	L
lnguyen1@myspace.com	Lillian	60.6036	15.626	3XL
devans2@yellowbook.com	Diana	-0.26492	109.12069	XS
laustin3@craigslist.org	Lisa	-3.99313	-79.20422	S
wcrawford4@state.tx.us	Willie	11.2889	124.5671	L
acooper5@typepad.com	Anne	49.74955	21.33665	L
fclark6@arizona.edu	Fred	14.71667	-88.1	L
dwest7@slideshare.net	Debra	32.19303	35.37127	M
dwallace8@angelfire.com	Donna	13.17603	-86.61234	XS
bcole9@hud.gov	Brenda	14.21667	120.85	2XL
jwheelera@dailymail.co.uk	Joyce	58.1881	12.716	2XL
adunnb@xinhuanet.com	Angela	27.7694	115.37857	3XL
jwelchc@amazonaws.com	Julie	43.68	15.91972	3XL
gcruzd@nature.com	Gary	-5.41667	38.01667	XS
jrileye@xing.com	Janice	36.21492	28.11487	S
hgonzalezf@foxnews.com	Helen	-28.35889	-49.29139	M
rcarrg@creativecommons.org	Richard	47.6	39.7	XL
ahamiltonh@elegantthemes.com	Ann	28.74677	118.26191	S
mmorrisi@howstuffworks.com	Melissa	15.44447	120.8007	XL

FIGURE 5-3: Data can help you choose what content to include in your marketing messages.

This level of customization is possible through Marketing Cloud's proprietary scripting language, AMPscript, covered in Chapter 11. This list only scratches the surface of what you can do with AMPscript and the right data.

Defining an initial data set

The worst thing you can do to yourself is to try to build all these scenarios at once. We recommend starting small and building toward more complexity over time. You'll have the opportunity to think of new uses for the data you have and to ask subscribers for new data that you can use to craft a delightful user experience.

It's tempting to store data just because you can. Despite your best intentions, though, you aren't going to find a use for every piece of information you have about your customers, products, or email interactions. Be objective and narrow the data you store in Marketing Cloud to what you will really use.

You can also run into trouble trying to store data that isn't easy to get or keep up to date. For example, data that is available in real-time thanks to an integration between Marketing Cloud and another business system is better than data you have to load into Marketing Cloud manually every month.

We recommend that your initial data look like what you would expect from a basic direct mail database:

>> Salutation (Mr., Mrs., Ms., and so on)

>> First name

>> Last name

>> City

>> State

>> ZIP code

>> Country (if you send internationally)

>> Birthday

If you have more than one list type (newsletter, discounts, random promotions), you should also capture which list each subscriber is on.

The data in the preceding list is the base level of information you need to start sending effective email marketing that is both personalized and potentially customized to fit your customer's needs and expectations.

Dealing with a data shortfall

What if you don't have the data to fill in all the fields for all your subscribers? Three options are available to you:

>> Proceed with what you have.

>> Change how you collect data.

>> Purchase supplemental data from third-party sources.

Let's examine each option.

Proceed with limited data

With the first option, you push on with your imperfect data, at least for the interim. You first messages might be less sophisticated and your results will likely be less impressive, but at least you are getting started. Many people find this approach acceptable, especially in the short term while filling in the data blanks.

Change how you collect data

People usually use the second option — changing how they collect data — with the first one. While leveraging the data you have available, you improve your process for collecting data.

Preference centers and surveys are tools you can use to ask your subscribers for data. As you build trust with your customers, customers will be willing to provide you with more information.

For example, you might send a periodic, dedicated email that asks subscribers to go to a survey tool and answer some questions. Another approach is a simple question at the bottom of every email you send asking whether the information was helpful. Figure 5-4 gives an example of such a question. Clicking yes or no shows the subscriber a "Thank You!" landing page while showing you what kind of content the subscriber likes to see from you.

Would you like fewer emails?

Instead of being removed completely from our email list, would you
like to receive email updates less frequently?

⊙ Yes, please send me email updates less frequently.

○ No thanks. Please remove me from your email list.

Beware of becoming too extreme in your data collection efforts. Requiring all fields on a sign-up page, for example, will inhibit list growth substantially. Instead, think about all the processes you have in place that interact with your subscribers and make minor adjustments. From call center operations to physical point-of-sale installations to your email programs, you have numerous opportunities to enhance the quantity and quality of your data *without scaring off your subscriber*.

Consider quick actions like the following to gather data without offending your subscriber base:

>> Send a "spring cleaning" email to encourage your subscribers to update their information in your preference center. This can be used with an incentive, as in Figure 5-5.

>> In your newsletters, insert links that ask subscribers if they want to see more of this type of content. By tracking the clicks on the links, you can build a profile of the interests of each subscriber.

20% OFF

YOUR NEXT PURCHASE WHEN YOU
COMPLETE YOUR PROFILE

FIGURE 5-5:
An incentive
for asking
subscribers to
update their
profile.

>> Publish incentives for people to update their profile and interests. These incentives don't have to cost you money. Just a statement such as "Update your profile today to receive more of the information you like" reminds subscribers that you want to send them relevant content. Just make sure you have enough content to support a statement like this!

Purchase supplemental data

If you have a list of only email addresses, you can pay a third-party data provider to match those email addresses in its databases and return other subscriber data. The provider can give you information such as the subscriber's name, address, and phone number.

The full scope of information available varies by the provider but can be quite extensive. Some claim to be able to offer an electronic change of address (ECOA) service, which gives you current email addresses for subscribers whose messages have started bouncing.

WARNING

The marketing community is full of stories of third-party data gone bad. As with anything, there are right and wrong ways to acquire and use third-party data. We've used these services with mixed results in the past. If you investigate each data provider appropriately, and are on the lookout for the best practices and red flags described next, you should be able to identify a quality data provider for your needs.

Data providers following best practices

>> Will email their proposed list from their servers

>> Perform an active opt-in process, where only people who have confirmed that they want to hear from you are included in the list you're buying

>> Provide references

>> Take a reasonable amount of time to provide results (two weeks is about right)

Watch out for these red flags from data providers who

>> Provide immediate results (indicates they did not ask permission from list members)

>> Want you to send from your server

>> Do not employ an opt-in process

>> Charge you for every match

Data after a send

Don't forget that you'll receive a wealth of new data from each message you send. This continual influx of data includes useful facts like the following:

>> **Bounces:** Emails that were returned to you undelivered. Subscribers who bounce might not be worth continuing to maintain information about.

>> **Open date and time:** The date and time the subscriber opened the email. You can use this information to get an idea about how prompt certain subscribers are about opening their email. In aggregate, you can even use this data to make decision about what day of the week or time of day to send future emails.

>> **URLs clicked:** The date and time the subscriber clicked a link in your email. You might be able to infer the success of particular kinds of links (images versus text), the subject matter of the link, or the position of the link in the page from which ones your subscribers click.

>> **Unsubscribes:** Recipients who no longer want to receive your emails. Obviously, it's important to know which subscribers to continue targeting.

Combine this information with your other useful data, and you have a powerful base of data to make immediate, intelligent decisions about the people you market to and how you market to them. It also gives you a solid foundation for testing.

Mapping Your Data to Your Objectives

It's great that you have all sorts of data available to you, but how do you take advantage of it? What is going to be the most helpful or effective? To figure this out, you first need to determine your marketing goals.

Marketing objectives

You decide the marketing objectives that make sense for you and your business. Just like professional development goals, your marketing objectives should be

» Specific so that everyone understands what needs to be accomplished

» Measurable so you know if your campaign met the objective

» Defined by time so you have a date that you plan to complete it by

» Pertinent so that the objective helps business performance

» Actionable so that there are clear steps to take to achieve the goal

Don't forget to be realistic. Too many objectives, timelines that are too short and goals that are too high can do more harm than good. Start slow and remember that you can always add more objectives later.

Data to fulfill your objectives

After you've decided on your objectives, you can start figuring out what data to gather to determine whether you've achieved those objectives.

Let's look at a sample goal. You have a newsletter that reaches 100,000 people. On average, 25 percent of the subscribers open the email and 5 percent click a link (*click through rate,* or *CTR*). One goal you might have is to increase the CTR to 10 percent over the next 12 months.

A lot of variables could be at play in determining the CTR of your email newsletter, and you can use data to experiment with each of them. For example:

» How many emails you send per week. You could experiment with sending more or fewer emails to see the effect on CTR. See information about A/B testing in Chapter 11.

» Whether a subscriber opens the email. A subscriber has to open an email to click a link, and adding personalization to the subject line is a proven way to improve open rates. Find information about personalization in Chapter 11.

» How many subscribers on your list are inactive — never open or click at all. You could remove inactive subscribers to increase the density of clicks among the subscribers who remain.

>> Number and placement of links in the newsletter. You could experiment with repeating a link at the beginning and end of a newsletter to raise the visibility of the link and improve CTR.

>> Time of day you sent the newsletter. You can evaluate what time of day you get the most opens and clicks and focus on sending at that time.

Data objective exercise

Let's wrap up this chapter by using data to solve a real problem:

1. **Take out a piece of paper (or open your favorite note-taking app on your device of choice). Write down a problem you're facing and your objective to improve the situation.**

   Is that objective specific, measurable, time-bound, pertinent to business performance, and actionable? If not, take the time now to mold it so it meets all those criteria.

2. **Brainstorm the factors that might be contributing to the problem.**

   Don't limit yourself to the obvious factors. You can even include the factors that influence the factors!

3. **Think about what data you could use to investigate each of the factors.**

   Is the data readily available? How can you access it?

Getting used to using this approach to problem-solving makes the data in your Marketing Cloud account immensely useful to you and your company.

Chapter **6**

Establishing Your Data Model

n Chapter 5, you searched far and wide for data you could consider using in your online marketing campaigns before mercilessly culling the data that didn't help you meet your marketing objectives. Now that you have a healthy, well-thought-out pool of data, you need to get it into a place where Salesforce Marketing Cloud can use it.

For a long time, Marketing Cloud had only one simple and effective approach to storing data. But new functionality demanded a more sophisticated — and more complex — model to store different kinds of data that you use in multimedia online marketing campaigns.

In this chapter, we discuss your data storage options and help you decide which one to use. Then we talk about how to set up your data model and how to import the data you already have into it.

Understanding Marketing Cloud Data Models

The two data models in Marketing Cloud are as follows:

>> **Subscriber/list model:** All data is stored in fields in a subscriber record and subscribers are grouped into lists for sending.

>> **Relational data model:** Data is stored in relational database tables called *data extensions.*

Subscriber-and-list model

The traditional way to store subscriber data in Marketing Cloud has been to use the subscriber-and-list model. This approach is simple, straightforward, and has some nice built-in conveniences.

In this model, Marketing Cloud considers each subscriber to be a complete entity. The email address identifies the subscriber entity, and profile and preference attributes contain the following kinds of data about the subscriber:

>> **Profile attributes:** Contain demographic data about the subscriber. Figure 6-1 shows the profile attributes that exist in your account by default.

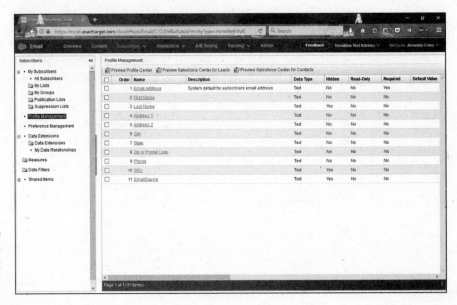

FIGURE 6-1:
Years of experience say most Marketing Cloud users need these attributes.

>> **Preference attributes:** Contain yes/no choices that subscribers communicate to you about how they want to hear from you. The only preference attribute delivered by default is called HTML Email. When subscribers select the check box next to this preference, they receive your emails in beautiful, full-color HTML. If they deselect this check box, they receive a text-only version of your email.

One of the little conveniences built into the subscriber-and-list model is Profile Center. For each subscriber, Marketing Cloud automatically generates a web page that you can link to in the footer of your email. When subscribers click the link, they go to a form where they can update their attribute values and change the lists to which they are subscribed.

Figure 6-2 shows an example of a profile center. It's an easy way to get to some of the subscriber data you've been after while making subscribers feel listened to and in control.

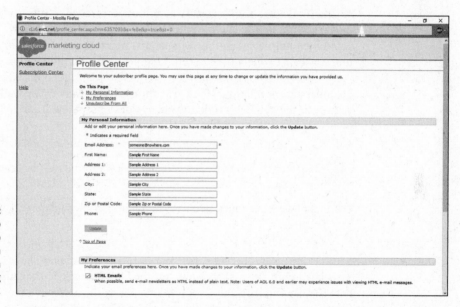

FIGURE 6-2:
Subscribers go to Profile Center to update their own information in your Marketing Cloud account.

Your Marketing Cloud account comes with basic profile and preference attributes already created. You can choose to create a few additional profile and preference attributes to store data that isn't part of the basic starter set.

It wouldn't make sense to use a powerful piece of online marketing software to communicate to only one subscriber at a time, so you use lists to group many subscribers so you can send to them all at once. Marketing Cloud automatically includes all your subscribers on the big All Subscribers list, and then you create other lists, each one of which containing a subset of your All Subscribers list. Often, a list corresponds to a message type. For example, you might have one list for your monthly newsletter and another for your weekly flier. A subscriber can exist in any number of lists.

The subscriber-and-list model is simple to understand and adequate as long as each subscriber has no more than one piece of relatively static data for each attribute. For example, if all you have is the subscriber's email address, first name, and last name, the fields on the subscriber entity are fine. However, when you begin capturing things such as purchase history, where each subscriber could have a different number of past purchases and the information could be changing every day, using just the subscriber attributes becomes unwieldy and inefficient.

Relational data model with data extensions

As the Marketing Cloud software continued to evolve, the subscriber-and-list model started falling short of the growing needs of increasingly customized and automated online marketing campaigns. Marketers needed the power of a tool that was being widely used in other high-tech fields: the relational database.

To understand a relational database, think of your wallet. The wallet as a whole is yours, but the data within that wallet resides in separate locations:

>> Your driver's license has your name, contact information, and demographics.

>> Your credit or debit card has your name and information you use to make purchases.

>> Your health insurance card has your name and information you use to get health care.

Each of these items serves a different purpose, so it makes sense to store the data associated with them separately, but they are also all tied together by a piece of data that is unique to you — your name. Using this name, you can figure out that the different cards go together and belong in the same person's wallet.

In relational database parlance, the different data storage locations (the cards in the preceding example) are called *tables*. In Marketing Cloud terminology, though, a table is called a *data extension*. In both cases, the unique identifier that ties the data together (your name in the example) is called a *primary key*.

To put this concept in practical terms, here is an example of data an online retailer wants to store about a customer. The retailer creates a Customers table with the following fields:

- » Customer ID (primary key)
- » Salutation
- » First Name
- » Last Name
- » Address
- » Address 2
- » City
- » State/Province
- » ZIP/Postal Code
- » Country
- » Phone Number
- » Email Address

After a customer makes a purchase, the retailer will have information that doesn't fit in the Customers table. So she creates a Shipping table with the following fields:

- » Customer ID
- » Order ID (primary key)
- » Ship To Name
- » Address
- » Address 2
- » City
- » State/Province
- » ZIP/Postal Code
- » Country
- » Phone Number

Now you might be thinking to yourself, "Wait a second. Customer ID was supposed to be the primary key." But the value of a primary key has to be unique within the table so it can definitively identify a single row in that table. Because a single customer could make more than one purchase, the same Customer ID could appear on many rows.

So you need a different value, the Order ID, to be the primary key of this particular table and to uniquely identify each row. The Customer ID is still available on each row, though, to connect the Shipping table with the Customers table. Using the Customer ID, you can get to the name and email address of the customer who placed the order.

Because an order may contain several items all being shipped to the same address, next the retailer needs an Orders table to identify the item or items to be shipped:

>> Order ID

>> Product ID

>> Order Date

>> Quantity

Note that this table has no single primary key field of its own but it associates the primary keys of other tables together. You might use a table like this to send a "Thank you for your order!" email at the end of each day. You could write a database query to collect all the information related to today's orders by starting from this table, using the Order ID to hop to the Shipping table, and then finding the Customer ID to hop to the Customers table.

As you can see in Figure 6-3, several files can be linked to build a useful relational data model.

Customers Table	Shipping Table	Orders Table
Customer ID (primary key) ——►	Customer ID	↗ Order ID
Salutation	Order ID (primary key)	Product ID
First Name	Ship To Name	Quantity
Last Name	Address	
Address	Address 2	
Address 2	City	
City	State/Province	
State/Province	Zip/Postal Code	
Zip/Postal Code	Country	
Country	Phone Number	
Phone Number		
Email Address		

FIGURE 6-3: You can link many data files together in a relational data model.

If your company has rules about how long you must keep data or how quickly you should delete it, you can set a data retention policy on a data extension to delete the content in the data extension automatically. You can choose among the following options for removing data:

>> **Individual records:** When you delete individual records, each time the system cleans out the old data, it deletes the rows in the table that have reached the required age.

>> **All records:** Deleting all records wipes out all the data in the data extension when any of the records has reached the required age. You usually use this option for data extensions in which all the content is the same age.

>> **All records and data extension:** Choosing this option removes the entire data extension, data and all.

You also have options when it comes to setting up the date to delete the data extension content. You can choose a specific date or enter a number of days. When you create the data extension, the system starts counting the days, and after that date or the number of days you chose elapses, it deletes the content according to your selection. You can tell the system to restart the count of days each time you import into the data extension, if you prefer.

Using data extensions to contain your subscriber data is both more difficult and more powerful than using the subscriber-and-list approach. Whereas the purpose of subscriber attributes and lists is clearly defined before you even open your Marketing Cloud account, a data extension is a blank slate that can be configured to any purpose. Some data extensions contain the data that would otherwise be held in attributes; others serve the same purpose as lists, defining which subscribers receive a message.

Adopting a relational data model has several benefits:

>> Easier maintenance of individual records or types of data within a larger set

>> Easier accommodation of new data — just add a new table

>> Reduced storage needs by eliminating duplicate data

>> Faster data processing at send time

Which data model will work for you?

Now that you have an understanding of the differences between the data structures you can employ, it's up to you to decide which best fits your needs. Consider the following questions when choosing whether to use the subscriber-and-list model or the relational data model:

>> **How confident are you with relational database concepts? Do you have any SQL knowledge? Can you map out data relationships, and then manipulate your source data to support those relationships? Do you feel comfortable with complex data relationships?** If you aren't comfortable with these concepts yet, you might want to start by storing your data in simple subscriber attributes.

>> **Are you going to be pulling information from a separate database to refresh Marketing Cloud data on a regular basis? Can you configure an automated synchronization of data between your primary database and Salesforce Marketing Cloud?** If so, a relational data approach is not required but will make things easier.

>> **Do you plan to implement Journey Builder (see Chapter 10)?** If so, you'll be better served by using a relational model with Journey Builder Decisions.

>> **How large is your data set, and how often will it be updated?** If the data set is large and has components that are updated frequently, a relational model is far more efficient.

Even if you start with subscriber attributes, you can move to a relational data model later, and you probably will. The relational model makes it possible to use the coolest functionality in Marketing Cloud.

Setting up a subscriber-and-list data model

If you decide to start by using the subscriber-and-list model to store your subscriber data, you have a short to-do list to get up and running. Start in the Email app by choosing Email from the Email Studio category on the app switcher.

Setting up your subscriber profile attributes

If you need additional profile attributes, use the following steps to create them. You might not need to perform this procedure if the profile attributes provided by default serve your needs:

1. **In the Email app, pause your mouse pointer over the Subscribers menu in the toolbar, and choose Profile Management from the menu that appears.**

   A list of the profile attributes defined in your account appears.

2. **Click the Create button to open the New Attribute Properties window.**

3. **Complete the information on the General tab:**

   - *Enter the name of the attribute.* Remember that the name appears in Profile Center for subscribers to see.

   - *Enter a description of the attribute.*

   - *(Optional) Change the order in which the attributes appear in Profile Center.* Click the Change button. In the window that appears, use Move Up and Move Down buttons to change the attribute's position.

   - *Select the appropriate check boxes to indicate if the attribute is Required, Hidden (does not appear in Profile Center), or Read-Only.* If, as part of your send process, you could be passing in subscriber information that differs from the value in this field, but you do *not* want Marketing Cloud to update the value in this field, select the Do Not Update Subscriber Values with Send Time Values check box.

4. **Complete the information on the Data tab.**

   The fields on this tab define what kind on information and how much information the attribute can contain. You can also set a default value.

5. **Complete the information on the Values tab.**

   On this tab, you can create a list of values for this attribute.

6. **Click OK.**

Setting up your subscriber preference attributes

Use the following steps if you want to set up additional preference attributes. You might be able to skip these steps if you're happy with the preference attribute delivered by default with your Marketing Cloud account.

1. **In the Email app, pause your mouse pointer over the Subscribers menu in the toolbar, and choose Preference Management from the menu that appears.**

   A list of the preference attributes defined in your account appears.

2. **Click the Create button to open the New Preference Properties window.**

3. **Complete the information on the General tab:**

   - *Enter the name of the attribute.* Remember that the name appears in Profile Center for subscribers to see.

   - *Enter a description of the attribute.*

- *(Optional) Change the order in which the attributes appear in Profile Center.* Click the Change button. In the window that appears, use the Move Up and Move Down buttons to change this attribute's position.

- *Select whether Yes or No is the default value.*

- *Select the appropriate check boxes to indicate if the attribute is Hidden (does not appear in Profile Center) or Read-Only.* If, as part of your send process, you could be passing in subscriber information that differs from the value in this field, but you do *not* want Marketing Cloud to update the value in this field, select the Do Not Update Subscriber Values with Send Time Values check box.

4. **Click OK.**

Creating lists of subscribers

Use the following steps to create a list of subscribers to whom you can send email messages:

1. **In the Email app, pause your mouse pointer over the Subscribers menu in the toolbar, and choose Lists from the menu that appears.**

2. **Click the Create button on the right side of the screen.**

   The Create List window appears with two tabs.

3. **Complete the fields in the Define Name & Location tab, and then click Next.**

   Most of these fields are self-explanatory, but the Public List check box merits some discussion. If you select this check box, this list appears in Profile Center for subscribers to choose to opt in or opt out. You should select this check box for any list used for ongoing communication, such as weekly deals or newsletters.

TIP

   Because the name of public lists appears in Profile Center for subscribers to see, choose your list name with care. The name should clearly describe the kind of email subscribers can expect to receive if they opt in. Using proper capitalization and avoiding abbreviations gives your Profile Center a more professional, polished look.

4. **Complete the fields in the Select Welcome Email tab, and then click Save.**

   If you choose to send a welcome email, Marketing Cloud sends the email you choose to each new subscriber who joins the list. For example, if a subscriber opts into the list via Profile Center, the system sends the subscriber the welcome email you choose here.

Setting up a relational data model

If you choose to dive right into a relational data model, you have more work to get things started. Much of what you need to do — before you begin any of the following procedures — involves planning the design of the database. When you're ready to implement your design, start in the Email app by choosing Email from the Email Studio category on the app switcher.

Setting up a data extension

Use the following steps to create a data extension to contain data in your relational data model. These steps set up the data extension but do not populate it with data. See the procedure later in this chapter for information on how to import content into your data extension.

1. **In the Email app, pause your mouse pointer over the Subscribers menu in the toolbar, and choose Data Extensions from the menu that appears.**

2. **Click the Create button, on the right side of the toolbar.**

3. **In the Create Data Extension window that appears, select Standard Data Extension and then click OK.**

4. **Complete the fields in the Properties tab of the Create New Data Extension window, and then click Next.**

5. **Complete the fields in the Data Retention Policy tab, and then click Next.**

   Using these settings, you can cause Marketing Cloud to automatically delete content from your data extensions after a period of time. This feature can keep you from using all your storage space and incurring fees.

6. **In the Fields tab, define each field in the data extension and click the Create button.**

Setting up a sendable data extensions

When you use the relational data model, you create sendable data extensions instead of lists of subscribers. The procedure for creating a sendable data extension is the same as the one for creating any other kind of data extension. Just make sure to select the Is Sendable? check box on the Properties tab of the Create New Data Extension window, shown in Figure 6-4, when you get to Step 4.

FIGURE 6-4:
Select the Is
Sendable? check
box to set up a
sendable data
extension.

Getting Data into Marketing Cloud

You've chosen the data you need for your online marketing campaigns and your Marketing Cloud data model is ready to accept that data. It's finally time to import the data!

The simplest way to import data into Marketing Cloud is to use *flat files* — text files that have one record per row and that use a character, usually a comma, pipe, or tab, as a delimiter that signifies where one field ends and another begins. Figure 6-5 shows a flat file. If you think of a flat file like a spreadsheet, a field is like a column and a record is like a row.

FIGURE 6-5:
Sample of a flat
data file that
could be used in
Salesforce
Marketing Cloud.

```
subscriber_import.csv - Notepad                                          —  □  ×
File  Edit  Format  View  Help
Email_Address,First_Name,Address_1,Address_2,City,State,Zip,Phone
acruz@example.com,Amelia,123 Main St,Appt A,Anytown,IN,99999,317-555-1234
glee@example.com,George,456 Broadway,,Anytown,MI,99999,616-555-5678
```

Later in this section, after the discussion of importing flat files, we touch briefly on integrating your Marketing Cloud account with your customer relationship management (CRM) system to systematically update your Marketing Cloud data.

Importing to subscriber attributes

This section is relevant if you've decided to start by using the subscriber-and-list model. If you'll be using a relational data model instead, you can skip this section and proceed to the next one, "Importing to data extensions."

Because the subscriber attribute model contains all necessary data in one big All Subscribers list, preparing the file to populate this table is straightforward.

You put the data you want to import into a single file, where each subscriber's data is a separate line in the file and each piece of data is delimited by a character, usually a comma or a tab. The file is actually a text file, but you might be able to open it in a spreadsheet program to help you review the content more easily. If you're exporting data from a different business system, that system might be able to generate a properly delimited file for you.

TIP

Marketing Cloud gets confused if the character you choose as a delimiter also appears in one of the fields. For example, if you have a comma-delimited file and a comma appears in the middle of an address, Marketing Cloud will think that the comma indicates the end of the address field. If the content of your data includes the delimiter character, choose a different character as the delimiter. Figure 6-6 shows the different delimiters you can choose and the field where you can enter a different delimiter.

Import Into Data Extension

① Upload File   ② Configure Mapping   ③ Review & Import

Data Extension	Salesforce Marketing Cloud for Dummies
File location	● My Computer ○ FTP
File*	[ ] Browse...
	☐ Compressed
Delimiter*	● Comma ○ Tab ○ Other [ ]
Date format	English (United States) ▾ Example: 11/26/2016 1:41 PM

FIGURE 6-6: Delimiter types for file import to Salesforce Marketing Cloud.

Use these steps to import your data:

1. In the Email app, pause your mouse pointer over the Subscribers menu in the toolbar, and choose Lists from the menu that appears.

2. **In the list, find the list you want to import to, and click the import icon in the Actions section, on the right side of the row.**

   The import icon is shown in the margin.

3. **Complete the steps in the Import Wizard that appears.**

   People have been importing to Marketing Cloud lists for a long time, so this wizard is a useful and time-tested aid to get your content into the system.

Importing to data extensions

This section is relevant if you've decided to use a relational data model. If you'll be using the subscriber-and-list model, see the preceding section, "Importing to subscriber attributes."

If you're using a relational data model, you must import more than one file of data; you import one file for each data extension. Other than that, the import process for data extensions is similar to the import process for subscriber attributes.

Use these steps to import your data:

1. **In the Email app, pause your mouse pointer over the Subscribers menu in the toolbar, and choose Data Extensions from the menu that appears.**

2. **In the list, find the list you want to import to, and click the import icon (shown in the margin) in the Actions section, on the right side of the row.**

3. **Complete the Import Wizard that appears.**

Utilizing a CRM integration

If your company uses a customer relationship management (CRM) system, it may be the single richest source of customer data that your Marketing Cloud campaigns can use. Obviously, if you use the Salesforce CRM, you have a prime opportunity to connect the two systems so that customer data can flow directly from one into the other.

Integrating your Marketing Cloud account with your CRM system has several benefits, such as the following:

>> Leverage knowledge of individual leads

>> Enable your sales team to reach out to individual leads but enforce your branding standards on their communication

>> Maintain customer data in a centralized location so you don't have to manage updates in two systems

>> Provide a more in-depth view of customer interactions within the CRM environment

The process to integrate your account may require additional configuration, but, if the company does a good job of keeping your customer information complete and current in your CRM system, you'll be glad to have access to it through Marketing Cloud.

Contact Builder

If you've elected to use a relational data model, you can use Contact Builder to manage the data you've imported. Contact Builder creates a single view of each contact in your database and allows you to easily tie other data points to that contact. Figure 6-7 shows Contact Builder.

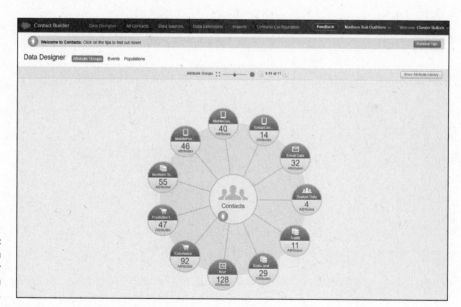

FIGURE 6-7: Sample Data Designer mapping in Contact Builder.

Contact Builder is required for any implementation of Journey Builder. Contact Builder allows you to visually build relationships between different data extensions, and these relationships support business rules and decisions in Journey Builder. Any data point used to make a decision or to support content in Journey Builder must be included in Contact Builder.

See Chapters 10, 16, and 17 for full details about Journey Builder.

3

Marketing Cloud Builders

Create the component parts of the marketing messages that you'll send to your customers.

Segment your contact list into audiences who will receive a specific message.

Set goals for your marketing communications and use analytics tools to make sure you're progressing toward them.

Automate sending your customers happy birthday messages and other simple communication series.

Chapter **7**

Content Builder

I n this chapter, we discuss the tools for creating and approving content. Content Builder is the central library of all the parts and pieces that go into your online marketing messages. It is the app in Salesforce Marketing Cloud where you store and create all your online marketing assets, such as the following:

» Images

» Videos

» Audio clips

» Code

» Documents

» Text

» Content blocks

» Email templates

» Emails

The Approvals app gives you the option to require approvals for the content that you store in Content Builder. By using this app, you can make sure that your content receives the okay from the right person in your company before subscribers receive it in email.

Currently, email is the only channel of content that can use Content Builder and Approvals. Marketing Cloud plans for all marketing channel apps to store content in Content Builder and process it through the Approvals app.

Using Content Builder

Figure 7-1 shows the Content Builder app. You can get to Content Builder in two ways. One, you can pause your mouse pointer on Content Builder on the app switcher and then click Content Builder. Two, you can click Content on the toolbar in the Email app. Once Marketing Cloud configures Content Builder to work with content from other channels, you'll probably be able to launch it from those apps as well.

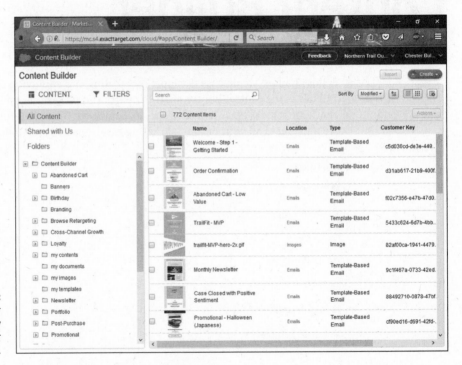

FIGURE 7-1: Content Builder is like a library for all your marketing assets.

Changing the display

You have some options about how you display assets in Content Builder. The light gray toolbar near the top of the app, shown in Figure 7-2, offers the following options:

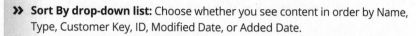

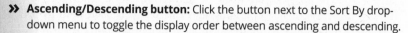

>> **Sort By drop-down list:** Choose whether you see content in order by Name, Type, Customer Key, ID, Modified Date, or Added Date.

>> **Ascending/Descending button:** Click the button next to the Sort By drop-down menu to toggle the display order between ascending and descending.

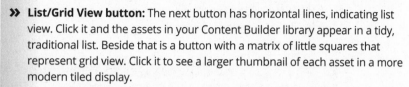

>> **List/Grid View button:** The next button has horizontal lines, indicating list view. Click it and the assets in your Content Builder library appear in a tidy, traditional list. Beside that is a button with a matrix of little squares that represent grid view. Click it to see a larger thumbnail of each asset in a more modern tiled display.

>> **Settings button:** The last button on the toolbar controls what information you see for each asset. Click the button and select or deselect Type, Customer Key, ID, Modified Date, and Added Date.

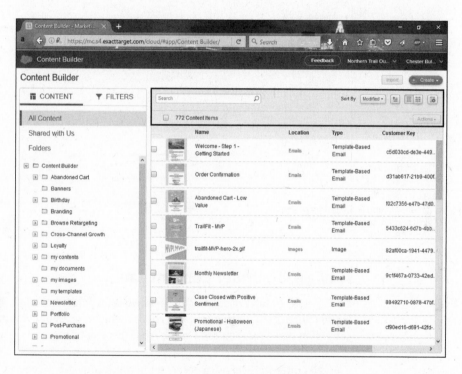

FIGURE 7-2:
Control what you see and how you see it in Content Builder.

TIP

If you access Content Builder from the Email app, a Use Classic Content link appears next to the app name. This link takes you back to the Email app's original content creation tools. Unless you've been using the Email app for a while and have become accustomed to those tools, there's no reason to go backward!

Finding content in Content Builder

The longer you work in Marketing Cloud, the more content you accumulate. It might not take long at all before you need help to find a particular piece of content. Fortunately, Content Builder contains several tools you can use to find what you're looking for. These tools are on the Content tab, the Filter tab, and the search bar, as shown in Figure 7-3.

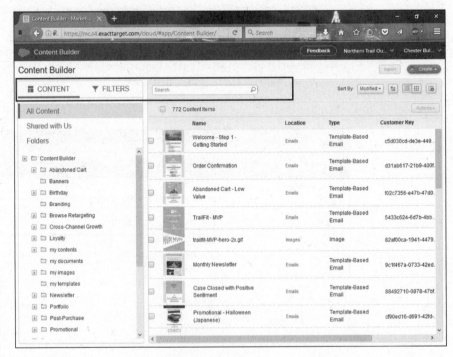

FIGURE 7-3:
This is where you access the tools that help you find content in Content Builder.

Navigation under Content tab

The Content Builder dashboard has a navigation pane on the left. The default view is the Content tab. In that tab, you choose which pieces of content to show in the canvas on the right. You can choose from these options:

>> **All Content:** Every piece of content to which you have access.

>> **Shared with Us:** Only pieces of content that other business units shared with you.

>> **Folders:** Your folder structure, which you can use to navigate to your desired piece of content. Click a folder to see the content in the canvas.

Filters

Next to the Content tab in the navigation pane is a tab called Filters. Click this tab to set criteria for the filter. The content objects that appear in the canvas on the right are those that match the criteria you set up in the filter. For example, the filter in Figure 7-4 causes the system to display all templates and template-based emails in Content Builder.

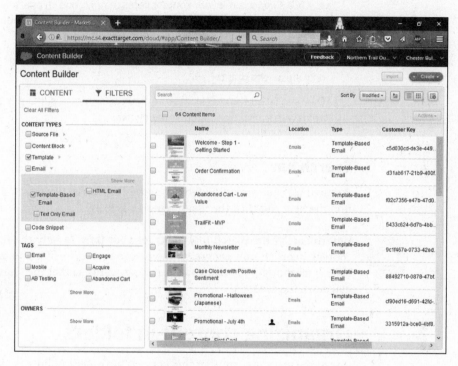

FIGURE 7-4:
This filter surfaces all your email templates and the emails you created using those templates.

You can filter with the following categories:

>> **Content Types:** The following content types are available as filters. If an arrow appears next to the name of a content type, click it to expand the category.

- *Source File:* Choose what kind of file was the source for the content items that you want to find. Examples include Image and Text.

- *Content Block:* Choose the kind of content block you're looking for. Examples include Free Form and Dynamic Content. See more information about content blocks later in this chapter, in the "Creating reusable content blocks" section.

- *Template:* Select the template that is the basis of the email you're looking for. Note that this filter returns not templates but emails based on the template you choose. More information about how you create emails from templates appears later in this chapter, in the "Templates" section.

- *Email:* Narrow the list to emails that are template based, HTML based, or text only.

- *Code Snippet:* Limit your content items to only code snippets. More information about code snippets is available later in this chapter, in the "Creating reusable code snippets" section.

» **Tags:** Select the check box next to a tag to limit the content items you see to only those with that tag.

» **Owners:** Select the check boxes next to one or more usernames to see only items with those users listed as the owner.

Search bar

A search bar appears in the toolbar above the canvas. To search for a term, enter it in the field and click the magnifying glass icon.

TIP

Unfortunately, the search tool looks for your term in only the file names of the content items. If you generally like to use search to find assets, make sure to choose meaningful file names with rich keywords so that the search will work for you down the road.

Organizing content in folders

One of the ways that you can find content in Content Builder is by navigating the folder structure. You collect a lot of content as you use Marketing Cloud, so having a good organizational strategy early can save you a lot of time and headaches later.

Use the following steps to create a folder:

1. **From the Content Builder app, click the Content tab in the left navigation pane.**

2. **Right-click the Content Builder folder and choose Create Folder from the menu that appears.**

   A dialog box appears, prompting you to enter a name for your folder.

3. **Enter a name for your folder and click OK.**

The system creates a folder that is a child folder (subfolder) of the Content Builder folder. You can also right-click another folder and the system will make your new folder a child of it. Regardless of where you create the folder, you can always move it to a new location.

TIP

When you create a folder inside another folder, the folder you create is called the *child* folder. The folder that contains the child is called the *parent*.

To move a folder, use these steps:

1. **From the Content Builder app, click the Content tab in the left navigation pane.**

2. **Right-click the folder you want to move and choose Move Folder from the menu that appears.**

   A window appears, prompting you to choose a new location for your folder.

3. **Select the folder that you want to be the new parent and click OK.**

Importing content from Classic Content

This section is relevant if you began storing content in the Classic Content tool in the Email app and now want to move it to Content Builder. If you don't have content in the old tool that you want to move, you can skip this section.

Any content you already have organized in the Classic Content tool of the Email app does not appear in Content Builder automatically. You have to import that content.

You don't have to import all the content at once, which is a helpful option if you've accumulated old folders in your content libraries that you don't want cluttering up Content Builder. In addition, you don't have to keep the previous organization structure when you import. You can map the folders from the Classic Content tool to new folders that you've already created in Content Builder.

TIP

The Content Builder folders to which you import must already exist, so be sure to follow the steps in the preceding section to create folders before you begin the import. After you begin the import, you can't stop or undo it; so it's worth your effort to put up-front time into the design of your folder structure.

To import content from the Classic Content tool, use these steps:

1. **From the Content Builder app, click the Import button, above the toolbar on the right side of the screen.**

   An Import Assistant window appears to walk you through the steps of importing content.

2. **Follow the instructions in each step of the Import Assistant:**

- *Introduction:* Simply welcomes you to the Import Assistant. Read the content and click Next.

- *Select Method:* Asks whether you want to import your old folder structure along with your assets. Either way, you have the opportunity to select the particular assets to import. Choose an option and click Next.

- *Select Content:* Offers check boxes next to each folder in your Classic Content tool. Select the check boxes next to the folders that contain the content you want to import. If you selected Content Only in the Select Method step, this step also offers the ability to choose the destination folder. When you're ready, click Import.

TIP

  The system moves everything you import to the same folder, so if you want to import to multiple folders in Content Builder, you must execute the Import Assistant once for each folder.

- *Import Progress:* Shows the progress of the import process. Depending on how many assets you chose to import, this process could take quite a while. You don't need to keep the Import Assistant open during the entire import. It will finish the import in the background and notify you when it is complete.

Uploading content outside Marketing Cloud

You create many kinds of content directly in Content Builder, as described in later sections of this chapter. But some kinds of content — especially images, videos, audio clips, and documents that you send as attachments — you create in other tools outside Marketing Cloud and then upload to Content Builder.

To upload a file, use these steps:

1. **From the Content Builder app, navigate to the folder that will contain the uploaded file.**

   You can move the file later if you need to.

2. **Click the Create button (above the toolbar on the right side of the screen) and choose Upload from the menu that appears.**

   A window appears to allow you to navigate your computer to find the files you want to import.

3. **Select the file that you want to upload and click Open.**

As shown in Figure 7-5, a box appears as a preview of the file to upload. The box contains a *Pending Upload and Publish* message. Not coincidentally, an Upload and Publish button appears above the preview box.

4. **Click Upload and Publish.**

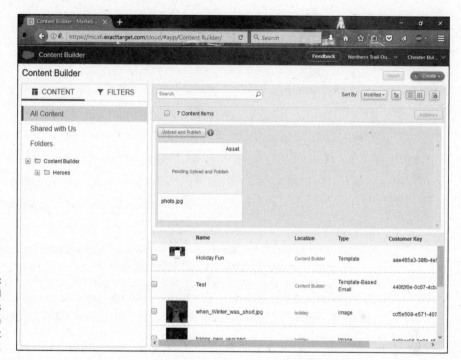

FIGURE 7-5:
Clicking Upload and Publish is the only action you can take at this point.

TECHNICAL STUFF

Salesforce Marketing Cloud uses a third-party content delivery service that specializes in delivering your assets quickly and reliably when your subscriber's email client requests them from the server. By clicking Upload and Publish, you're instructing Marketing Cloud to send your assets to that content delivery service.

Managing content in Content Builder

Content Builder enables you to perform several actions on a piece of content. One method is to use the Actions menu, which appears on the far right of the Content Builder toolbar, as shown in Figure 7-6. You use this menu when you want to move or delete multiple pieces of content at once. Select the check box on each item you want to move or delete, and then click Move or Delete on the Actions menu.

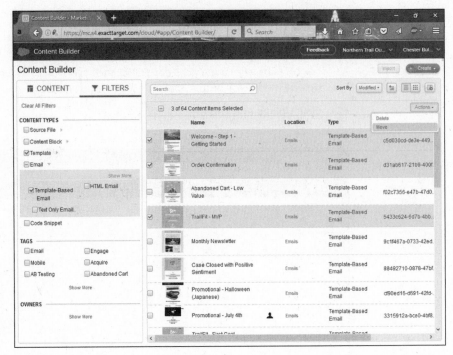

FIGURE 7-6:
Select the check box next to multiple pieces of content to move or delete them at the same time.

You can also use the down-arrow button on each piece of content to display a drop-down menu. This menu provides the Move and Delete actions plus a lot more. In the grid view of the content (see Figure 7-7, left), the button appears near the bottom of the icon for the piece of content. In the list view (see Figure 7-7, right), the button appears on the far right of the row.

FIGURE 7-7:
The button where you can find the actions menu in both the grid and the list view.

The drop-down menu on a piece of content has the following options: Edit, View Properties, Share, Replace, Duplicate, and Delete.

Edit

The Edit option opens the piece of content in the editing tools for you to edit. This option is only for content you build in the builder, such as emails, templates, and content blocks. It is not available for files you upload, such as images.

View Properties

The View Properties option displays a window that shows you the following details about the content:

>> **The file name of the content.** You can change the file name here by clicking the current name and typing a new name in its place.

>> **The folder where the content resides.** From this screen, you can move the piece of content to a different folder by clicking the current location and selecting a new location.

>> **Whether the content has been shared with other business units.** You can also share the content from this screen by clicking the Share link.

>> **The ID number Marketing Cloud assigned to the content.**

>> **The customer key.** You assign this unique value to the piece of content, and then use the key to refer to the content from API scripts that you write. You can edit the customer key value here by clicking the current value and changing it.

>> **Tags, which are keywords that you assign to a piece of content.** You can filter or search for content based on tags. You can also add tags to a piece of content from this screen by clicking the Add Item link.

>> **The content owner.** This value defaults to the user who created or uploaded the piece of content. You can change this value by clicking the current owner and selecting a different one.

>> **The date and time the piece of content was last modified and by whom.**

>> **The date and time the piece of content was created and by whom.**

>> **The description you entered when you created or uploaded the piece of content.**

>> **The static URL of the piece of content.** You can click the Copy button to copy the URL to your clipboard so you can reference the piece of content in HTML.

Share

If your Marketing Cloud account has multiple business units, you can use the Share option to share a piece of content with other business units. Select the Shared radio button to display the tool you use for sharing, as shown in Figure 7-8.

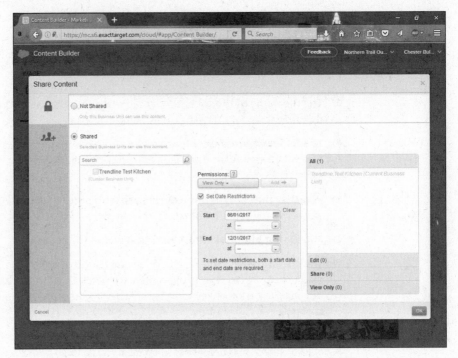

FIGURE 7-8:
Use sharing to
make your most
awesome content
available for
other business
units to use.

To share the piece of content, follow these steps:

1. **In the box on the left, click the business unit with which you want to share the piece of content.**

2. **In the Permissions drop-down menu, choose a value.**

   You can choose All, Edit, Share, or View Only. The value you choose determines what the people in the business unit can do with this piece of content.

3. **If you want to make the piece of content available to other business units for only a set period, select the Set Date Restrictions check box.**

   A panel appears where you can choose the start date and time and the end date and time of the period when you want the content to be available to the business unit.

4. **Click Add.**

The business unit appears in the box on the right. The box on the right contains panels for All, Edit, Share, and View Only so you can see which business units have each level of permission with this piece of content.

Move

Select the Move option to change where you store this content in the Content Builder folder structure.

Replace

The Replace option is only for content you upload to Content Builder, such as images and video. Using this option, you can replace the file with an updated version of the same file. Any email or template that contains this content automatically displays the updated version. This option is not available for content items that you build in the builder, such as emails, templates, and content areas.

Duplicate

Use the Duplicate option to create a copy of the piece of content in the same folder.

Delete

Choose the Delete option to delete the piece of content permanently. Beware! If the piece of content appears in any of your emails, it will disappear from those emails.

Images and More

Images are simple in Content Builder because the hard work of creating excellent images happens well before you upload them to Marketing Cloud. The same is true for videos, audio clips, and other kinds of documents you might want to upload, such as PDFs. You just upload your finished files to Content Builder, and they are available for you to use when you're creating your email templates and messages.

To upload files to Content Builder, use the steps in the previous section "Uploading Content outside Marketing Cloud." After uploading the files, you can use any of the procedures discussed in the preceding section, "Managing content in Content Builder."

Templates

Content Builder takes the place of the old template creation tools that were available via the Email app. The template editor screen in Content Builder is shown in Figure 7-9.

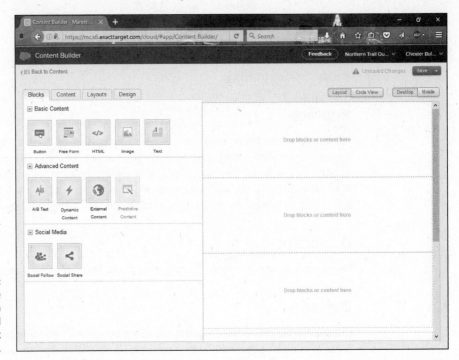

FIGURE 7-9:
A template
ensures that a
series of related
emails look
related.

An email template is a starting point for your email messages. The template contains multiple content areas where you can drag and drop images, content blocks, or other kinds of content. You can save time and ensure consistency across email messages by filling in some of those content areas on the template with boilerplate options.

Use these steps to create a template:

1. **From the Content Builder app, navigate to the folder that will contain the template.**

   You can move the template later if you need to.

2. **Click the Create button (above the toolbar on the right side of the screen) and point to Template. Choose one of the following options from the flyout menu that appears:**

   - *Paste HTML:* If you're skilled with HTML and become accustomed to the conventions used in Marketing Cloud, you can paste HTML into an editor window to create customized templates.

   - *From Existing Template:* Beginners should choose this option. Marketing Cloud offers numerous layouts that you can use as the basis of your template. The following steps in this procedure assume that you chose this option.

3. **From the list of layouts that appears, click the one that you want to use, and then click Select.**

   The template appears for you to edit.

4. **Create *boilerplates,* those sections of the template that you want to be the same for every email message that uses this template.**

   For example, you might choose the image that appears at the top and add a button to share the email on Twitter somewhere near the bottom, but leave the middle section to populate when you create the individual emails.

   See Chapter 11 for information on how to create an email from a template.

Messages

Email is the only message type currently available to create and manage in Content Builder. Sending an email message is a multistep process. You might jump right into creating an email, but you'll probably create a template and reusable content — content blocks and code snippets — to go inside that template before you even start the email itself. Beyond that, sending the email is a separate process.

The following sections describe how to create the content blocks and code snippets that you can reuse across multiple templates and emails. See Chapter 11 for information on creating emails.

Creating reusable content blocks

Email and email templates are comprised of content areas arranged in different layouts, depending on the template. You can drag content blocks to those content areas, as shown in Figure 7-10. Reusable content blocks store content that you want to use in multiple emails and email templates.

To create a reusable content block, use these steps:

1. **From the Content Builder app, navigate to the folder that will contain the content block.**

   You can move the content block later if you need to.

2. **Click the Create button (above the toolbar on the right side of the screen) and point to Content Block.**

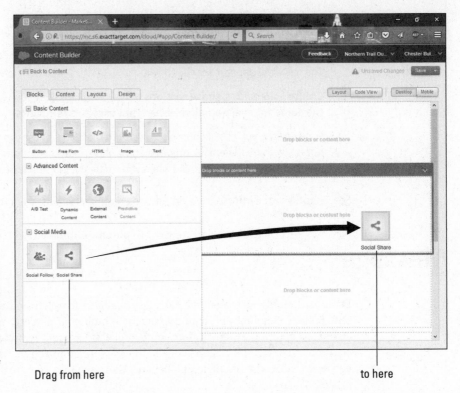

FIGURE 7-10:
Dragging a reusable content block in to a content area makes creating an email the easiest part of the process.

Drag from here   to here

3. **Click the type of content block you want to create from the flyout menu that appears:**

- *Free Form:* Enter anything you want. This is a blank slate where you can feel free to include all kinds of content, such as text, HTML, or images.

- *Text:* Type text only.

- *HTML:* Paste HTML that you created in an outside tool.

- *Image:* Choose an image. Using an image-only content block in an email or a template is similar to using an image, but you have more control. For example, you can add a hyperlink to the image in the content block.

- *A/B Test:* Select two pieces of content to compare and determine which performs better. Marketing Cloud tracks the number of subscriber clicks for each piece of content.

- *Dynamic Content:* Create rules to show a different piece of content based on information you have about the subscriber. For example, you could set up a dynamic content block to show an image from the subscriber's state of residence.

- *Social Share:* Invite the subscriber to share the email on social media.

- *Social Follow:* Encourage the subscriber to follow you on social media.

- *Button:* Create a hyperlink that looks like a button.

- *Layout:* Choose a mini template within the content block. For example, you can create a have a two- or three-column layout for the content block, and then enter text or images in those columns.

- *External Content:* Pull information from your website or other external source. For example, you could create a web page that always has the latest headlines about your company. Then you can pull the content from that web page into your content area when you send the email.

4. **Use the editing tools to create the content in your content block.**

    See more information about the editing tools in Chapter 11.

5. **Click Save, on the right side of the toolbar.**

Creating reusable code snippets

When you're using the HTML editor tools to create an entire email, populate a content area within an email, or develop an email template, you have an option on the toolbar to Insert Code Snippet. When you choose this toolbar option, a drop-down list appears with several code snippets that were delivered with your Marketing Cloud account. The drop-down list also contains code snippets that you've created in your account.

Follow these steps to create a reusable code snippet that you can later insert using the Insert Code Snippet toolbar option:

1. **From the Content Builder app, navigate to the folder that will contain the code snippet.**

    You can move the code snippet later if you need to.

2. **Click the Create button (above the toolbar on the right side of the screen) and point to Code Snippet.**

3. **Paste the code into the editor window or upload the code.**

4. **Click Save, on the right side of the toolbar.**

Approvals

This Approvals app lets you create an *approval workflow*, a simple review and approval process for your content. You can get to the Approvals app from the Content Builder category on the app switcher, as shown in Figure 7-11. You can also get to Approvals from any screen where you create an email or from the Content Builder grid.

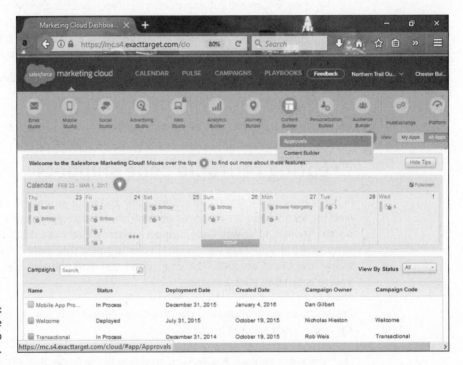

FIGURE 7-11:
Getting to the Approvals app dashboard.

As of this writing, the Approvals app works only with email-related content, though the plan is to make it work with content related to other communication channels in the future. The Approvals app is not available in your account by default: You have to contact your account executive to have it turned on. There may be an additional charge for using this app.

How the Approvals app works

The Approvals app is a relatively uncomplicated tool. You can choose to create one of two kinds of workflow:

- » A **standard workflow** incorporates three kinds of roles:

  - A *submitter,* who creates the content and submits it for approval. A submitter can perform test sends of emails before approval but not actual live sends.

  - One or more *reviewers,* who look over the content and then give it the okay or send it back with annotations to the submitter.

  - An *approver,* who looks over reviewed content and provides the final approval.

- » A **two-step workflow** combines the reviewer and the approver functions so that the person doing the reviewing is also the one to give the final okay.

Throughout this process, the system generates notifications that pass back and forth among the submitter, reviewers, and approver. If approved content is edited, it goes back to submitted status, at which point the approval process starts again.

When you turn on this functionality in your account, every message must receive approval before it is sent. You cannot choose which emails are subject to the approval process.

After you turn on your approval workflow, you see the progress of your emails through the workflow on the Approvals dashboard. Emails that have been submitted but not approved appear on the In Progress tab, and approved emails appear on the Approved tab.

Setting up an approval workflow

After you contact your Marketing Cloud representatives to enable the Approvals app in your account, you have to set up the users, set up the workflow, and turn it on. Figure 7-12 shows an example workflow setup.

REMEMBER

Don't forget to warn all your Marketing Cloud users before you turn on your approvals workflow. After you turn it on, it affects every single email in your account.

Use the following steps to set up your approval workflow:

1. **From anywhere in Marketing Cloud, pause your mouse pointer over your name on the right side of the toolbar and click Administration.**

2. **On the Applications menu in the toolbar, select Approvals.**

   The Approvals screen appears.

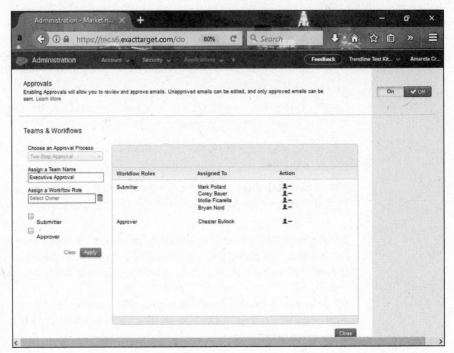

FIGURE 7-12:
In this two-step
approval
workflow, many
people can
submit content
but only Chester
can approve it.

3. Click the Create a Team button.

4. Choose your approval process type.

Decide whether you want a standard approval process (the one with separate reviewers and approvers) or a two-step approval process (the one where the approver does the reviewing as well).

5. Enter a team name.

After you enter a team name and move on to the next field, the system saves the team and you can no longer change the type of approval process that you selected in Step 4.

6. Add members to the team.

a. *In the Assign a Workflow Role field, begin entering the name of a user. Then click the correct name in the list of suggestions that appears.*

b. *Select one or more check boxes next to the role or roles you want to assign that user.*

c. *Click these steps for each user involved in the workflow.*

The name of the user appears in the grid on the right side of the screen so you can see which users you've already assigned.

7. **(Optional) After assigning roles, click the On button (on the right side of the screen) to make the workflow process effective for all emails in the account.**

You might want to wait to turn on the workflow if you need to update the user's permissions.

8. **Click Close.**

As you can see, the meat of the work to set up your approval workflow is assigning users to roles. A user must have certain user permissions to participate in the approval workflow. Use the procedures for editing users in Chapter 3 to make sure all users mentioned in your workflow have the following permissions:

>> Approval ➪ Approval Items ➪ Add/Remove Users

>> Approval ➪ Approval Items ➪ Create and Edit

>> Approval ➪ Approval Items ➪ Delete

Who should use the Approvals app?

One of our clients is a national restaurant chain with hundreds of locations, most of them corporate-owned but many franchised. The chain hired a separate agency to design content for the franchised locations when they did local promotions.

The designs of the separate agency had to be approved by corporate before the emails were sent to subscribers. The Approvals app made it easy for the agency to submit its designs for approval and helped the restaurant chain keep an eye on all its messaging and make sure it reflected well on the brand.

The Approvals apps is helpful for large, dispersed companies that need technology to enforce rules about who has to see content before it arrives in subscribers' email inboxes. Approvals is not a tool for everyone, though, and it doesn't completely address the need for approval processes.

Shortly after the Approvals tool was introduced, we tried turning it on for a smaller client and quickly discovered that it can create an unnecessary bottleneck. You probably don't need the Approvals app if the following two items apply to you:

>> Your marketing effort is small and centralized

>> Just dropping someone a note to look over your message content before you send it has been working so far

WARNING

Very importantly, the workflow in Approvals reviews *only content*. During the process of submitting content for review, the submitter does choose an audience, but the email is not limited to that audience after approval. The Approvals app does not have steps to ensure that the audience, the send date, or the send time are what you want.

WARNING

Even if you decide to use the Approvals app, you'll still need a separate process to make sure your emails are going to the right people at the right time.

Chapter **8**

Audience Builder and Contact Builder

Contact Builder and Audience Builder, the apps that appear under the Audience Builder category on the app switcher, are the future of the data model for keeping and finding information about the people who are the target of your marketing campaigns.

The first app we talk about in this chapter, Contact Builder, is still a young addition to Salesforce Marketing Cloud, but it's important to get the most out of Journey Builder. You can read more about Journey Builder in Chapters 10, 16, and 17.

Marketing Cloud designed Audience Builder to handle the variety and complexity of contact data. Even if you have millions of contacts and manage hundreds of attributes about each one, Audience Builder can tell you, in real time, how many of your subscribers meet the filter criteria you set up. Marketers use Audience Builder to investigate the composition of their subscriber lists, analyze customer behavior, and create lists for sending marketing messages.

Contact Builder

Contact Builder is the data hub of Marketing Cloud, through which data moves back and forth between other apps, as well as back and forth with other integrated systems, such as your customer relationship management (CRM) system. Through Contact Builder, you have a single, centralized place where you can see all the data you have about each person in your database.

Contact Builder is not just a viewing tool, though. It includes tools that you can use to create and manage the sophisticated database structures that you design when you imagine your data model (see Chapters 5 and 6).

TIP

At the time of this writing, Marketing Cloud had not yet fully integrated Contact Builder into all the Marketing Cloud apps where it will eventually be useful. Its primary practical use is to create attribute groups that Journey Builder (Chapters 10, 16, and 17) uses. Mobile Connect (Chapter 12) also uses Contact Builder for list management. Plus, you can use it as an alternative method to create data extensions (Chapter 6) that you use in your Email app (Chapter 11).

Menus

You open Contact Builder by pausing your mouse pointer on the Audience Builder category in the app switcher and choosing Contact Builder. Contact Builder appears, open to the first menu option: Data Designer. The other menu options are All Contacts, Data Sources, Data Extensions, Imports, and Contacts Configuration.

Data Designer

Data Designer contains a visual representation of all your attribute groups. Each attribute group appears as a spoke off the center Contacts hub, as shown in Figure 8-1. From this screen, you can create new attribute groups.

By default, Data Designer shows you attribute groups, but you can switch to see events and populations by clicking the links in the white toolbar near the top of the screen.

The events view is where you can define an event data extension for the Marketing Cloud API to use. The API is a set of developer tools that programmers can use to make Marketing Cloud functionality available to external systems. The API is outside the scope of this book.

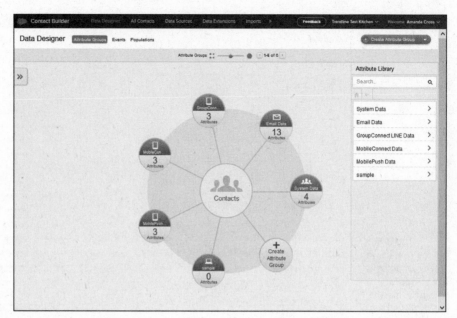

FIGURE 8-1:
Attribute groups
appear as
spokes off the
Contacts hub.

The Populations view is where you can associate a master data extension that holds a very large number of a particular type of contact to the All Contacts list. For example, you could create a data extension of all customers and another one of all prospects, and then set up each as a population to make the columns in the data extension available to Journey Builder. Salesforce recommends that you create no more than two or three populations. In any event, now that audiences are the recommended journey entry method, the concept of a population is less significant.

All Contacts

The All Contacts screen, shown in Figure 8-2, displays all the contacts in your account. You can search for a particular contact or filter the entire population using the filter options on the left.

TIP

You can click the Contact Key value to see more details about a contact, including all the messages you sent the contact up to the past 365 days. For each message, you can see whether the contact opened or clicked any links in the message. This view of data is much more robust than the one you get by looking up a subscriber's history using the properties available from the Email app's All Subscribers list.

Data Sources

You can use data sources when integrating Marketing Cloud with other Salesforce platform accounts, such as Service Cloud. However, integrations are outside the scope of this book, so we'll skip this menu.

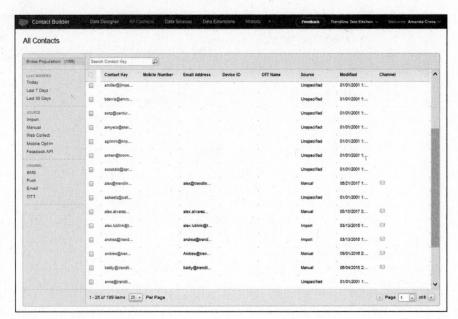

Data Extensions

The Data Extensions screen is similar to the screens you use to work with data extensions in the Email app. You can access existing data extensions, build new ones, and import or export data.

Looking at a list of data extensions through Contact Builder versus Email differs somewhat. If you're accustomed to using the Email app to manage data extensions, you'll immediately notice that the number of rows doesn't appear next to the name of the data extension. You have to use the detail view of the data extension to see the row count.

However, there are advantages to accessing data extensions through Contact Builder. From the record view tab, you can search in the data extension as long as the data extension has a primary key value set (see Chapter 6). Additionally, you have to view your data extensions through Contact Builder if you want to

>> Edit a selected row.

>> Clear (delete) a selected row.

>> Manually add additional rows.

These options can be tremendous time-savers when creating data for testing.

Imports

The Imports screen offers identical functionality to the Import File activity available in Automation Studio. See Chapter 10 for information about the Import File activity and Automation Studio.

Contacts Configuration

The Contacts Configuration menu contains some configuration settings that control how the system deals with contacts that have more than one email address. At this point in your experience with Marketing Cloud, it's probably best to use the default settings. Even after you're very experienced, you'll almost always use the defaults here anyway.

Contacts

TIP

The concepts we talk about in this section rely heavily on the relational data model concepts introduced in Chapter 6. If you're not already comfortable throwing around terms like *data extension* and *primary key,* you should review that chapter before you proceed.

Contact Builder is, intuitively enough, where you build contacts. In this context, a *contact* is a person whom you keep data about. It might be a person who has subscribed to your emails, someone who receives your SMS messages, or a prospect who doesn't receive any communications from you.

Marketing Cloud parlance refers to making the contact the central concept of your database design as using a *contact model* or a *person model.* As opposed to thinking about your data as a bunch of channel-specific lists that contain people, you think of it as a bunch of people with whom you communicate in various ways.

In a person-model data structure, each person has a row in the All Contacts list. That row contains a unique identifier, the Contact Key, for the person. Other fields, called attributes, in the All Contacts list contain demographic information and contact information.

You may have data extensions that contain information about the person, such as which lists they have subscribed to or what orders they have placed. In those data extensions, a Subscriber Key identifies the person. For the system to know that the Subscriber Key in the Orders data extension is the same as the Contact Key in the All Contacts list, you need to create a relationship between the two.

Relationships and cardinality

Data Designer is the feature in Contact Builder where you create relationships between data extensions. An *attribute group* is the result when you create relationships among multiple data extensions.

When you create an attribute group, you choose a data extension that contains the Contact Key field or another data field that matches a value in the Contacts list. You indicate which fields correspond to each other in each data extension and set the cardinality.

The *cardinality* of the relationship is a description of how many of the values you can expect to find in that data extension. In Marketing Cloud, the cardinality can be one to one, one to many, or many to many.

In a *one-to-one relationship*, a single row of data in one data extension corresponds to a single row of data in another data extension. For example, if you created a separate data extension to contain your contacts' email subscription preferences, it would have a one-to-one relationship with the All Contacts list. The All Contacts list and the Email Subscriptions data extension each contain no more than one row for each contact.

In a *one-to-many relationship*, a single row of data in one data extension corresponds to one or multiple rows in the other data extension. For example, in a data extension that contains an order history, the contact may appear many times, depending on how many times the contact ordered from you.

In a *many-to-many relationship*, you can match on multiple instances of data occurring in both data extensions. For example, your order history data extension containing the details of multiple orders for a contact could be matched to a data extension that contains more details about the items included in each order.

You can add more than one data extension to your attribute group. For example, your Orders data extension can connect back to the Contacts data extension using the Contact ID but also connect to a ZIP code look-up table using a ZIP code value. If you needed any fields from the ZIP code look-up table to use in your Journey Builder journeys, you would need to make sure to include the data extension in an attribute group this way.

Creating attribute groups

To link data extensions in an attribute group, you must first establish a one-to-one relationship between the Contacts data extension and your data extension. From there, you can add additional data extensions as you need them.

WARNING

You must add a data extension to an attribute group before the data in that data extension is available to Journey Builder's filters as contact data.

Use the following steps to link data extensions:

1. **In Data Designer, click Create Attribute Group.**

   You can click either the button on the top right or the Create Attribute Group spoke on the data map. The Create New Attribute Group window appears.

2. **Name your new attribute group and choose an icon to represent the attribute group on the data map.**

3. **Click Create.**

   A workspace appears with the Contacts data extension already available on the left side of the workspace.

4. **Click Link Data Extension.**

   The Link Data Extension window appears with your Contacts fields on the left (under the Customer Data heading) and a navigation tree on the right.

TIP

   You can create a new data extension from this screen if the one you want to link doesn't exist. Click Create New Data Extension instead of Link Data Extensions.

5. **Navigate to the data extension that you want to link and click it.**

   A list of the columns in that data extension appears on the right.

6. **Click the fields from each list that correspond to each other.**

7. **Select One in the drop-down list next to the name of each data extension.**

   The system doesn't restrict you from using a one-to-many relationship, but the initial mapping of a data extension to the contact record should always be a one-to-one relationship. A typical use case would be to link the email address or subscriber key from your data extension to the Contact ID field in Contacts.

8. **Click Save.**

   The screen shows a representation of the data extension with a linked path connecting it to Contacts.

You can add an additional data extension to the attribute group by clicking the link icon with a plus sign that appears on the right side of the data extension and then repeating the mapping sequence just described.

After you add a data extension to an attribute group, you can no longer edit the data extension in the Email app. You must make any updates, including adding fields, from the Data Extensions link in Contact Builder. If a data extension is part of an attribute group, it must be removed from that attribute group to delete a field. This can have consequences to your data model, especially if Journey Builder is using the data extension, so deleting fields isn't recommended.

Audience Builder

Audience Builder starts with your entire population of contacts for a channel. You add filters to limit that population based on the contacts' attribute values and ultimately build an *audience.* For example, you can create a filter to cut the population of all the contacts for whom you have email addresses to only the contacts who live in Indiana.

You might use Audience Builder for data analysis, in which case the audience you build might never leave Audience Builder. However, if you want to send a message to an audience, you need to publish the audience. Some Marketing Cloud users like to use the feature in Audience Builder that shows a real-time count of contacts that satisfy the filter criteria to continue filtering only until the audience contains the desired number of subscribers to receive a particular email promotion.

Audience Builder deals with contacts, not subscribers. Whereas a subscriber has made a point of indicating a willingness to receive messages from you, a contact can be anyone about whom you have contact information. Whenever you create an audience that you intend to use for sending, make sure to include filter criteria to limit the list to only those people who have said they want to receive messages from you.

When you publish your audience, Marketing Cloud takes a snapshot of the data for the contacts in the audience at that moment and puts it in a data extension for you to use for sending. See Chapter 6 for more information on data extensions.

Because the published audience is just a snapshot of the contact data, any updates to the contact after you publish don't appear in the data extension with the audience data. You need to update your audience if you want to have the latest data.

Audience Builder requires substantial setup initially, but Marketing Cloud has a special team dedicated to configuring the data. You can choose among a variety of dimension packages that make specific contact attributes available to use in Audience Builder. In addition, your own contact attributes appear in Audience Builder. The experience of using Audience Builder is specific and personalized for each account.

Dashboard

You get to Audience Builder by clicking Audience Builder from the app switcher. The first screen you see is the dashboard, shown in Figure 8-3.

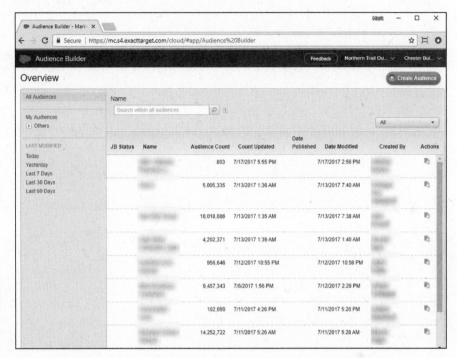

FIGURE 8-3: The dashboard offers an overview of the audiences you've already created.

On the Audience Builder dashboard, you see all your existing audiences. For each audience, you see the following:

>> Name of the audience

>> Number of subscribers in the audience

>> Date and time of the last update of the contact data in the audience

>> Date and time the audience was published

>> Date and time of the most recent changes to the filter rules that define the audience

>> User who created the audience

An Actions column also appears on this screen. This column contains buttons you can use to edit the audience or create a copy that you can modify without affecting the original.

Audience workspace

When you create a new audience or open an existing audience to edit, you see several tabs, as shown in Figure 8-4.

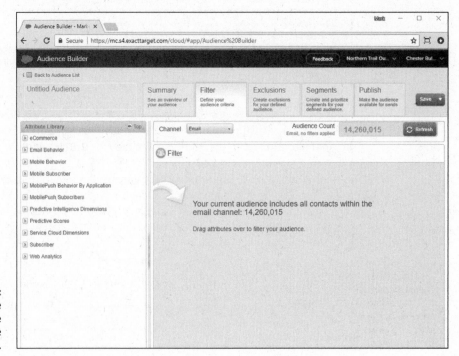

The following tabs contain tools you use to create your audience:

» **Summary:** Information about the audience itself, such as its creation date and who created it. You don't use this tab when creating an audience; the system populates it with information about the audience. You can refer to it later when you need a quick overview.

» **Filter:** The canvas where you create the audience. This tab is the most important one because this is where you define the filter criteria that narrow down your entire population to just the contacts whom you want to target. The attributes that you set up in your particular account appear in the Attribute Library on the left, and you drag them into the work area on the right to filter based on that attribute.

» **Exclusions:** The canvas where you choose contacts to leave out of the audience. For example, you could create a filter that includes all contacts in Indiana, and then create an exclusion to suppress all contacts with an email address that matches your competitor's company name.

>> **Segments:** The canvas where you divide the audience into subsections. You can use the segments for things such as A/B testing.

>> **Publish:** The tool to take a snapshot of the data for the contacts in the audience, put it in a data extension, and make the data extension available for other apps to use. For example, you might publish an audience so that your email app can send an email using the email addresses in the published audience data extension.

The tabs act as a wizard to take you through each step of the process of creating an audience and making it available for apps in Marketing Cloud to use.

The Filter, Exclusions, and Segments tabs use a canvas where you can drag attributes from the Attribute Library on the left into the workspace on the right. Some attributes are preconfigured, but usually the Edit Criteria window appears.

Although the fields in this window may vary depending on the nature of the attribute you select, generally you enter the value that you want the attribute to equal. For example, to filter your audience to include only contacts in Indiana, you drag the State attribute to the workspace and use the Edit Criteria window to indicate that State must equal IN for a contact to be included in the audience.

When you save the Edit Criteria window, Audience Builder immediately applies the filter to let you know how many contacts met the criteria. While the system is calculating, an updating icon appears next to the count on the Filter tab. When the calculation is complete, the updated number appears and a green check mark replaces the orange updating icon, as shown in Figure 8-5.

When you add more than one attribute to the canvas, an AND button appears to the right of both attributes to indicate that only contacts who match both criteria appear in the audience. You can click the AND button to change it to OR or INC (includes).

You can reorder the attributes on the canvas. Click an attribute and drag it to the new position in the list. Reordering is particularly relevant on the Segments tab because the system adds the contact to the first segment for which the contact qualifies. For example, if you created one segment for all email subscribers and a second for only email subscribers in Indiana, none of the contacts would make it to the Indiana segment because they all already qualified for the first segment. Instead, move the more restrictive segment to be first so it can contain some contacts and the rest can end up in the all-subscribers segment.

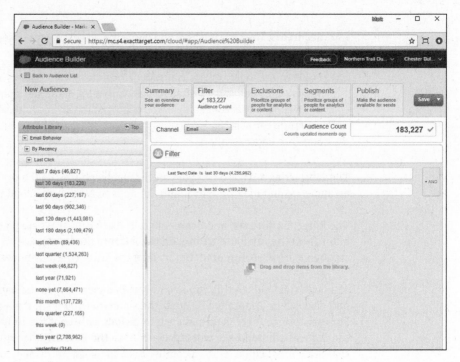

FIGURE 8-5:
The system has
calculated the
number of
contacts in your
audience.

Creating an audience

Use the following steps to create an audience:

1. **From the Audience Builder overview screen, click the Create Audience button.**

   The Audience Builder canvas appears with the Filter tab open.

2. **Click the words Untitled Audience (in the upper-left corner) and type a name for your audience. Then click Done.**

3. **Select the channel of contacts that you want to start with.**

   Choose a value from the Channel drop-down menu near the top of the screen.

4. **In the Attribute Library on the left, navigate to the attribute you want to use in your filter.**

   You may need to open multiple categories to find the attribute that you want. The exact attributes and attribute categories that you see in the Attribute Library vary depending on your Audience Builder configuration.

5. **Click the attribute in the Attribute Library and drag it to the workspace on the right side of the screen.**

TIP

If a number in parentheses appears next to the attribute name, the attribute is preconfigured and you can skip to Step 8. The number indicates how many contacts satisfy that filter.

6. **Complete the Edit Criteria window that appears, and click Done.**

7. **Repeat Step 6 for as many filter criteria as you want to add to the audience.**

8. **Click the Exclusions tab.**

9. **In the Attribute Library, click each attribute that you want to exclude from the audience, and drag the attribute to the workspace. Click Done.**

TIP

You may need to click the Refresh button that appears above the workspace, on the right side of the screen, to see the updated audience count after applying your exclusion. The number of contacts excluded by the exclusion criteria that you added appears on the right side, as shown in Figure 8-6.

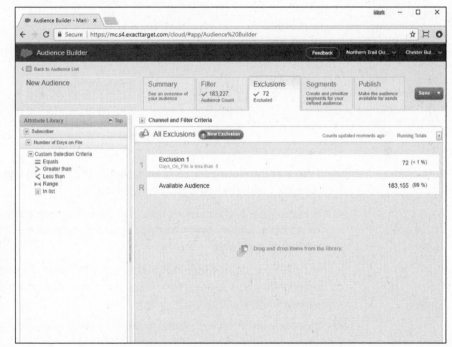

FIGURE 8-6:
The number of contacts excluded by a filter criterion can give you an idea of whether your exclusions are too restrictive.

10. Click the Segments tab.

11. Click the New Segment button.

The Segments workspace appears with the Segments tab open, as shown in Figure 8-7.

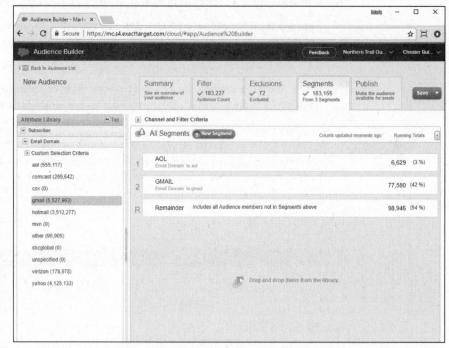

FIGURE 8-7:
The Segments workspace is a mini-dashboard, where you can see the list of segments you already created, edit the segment definitions, and create new segments.

12. If you want to name your segments, click in the field and replace Segment 1 with the name you want to use.

13. As in the Filter and Exclusions tabs, click and drag each attribute from the Attribute Library to the workspace and complete the Edit Criteria window, if applicable.

You may need to click the Refresh button to see how many contacts from the audience qualify for this segment. The number of contacts in the segment appears on the Segments tab.

14. Click Done after you've finished defining the first segment.

Alternately, if you want another segment, repeat Steps 11–14.

15. **Click the Publish tab.**

A summary of the audience definition appears, as shown in Figure 8-8.

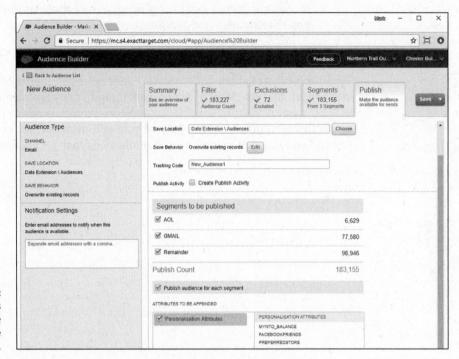

FIGURE 8-8:
Check the details
of your audience
definition before
publishing it.

16. **Complete the fields on the Publish tab.**

- *Save Location:* Choose the folder where you want to save the audience.

- *Save Behavior:* Select the option of overwriting the records in existing data extensions or generating new data extensions.

- *Tracking Code:* Enter a value to use to track this audience. When the system generates the data extension with the audience, this value appears in a column in the data extension.

- *Publish Activity:* Select this box to create a publish activity for the audience. Later, you can schedule the publish activity by adding a Publish Audience activity to a step in Automation Studio. (See Chapter 10 for details on Automation Studio.) Each time the automation runs, the system will republish the audience.

- *Segments to be published check boxes:* If you've created multiple segments as part of the audience setup, you use these boxes to select which ones to publish.

- *Attributes to be appended:* Choose which contact attributes you want the system to include in the data extension.

17. **Click Save and Publish.**

Together, Contact Builder and Audience Builder give you control of all the data you store about the people with whom your brand communicates online. Contact Builder is where you put the data in; Audience Builder is where you get the data out. With this information safely stored but easily available, you are ready to focus on excellent, targeted marketing communications that get measurable results.

Chapter **9**

Analytics and Personalization Builder

Management guru Peter Drucker is famously quoted as saying, "you can't manage what you can't measure." Your company has essential business goals that your online marketing campaigns need to address. Analytics are key to managing those campaigns and making sure that you're accomplishing those goals.

Whether it's to prove that your campaigns are reaching the right potential clients, to demonstrate that your work is driving new business, or just to help your higher-ups feel good about the money that your company is already putting into your projects, you need powerful analytic tools.

Salesforce Marketing Cloud has always provided a robust suite of reports you can use to measure and manage your efforts. Recently, it has also introduced an interactive reporting tool. We discuss both the interactive reporting tool and the traditional reports in this chapter. We also briefly touch on the predictive analytics capabilities of Marketing Cloud.

Discovering Discover

Discover is the feature name for the interactive reporting tool in Marketing Cloud. Essentially, it helps you easily modify existing reports or design your own reports to get at exactly the analytics you need.

To get to Discover, log in to your Salesforce Marketing Cloud account, pause your mouse pointer over Analytics Builder, and select Reports from the list that appears. Discover reports and Standard reports are available in the same catalog, but you can filter based on whether a report is a Discover report.

TIP

If you've used other business intelligence tools, the design and functionality of the Discover interface will be familiar: You drag and drop combinations of data attributes and measures onto a table layout canvas. The data attributes can be things such as dates, device types, and segments; the measures are things such as counts, rates, and actions. Figure 9-1 shows a sample of the lists of fields you can use and the canvas where you drop them.

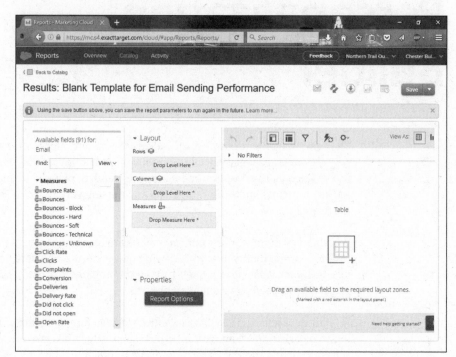

FIGURE 9-1:
The Discover canvas.

Modifying an existing report

Adjusting an existing report template for your own needs is an easier way to begin using the Discover tool. Report templates are included in Discover that can help you get started. You can change the parameters that control how the report works and also the look and feel of the report to really make it your own.

To start getting to know the Discover feature, try practicing with the Discover version of a standard report that you already understand. The Recent Send Summary report is a good choice. This report displays detailed statistics about email sends over the last 30 days, and people use it to identify trends in audience behavior in response to their email sends.

You can find the Recent Send Summary report in the Report catalog. Click Catalog on the toolbar at the top of the screen. You can use the search field or the filters to help you find the right report. Make sure you open the version with the cube icon, which indicates that the report is a Discover report. Figure 9-2 shows the search field and filters in the Report catalog.

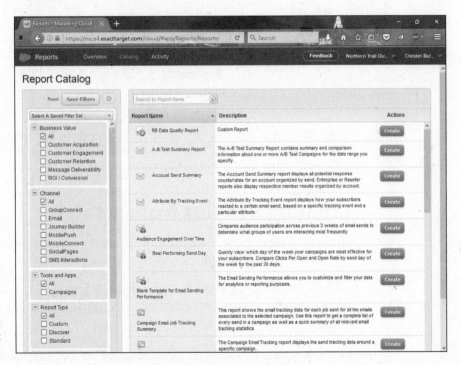

FIGURE 9-2:
The Report Catalog screen.

Looking at a standard report like Recent Send Summary gives you an idea of how a report is structured. You can play with the various measures and attributes to manipulate the criteria and the design. Figure 9-3 shows the Recent Send Summary report in the Discover editor.

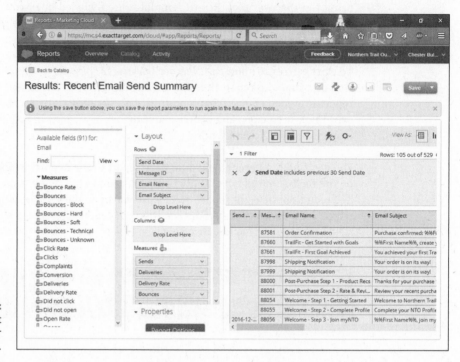

FIGURE 9-3:
A standard report in the Discover canvas.

REMEMBER

To get an idea of the options available for filtering and manipulating data displays, right-click any data field in the Layout column. To apply a filter before you add a field to the report, right-click the field in the field list (on the left).

Creating a report from scratch

After you've experimented with modifying existing reports to make them do what you want, you can try creating a new report that is all your own.

The key to building your own report in Discover is the Blank Template for Email Sending Performance. As the name suggests, this template gives you an empty canvas.

In the very simple example in Figure 9-4, we created a report that shows how *open rates* (the percentage of the recipients who opened the email) on different days of the week have performed over the years.

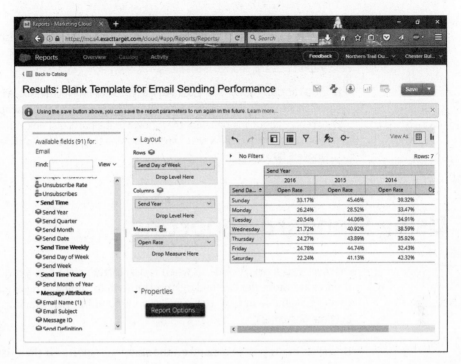

FIGURE 9-4:
A simple Discover report.

To create this report, we used the following steps:

1. **In the toolbar on the Reports screen, click Catalog.**

2. **Click the Create button for the Blank Template for Email Sending Performance report.**

3. **In the field list on the left, scroll to the Event Time Weekly section. Drag the Event Day of Week field to the Rows area (under Layout).**

4. **In the field list, scroll to the Event Time section. Drag the Event Year field to the Columns area (under Layout).**

5. **Again in the field list, scroll to the Measures section. Drag the Open Rate field to the Measures area (under Layout).**

You can save the report you create in Discover so that you can come back later and run the report again.

Be aware of the following:

WARNING

>> By default Discover refreshes the report display every time you add or modify an element. All this refreshing can slow down or even time-out your report generation if you apply a bunch of filters while you're initially building the report. A quicker approach is to use broader criteria while designing the layout, and filter later.

TIP

>> If the report is still slow to generate, click the Disable Auto Refresh button (lightning bolt icon) on the toolbar to toggle the function that refreshes the report as each change is made.

>> You can't drill down in the data to the subscriber-level metrics. All data available in this tool is aggregated up to the send-level. For example, if you run a report about link behavior that shows that a particular link in the email send had 5,000 unique clicks, you can't determine the people who clicked each of those 5,000 times.

Using Standard Reporting

Discover was a pricey add-on when it was introduced a few years ago because its reports are more flexible and customizable than standard reports. Now that Discover is available out-of-the-box, you might think that standard reports would become obsolete.

However, many people depend on the standard reports for their day-to-day work, and the standard reports will remain available. Even for a new user, standard reporting can be a useful tool. Although not as flexible and customizable as Discover reports, the standard reports are a convenient way to quickly get to tried-and-true metrics that marketers have been using for years.

To get to the standard reports, log in to your Salesforce Marketing Cloud account, pause your mouse pointer over Analytics Builder, and select Reports from the list that appears. Standard reports and Discover reports are available in the same catalog, but you can filter based on whether a report is a standard report.

There are too many standard reports to list here, but a description of each report appears next to the report name in the report catalog. We describe some of the most commonly used reports in this section.

Running a report

You run the standard reports in the same way, regardless of the actual type of report:

For numbered lists, we have one action or one related group of actions per step. So, for example, Step 1 has two actions but there's no intervening text so we're okay. You also need to keep the steps linear, without having the reader jump over a step (as happens in Step 2).

1. **In the toolbar on the Reports screen, click Catalog, and then click the Create button for the report you want to run.**

2. **In the Create Report window, fill out the parameters of the report.**

   You usually indicate a date range and possibly other limits. All reports with dates ask you to specify the time zone and culture code. These fields control the display of dates on the report. Dates on the report appear converted to the time zone that you indicate and in the format used by the culture you indicate with the culture code. For example, in the United States, we use MM/DD/YYYY, but another country might use DD/MM/YYYY.

   If the following message appears at the top of the Create Report window, the report is too large for your browser window or takes too long to generate:

   This report cannot be viewed as a web page. You must choose another delivery option from the Results page after submitting these parameters.

   You can get the report by email or FTP, as shown in Step 4.

3. **Click Submit.**

   If you didn't receive the message in Step 2, the report appears in your browser window and you're finished. If you did receive the message, continue with Step 4.

4. **Decide whether you want to receive the report by email or by FTP:**

   - For email, click the Email Results button (envelope icon). The Email Report Results window appears. Complete the information in this window and click Save.

   - For FTP, click the FTP Results button (two arrows icon). The FTP Report Results window appears. Complete the information in this window and click Save.

Subscriber Engagement report

The Subscriber Engagement report shows which subscribers are most engaged with your emails by listing the number of emails delivered to, opened by, and clicked by the subscriber. Figure 9-5 shows a sample Subscriber Engagement report.

You tell the report the following:

» The date range for which you want to see data.

» The lists to which you want to limit the data. You can choose All Subscribers if you don't want to limit the report to a particular list.

» The percentage of the subscribers to include in the report.

» How many emails the subscriber must have received to be included in the report. (Subscribers who have received only a few emails can look like they have high engagement, but it is an anomaly from a small sample size.)

	A	B	C	D	E	F
1	EmailAddress	Delivered	ClickedOn	ClickedToDeliveredRatio	Opened	OpenedToDeliveredRatio
2	al @trendlineinteractive.com	1	1	100.00%	1	100.00%
3	mi @trendlineinteractive.com	1	1	100.00%	1	100.00%
4	mo @trendlineinteractive.com	1	1	100.00%	1	100.00%
5	al @trendlineinteractive.com	1	1	100.00%	1	100.00%
6	al @trendlineinteractive.com	1	1	100.00%	1	100.00%
7	an @trendlineinteractive.com	1	1	100.00%	1	100.00%
8	An @trendlineinteractive.com	1	1	100.00%	1	100.00%
9	br @trendlineinteractive.com	1	1	100.00%	1	100.00%
10	cy @trendlineinteractive.com	1	1	100.00%	1	100.00%
11	em @trendlineinteractive.com	1	1	100.00%	1	100.00%
12	he @trendlineinteractive.com	1	1	100.00%	1	100.00%
13	je @trendlineinteractive.com	1	1	100.00%	1	100.00%
14	je @trendlineinteractive.com	1	1	100.00%	1	100.00%
15	kr @trendlineinteractive.com	1	1	100.00%	1	100.00%
16	la @trendlineinteractive.com	1	1	100.00%	1	100.00%
17	ma @trendlineinteractive.com	1	1	100.00%	1	100.00%
18	mo @trendlineinteractive.com	1	1	100.00%	1	100.00%
19	Ro @trendlineinteractive.com	1	1	100.00%	1	100.00%
20	so @trendlineinteractive.com	1	1	100.00%	1	100.00%
21	st @trendlineinteractive.com	1	1	100.00%	1	100.00%
22	od @trendlineinteractive.com	1	1	100.00%	1	100.00%
23	ti @trendlineinteractive.com	1	1	100.00%	1	100.00%
24	sa @trendlineinteractive.com	1	1	100.00%	1	100.00%
25	ch @trendlineinteractive.com	1	1	100.00%	1	100.00%
26	gi @trendlineinteractive.com	1	1	100.00%	1	100.00%
27	be @trendlineinteractive.com	1	1	100.00%	1	100.00%
28	br @trendlineinteractive.com	1	1	100.00%	1	100.00%
29	ma @trendlineinteractive.com	1	1	100.00%	1	100.00%
30	li @trendlineinteractive.com	1	1	100.00%	1	100.00%
31	kr @trendlineinteractive.com	1	1	100.00%	1	100.00%
32	ja @trendlineinteractive.com	1	1	100.00%	1	100.00%

Subscriber Engagement

FIGURE 9-5: A sample Subscriber Engagement report.

The report displays the subscribers, listed in high-to-low order by the click-to-sent ratio. Marketers use this report to identify their rock-star subscribers. This is a good group of subscribers to reward with exclusive special offers, for example.

Because of its size, this report can't be viewed in your browser window, so you need to send it to your email address or to an FTP site. (See the previous section, "Running a report," for details.)

Recent Email Sending Summary report

The Recent Email Sending Summary report shows high-level information about your email sends over a certain period of time. Figure 9-6 shows a sample Recent Email Sending Summary report.

For this report, you specify the following:

- What date range for which you want to see data.
- Whether to include single sends. A *single send* is the sending of an individual email by the API, such as a confirmation message after a person fills out a form on your website.

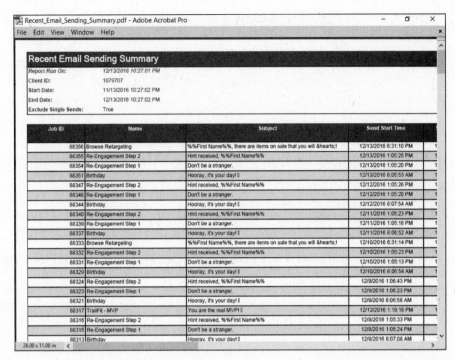

FIGURE 9-6:
A sample Recent
Email Sending
Summary report.

The report displays all your email jobs for the date range you specified. Marketers use this report periodically to establish a benchmark and to check progress against that benchmark over time. It's also a useful diagnostic tool if you suspect that your email sends are completing too slowly or not at all.

Account Send Summary report

The Account Send Summary report shows a count and a rate of every possible kind of response a subscriber can have to your emails. Figure 9-7 shows a sample Account Send Summary report.

You tell the report the date range, whether to exclude single sends, and whether to exclude jobs in which tracking was suppressed.

The report displays 40-some fields of information about deliveries, bounces, opens, clicks, forwards, and more. Because of its size, this report can't be viewed in your browser window, so you need to send it to your email address or to an FTP site. (See the previous section, "Running a report," for details.)

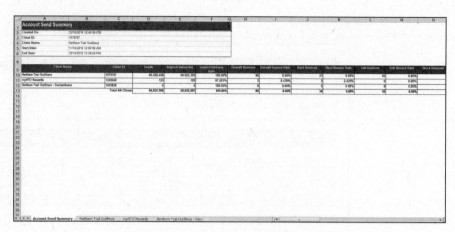

FIGURE 9-7:
A sample Account
Send Summary
report.

Email Performance for Domains report

The Email Performance for Domains report lets you evaluate email send results for each domain sent to in a single send. Figure 9-8 shows a sample Email Performance for Domains report.

You tell the report which email send you want to evaluate. The report displays a circle graph that shows you to which domains the email was sent. You can also see the open, click, bounce, and unsubscribe rates for each of the domains.

Email_Performance_for_All_Domains.pdf - Adobe Acrobat Pro

File   Edit   View   Window   Help

Email Performance for All Domains

Report Run On:	12/13/2016 10:30:20 PM
Member ID:	1079707
Email Send ID:	36767
Email Threshold	1
Email Name:	Abandoned Cart - High Value 1
Email Subject Line:	How can we help?
Date Sent:	5/9/2013 11:35:00 AM

Domain Name	Emails Sent	% of Total Sent	Delivered	Bounced	Bounce %	Opened	Open %	Cl
gmail.ntodemo.com	838	38.06 %	838	0	0.00 %	0	0.00 %	
yahoo.ntodemo.com	632	28.70 %	632	0	0.00 %	0	0.00 %	
hotmail.ntodemo.com	551	25.02 %	551	0	0.00 %	0	0.00 %	
aol.ntodemo.com	95	4.31 %	95	0	0.00 %	0	0.00 %	
comcast.ntodemo.com	46	2.09 %	46	0	0.00 %	0	0.00 %	
verizon.ntodemo.com	24	1.09 %	24	0	0.00 %	0	0.00 %	
work.ntodemo.com	16	0.73 %	16	0	0.00 %	0	0.00 %	
All other domains	0	0.00 %	0	0	0.00 %	0	0.00 %	
Totals	2,202	100.00 %	2,202	0	0.00 %	0	0.00 %	

13.00 x 11.00 in

FIGURE 9-8:
A sample Email
Performance for
Domains report.

Viewing Web and Mobile Analytics

The Web & Mobile Analytics screen in Marketing Cloud is beautiful, overflowing with colorful charts, maps, and diagrams about every aspect of how visitors are interacting with your website and mobile app. Figure 9-9 shows just one screen's worth of the analytics panels available in this tool.

FIGURE 9-9:
The Web &
Mobile Analytics
dashboard.

One panel displays a world map indicating which countries your visitors are from. Other panels (not shown in the figure) display a circle graph indicating which of your site pages are most popular and a line graph of the number and value of your abandoned shopping carts. The dashboard containing all these panels seems to scroll on and on.

REMEMBER

There are far too many panels to list them all, but fortunately each panel has individual controls you can use to orient yourself:

>> The What Am I Seeing? button (question mark icon) provides a rundown of what the current panel does.

>> The What Can I Do with This? button (arrow icon) suggests how to proceed with your new insight and data.

>> Date drop-down list enables you to choose the date range for the data shown in that panel.

Figure 9-10 shows the controls on each panel.

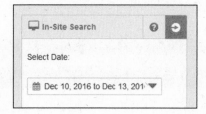

FIGURE 9-10:
Helpful controls
on the analytics
panels.

To get to Web & Mobile Analytics, log in to your Salesforce Marketing Cloud account, pause your mouse pointer over Analytics Builder, and select Web & Mobile Analytics from the list that appears.

You can use the data you see in the Web & Mobile Analytics screen in your ongoing marketing efforts. The most obvious benefit of using this tool is being able to segment your audience and execute follow-up messaging based on subscriber behavior on your website.

Since the analytic breakdowns can be tied back to subscriber data in your account, the behavioral data is available to other tools in your Marketing Cloud account, such as Audience Builder, Email, Subscriber Lists, and Journey Builder. The Data Extensions feature must be enabled in your account to act on the behavioral data because Marketing Cloud uses data extensions to hold the data. For details on enabling the data extensions feature, see Chapter 6.

The tricky part, of course, is setting up your website and mobile applications to collect behavioral information and to send the information to the Web & Mobile Analytics app in the first place. You must install the code on every website and mobile app from which you want to collect behavioral information about its visitors. The basic installation of the code to gather data from your websites may be something you can do yourself, but more advanced tracking on websites plus tracking in your mobile app may require the help of a developer.

Setting up web analytics

Marketing Cloud uses a tool called Collect to gather behavioral data from your websites. By default, Collect monitors the following details, but you can enhance your configuration to collect more data:

>> Browser type

>> User location

>> Session time and length

>> Page URL and title of the page that the visitor is viewing

>> Referrer URL of the page from which the visitor came

To get started with a basic implementation, you copy a snippet of JavaScript to your clipboard and paste it into the HTML of every individual page of your website where you want information to be collected. The process isn't difficult but can be tedious.

You can find the JavaScript snippet in the Web & Mobile Analytics interface:

1. **On the Web & Mobile Analytics screen, click the gear icon in the upper-right corner and select Configure Data Source.**

2. **Click the Configure Collect button.**

3. **Highlight the code snippet that appears on the screen and copy it to your clipboard.**

Now you can paste the code into your HTML. You should paste the code immediately before the closing </body> tag of the page.

Setting up mobile analytics

The process for setting up Collect in your mobile app is conceptually similar to setting it up on your web pages, but it's more difficult. Getting into the source code of your mobile app is less straightforward than opening up the HTML of your website pages to drop in a little JavaScript snippet.

Without getting into detail, Marketing Cloud provides the Journey Builder for Apps SDK, which your mobile app developer can install in your iOS or Android app. By installing this SDK, your app can work with the Web & Mobile Analytics tool.

Using Predictive Intelligence

Of all the tools in the Marketing Cloud platform, the predictive intelligence tools are probably the least known. Recently, Salesforce has begun integrating AI tools in all its products in an effort called Einstein. We are beginning to see how features currently in development as well as some long-standing capabilities fit into this overall direction of the software.

The main tools that already exist in Marketing Cloud for predictive intelligence capabilities are the Personalization Builder tools for email and the web. These tools can dynamically select content in an email or a web page based on the subscriber's purchase history, items viewed, shopping cart, and more.

To get to Personalization Builder, log in to your Salesforce Marketing Cloud account, pause your mouse pointer over Personalization Builder, and select Predictive Web or Predictive Email from the list that appears.

Personalization Builder needs to know the following to make an intelligent decision about what content to use:

>> Data about the subscriber's behaviors and preferences. Like Mobile & Web Analytics, Personalization Builder makes use of the Collect feature to monitor events on your website and gather this information.

>> A catalog of content from which to select just the right piece for this particular subscriber. You can upload three kinds of catalogs:

- Product catalog with a list of your products

- Content catalog with articles, videos, or whatever content you have available to view

- Banner catalog with heroes, calls to action, and offers

>> Rules that you define in Personalization Builder to decide what content to present to the subscriber in what circumstances.

Implementing Personalization Builder is not a casual task, and you might need to enlist the help of a developer. And you won't be able to do it quickly: Marketing Cloud's best practice is to observe your website behavior for at least 30 days before introducing content based on predictive intelligence.

However, these exciting tools will see continued emphasis and development from Salesforce. They are a powerful way to make your customers feel like you know them — even when you aren't available to talk to each one of them personally.

Chapter **10**

Journey Builder

As a digital marketer, you know that your campaigns contain many repetitive tasks that you need to perform. Tasks such as importing and exporting data, running reports, and executing recurring campaigns have a legitimate place on your agenda, but they take up time and energy that you could be using to solve problems.

Salesforce Marketing Cloud can save you some of the busywork by automating the simple tasks that you must repeat exactly the same way every day. Not only does automation make it possible for you to set up a lot more campaigns, but it also prevents the human error that tends to happen when a person is asked to do the same mundane task over and over again.

Salesforce Marketing Cloud has developed multiple tools for process automation over the years. The Journey Builder category on the app switcher contains two powerful automation tools: Automation Studio and Journey Builder.

Automation Studio is Marketing Cloud's digital workhorse. With it, you set up automated processes to run on a schedule or as a result of an event trigger. For example, you could set up a daily automation that creates a list of subscribers who are having a birthday that day and then sends them a happy birthday email. Or you could set up an automation to detect when a file has been added to an FTP site and then to import that file.

Journey Builder is the application you'll use for multiple component campaigns. It enables you to take advantage of channels from across Marketing Cloud to build comprehensive, dynamic experiences for your subscribers.

Even though this chapter is titled "Journey Builder," the Journey Builder app is so central to your online marketing efforts in Marketing Cloud that just one chapter cannot contain it! See Chapters 16 and 17 for additional information about Journey Builder.

Automation Studio versus Journey Builder

Automation Studio and Journey Builder are both powerful automation tools. But how do you decide when to use each one? Each has strengths, so you want to choose the tool that best matches the requirements and complexity of your campaign.

Automation Studio is simpler and more straightforward to use, and it is best suited to campaigns that proceed in a linear fashion. For example, a linear campaign might contain the following steps:

1. You upload a file of subscriber data to an FTP location, which triggers the campaign.

2. The campaign uploads the content of the file to your data extension.

3. The campaign segments the data extension for sending.

4. The campaign sends a series of messages to the subscribers on that data extension, with a fixed time interval between each message.

Figure 10-1 illustrates what this simple linear campaign would look like in Automation Studio.

On the other hand, if your campaign is more complex, you should probably use Journey Builder. Although Journey Builder is more complicated to set up, it has more power and flexibility, so it's the better choice when your campaign includes variable paths.

FIGURE 10-1:
Automation Studio is best suited to campaigns where only one path is possible.

In Journey Builder, you can set up a journey, which is a tool to decide when, what, and whether to send a subscriber a message based on conditions such as the following:

>> Random segmentation of your audience

>> Value of a subscriber attribute

>> How the subscriber interacted with a message sent earlier in the sequence of events

Journey Builder uses a drag-and-drop interface in which you model a subscriber's path through the journey. Figure 10-2 shows the interface.

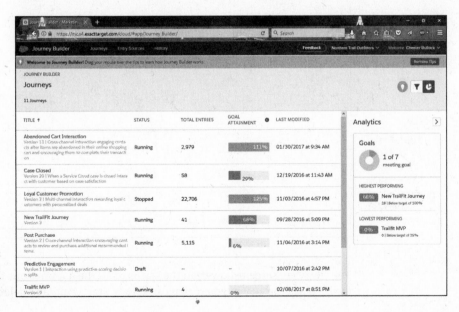

FIGURE 10-2:
A view of a Journey Builder canvas.

You can also use both Automation Studio and Journey Builder together on the same campaign. For example, you might want to use Automation Studio to import subscriber records before inserting them into a Journey Builder interaction. In this situation, you can create an automation in Automation Studio in which the last step is to load subscribers into a journey.

Understanding Automation Studio

In Automation Studio, you create an *automation*, which is a linear progression of steps to complete, one after the other. A step contains one or more *activities* that the system completes before moving to the next step. Previously, you had to create activities in the Email app before you could include them in your automations, but now you can create activities directly in Automation Studio.

To get to Automation Studio, pause your mouse pointer on Journey Builder in the app switcher and click Automation Studio. The Overview screen appears, as shown in Figure 10-3.

FIGURE 10-3: The Overview screen in Automation Studio is where you view all automations and activity.

The Overview screen shows you the status of all the automations that you've created. This is the screen where you can create, start, edit, and delete automations.

On the left side of this screen is a navigation pane, where you can browse for an automation within the folder structure. Click a folder, and its subfolders appear in the navigation pane and the automations in that folder appear to the right, in the list pane. You can search for a particular automation using the search field that appears above the navigation pane.

As mentioned, the list pane (see Figure 10-4) is where the automations in the folder you chose or that match your search criteria appear. You can filter the list of automations by using the View by Status drop-down menu, which appears above the list, on the right side. The two buttons next to the menu — Detail View and List View (both shown in the margin) — help you control the information you see about each automation in this list. Use the page selector in the bottom right of the screen to advance through the listings.

FIGURE 10-4:
Find your desired automation.

Click the name of an automation to open the editor view. Pause your mouse pointer over the name to see Run Once and Delete buttons.

On the right side of the Overview screen, you can see a Summary pane of the automations that are running or scheduled to run, as shown in Figure 10-5. You can use the buttons and fields near the top of the pane to set parameters for what to display. You can control whether you see information for a single day or an entire week, the day or week for which you want to see information, and what kinds of activities appear in the pane. Click the Update button to refresh the summary to reflect the parameters you chose.

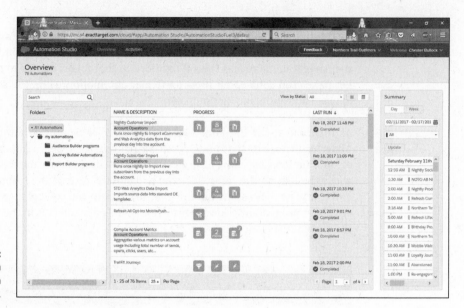

FIGURE 10-5:
Detail view of a daily automation activity summary.

Creating Activities

With a few exceptions, you must create activities in a separate process before you can include them in an automation. After you create an activity, it becomes available to select and include in any number of automations. Eventually, Marketing Cloud plans for activities to replace the Interactions tab in Email Studio for creating user-initiated sends, file imports, exports, extracts, and other automations.

The kinds of activities that you can create vary based on your account configuration; this section covers the core activities that appear in any account. To access the screen where you can create an activity from Automation Studio, click the Activities menu on the toolbar. The Activities screen appears, as shown in Figure 10-6.

Testing activities

It's possible to run an activity without including it in an automation, but you should do that only when you're testing the activity. Except for a few activities that alert you when they are complete, such as file imports, monitoring the progress of an activity running outside an automation is difficult or even impossible.

For example, if you run a query activity outside an automation, the only way for you to know when the activity is complete is to check whether the results of the query have appeared. This isn't a practical approach because, depending on the query's complexity, it could finish in as little as a few seconds or as much as many hours. You might find yourself checking for results over and over, never knowing whether they haven't appeared because an error caused the query to stop prematurely or simply because it hasn't completed yet.

FIGURE 10-6:
The list of activities you've created appears in the Activities screen.

By executing the query in a step in an automation, even if it's the only step in the automation, you can easily see whether the step is failing to progress or has encountered an error.

File-naming patterns

Some activities, such as the file import, file transfer, and data extract activities, require you to specify a file name when you're setting them up. However, because automations run periodically on their own, you might need to include a date in the file name so you can tell at a glance whether the file is the right one.

To help you have unique names for your files, Marketing Cloud lets you indicate a file-naming patterns instead of a static file name when you're setting up activities that need one. In the naming pattern, you include placeholders for the year, month, and day in the file name. The system replaces the placeholder with the current year, month, and day (as needed) so you can have different file names on different days.

For example, instead of entering subscribers.csv in the file name field, you would enter subscribersMMDDYYYY.csv. When the system processes the file name, it replaces the MM with the two-digit month, the DD with the two-digit year, and the YYYY with the four-digit year of the current day.

Data extract activity

Use the data extract activity to bundle a file of Marketing Cloud data to transfer it out of Marketing Cloud so you can use it in a different business system. For example, you might extract tracking data to import it into a separate analytics system.

Interestingly, you can use this activity also to transform an XML file to a comma-delimited, tab-delimited, or pipe-delimited file. This can be a convenient activity to use before importing an XML file into your Marketing Cloud account.

To create a data extract activity, use the following steps:

1. **From the Activities screen, click the Create Activity button, near the top right of the screen.**

2. **In the Create New Activity window that appears, select Data Extract and then click Next.**

   The Create New Data Extract Activity window appears.

3. **Complete the information on the Properties tab, and then click Next.**

   Specify a name and description for the activity, and also a file-naming pattern for the file that results from the extract. Don't forget to include the file extension (for example, CSV, ZIP, or TAB) in the file-naming pattern.

   The list of extract types that you can choose from depends on what is available in your account. Commonly available types include tracking data and data extensions.

TIP

   For the file transfer activity to find and move the file that results from a data extract activity, you must use the same file name when you're setting up both activities.

4. **Complete the information on the Configuration tab, and then click Next.**

   The fields on this tab vary depending on the extract type you chose in the preceding step.

5. **Review the information on the Summary tab, and then click Finish.**

File transfer activity

You can use the file transfer activity to upload to Marketing Cloud a file that you created elsewhere, or to download a file from Marketing Cloud. For example, you might use this activity right after the data extract activity to move a file of analytics data to a transfer location.

When you're using the file transfer activity to upload a file, the same activity can decrypt the file, or decompress the file, or both.

REMEMBER

This activity only makes the file available to Marketing Cloud; it does not update your subscriber data with the information from the file. See the "Import file activity" section, later in this chapter, for instructions on updating your subscriber information.

To create a file transfer activity, use the following steps:

1. **From the Activities screen, click the Create Activity button, near the top right of the screen.**

2. **In the Create New Activity window that appears, select File Transfer, and then click Next.**

   The Create New File Transfer Activity window appears.

3. **Complete the information on the Properties tab, and then click Next.**

   Specify a name and description for the activity. Also choose one of the following for the file action:

   - *Manage File:* Choose this option to use the activity to get content *into* Marketing Cloud from an outside file.

   - *Move a File from Safehouse:* Choose this option to use the activity to get a file *out* of Marketing Cloud.

4. **Complete the information on the Configuration tab, and then click Next.**

   Indicate the file-naming pattern and the location where you want to transfer the file to or from. Don't forget to include the file extension (for example, CSV, ZIP, or TAB) in the file-naming pattern.

TIP

For the file transfer activity to find and move the file that results from a data extract activity, you must use the same file name when you're setting up both activities.

For Manage File activities (file *into* Marketing Cloud), the Configuration tab is also where you tell Marketing Cloud if you want it to decompress and decrypt your file. A few additional controls help you prevent importing old data or overwriting data in your Marketing Cloud account too soon.

For Move a File from Safehouse activities (content *out* of Marketing Cloud), the Configuration tab is also where you tell the activity how to encrypt your file.

5. **Review the information on the Summary tab, and then click Finish.**

Filter activity

To create a group from a subscriber list, you set up the filter logic in a filter activity. When the automation runs, the system applies that logic to the subscriber list you've indicated and creates a group of subscribers that satisfy the criteria.

REMEMBER

You have to set up your data filter separately before you can use it as part of an activity. See Chapters 11 and 17 for more information about filters.

To create a filter activity, use the following steps:

1. **From the Activities screen, click the Create Activity button, near the top right of the screen.**

2. **In the Create New Activity window that appears, select Filter, and then click Next.**

   The Create New Filter Activity window appears.

3. **Complete the information on the Properties tab, and then click Next.**

   Specify a name and description for the activity, as well as the location of the data filter that you want to use.

4. **Complete the information on the Configuration tab, and then click Next.**

   Choose the list to which you're going to apply the filter logic. Also choose the name you want to give the resulting group and where you want to store that group.

5. **Review the information on the Summary tab, and then click Finish.**

Import file activity

You use the import file activity after you've transferred a file into Marketing Cloud using the file transfer activity. The import activity uses the information from the file you transferred to update your subscriber data.

To create an import file activity, use the following steps:

1. **From the Activities screen, click the Create Activity button, near the top right of the screen.**

2. **In the Create New Activity window that appears, select Import File, and then click Next.**

   The Create New Import Definition window appears.

3. **Complete the information on the Properties tab, and then click Next.**

   Specify a name and description for the activity as well as the file-naming pattern of the file to import. Also specify information about the file, such as where Marketing Cloud can find it and which delimiter it uses. You can use the other options to prevent the import from importing bad or old data. You can also set up the activity to alert you when the import is complete.

TIP

   If you set up your automation to import files on a schedule, problems can occur outside your control that cause the file you're importing to not post to the FTP site on time. The options on this tab are great safeguards to prevent duplicate imports of the same file if that happens.

4. **Complete the information in the Destination tab, and then click Next.**

   Choose the subscriber list or data extension to import the data into. Also choose whether you want to add, update, or overwrite the information you already have.

5. **Complete the information on the Destination tab, and click Next.**

   Map the columns from your import file to the columns in your subscriber list or data extension:

   - *If you choose Map by Header Row,* the names of the columns in your source file must match the names of the fields in your subscriber list or data extension.

   - *If you choose Map by Ordinals,* you can choose to map the first, second, third, and so on field in your import file to the field that you want the content imported to.

   - *If you choose to Map Manually,* you upload a sample file so that the system can show you all the columns to map to the subscriber attributes or data extension columns.

6. **Review the information on the Summary tab, and then click Finish.**

Refresh group activity

In the Email app, you can create a group to contain a subset of a subscriber list. The system populates the group based on either a data filter or a number of randomly selected subscribers. However, the group you create remains static; you need to use the refresh group activity to reapply the logic and generate an up-to-date subset of the list.

For example, if you create a group of subscribers whose birthday is today and send them a happy birthday message, you should refresh the group tomorrow to get the new subset of subscribers who should receive the birthday greeting.

REMEMBER

You have to set up your group separately before you can use it as part of an activity. See Chapters 8 and 11 for more information about groups.

Because of the simplicity of this activity, you do not create a stand-alone refresh group activity. Instead, you specify the details of the activity directly in the automation. See the procedure for creating an automation in the following section.

To create a refresh group activity, use the following steps:

1. From the Automation Studio Overview screen, create or open an automation, and then click the Workflow tab.

2. Drag the Refresh Group activity from the Activities list to a step on the automation canvas.

3. Click the Choose button, select the group you want to refresh, and then click Done.

SQL query activity

The SQL query activity is similar to the filter activity: Both create a subset of records based on logic that you've set up. The SQL query activity must be used with data extensions, though; you can't use it to filter subscribers in a subscriber list. The SQL query activity can filter any data extensions, not just those that contain subscriber records.

TIP

Before you begin, make sure you have nearby the name of the data extension you're going to query. You can't easily look up the name of a data extension when you're creating the activity.

REMEMBER

You have to set up your data extensions separately before you can include them in this activity. See Chapter 6 for more information about data extensions.

To create an SQL query activity, use the following steps:

1. From the Activities screen, click the Create Activity button, near the top right of the screen.

2. **In the Create New Activity window that appears, select SQL Query, and then click Next.**

    The Create New Query Activity window appears.

3. **Complete the information on the Properties tab, and then click Next.**

    Specify a name, description, and storage location for the activity. Also enter the SQL of the query.

4. **Complete the information on the Target Data Extension tab, and then click Next.**

    Choose the data extension where you want the system to put the results of the query. You can choose to add, update, or overwrite the information that's already in the data extension.

5. **Review the information on the Summary tab, and then click Finish.**

Send email activity

Use the send email activity to automatically send an email that you've created previously. See Chapter 11 for information about creating emails.

To create a send email activity, use the following steps:

1. **From the Activities screen, click the Create Activity button, near the top right of the screen.**

2. **In the Create New Activity window that appears, select Send Email, and then click Next.**

    The Create New Send Email Activity window appears.

3. **Complete the information on the Choose & Configure Email tab, and then click Next.**

    Select the email message you want to send, specify the subject line, and select the sender and delivery profile.

4. **Complete the information on the Choose Recipients tab, and then click Next.**

    Choose the lists and groups to which you want to send the message.

5. **Review the information on the Summary tab, and then click Finish.**

Wait activity

The wait activity tells Marketing Cloud to wait for a period of time before proceeding to the next step in an automation. Because this activity makes sense only in the context of an automation, you can't create a stand-alone wait activity. See the procedure for creating an automation in the following section.

To create a wait activity, use the following steps:

1. **From the Automation Studio Overview screen, create or open an automation, and then click on the Workflow tab.**

2. **Drag the Wait activity from the Activities list to a step on the automation canvas.**

3. **Complete the Wait window that appears, and then click OK.**

   Specify an amount of time to wait or a time of day to resume the automation.

Creating an Automation

You can include all the activities described in the preceding section in your automation. The editor view, where you create or edit automations, offers a drag-and-drop interface to add activities to steps in your automation.

The edit view of a scheduled automation appears in Figure 10-7.

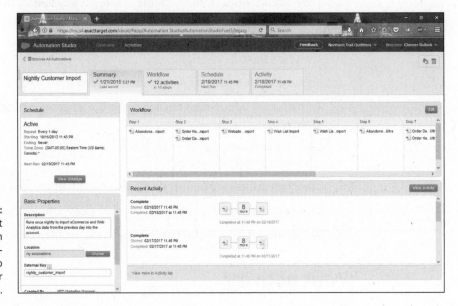

FIGURE 10-7:
Tabs on the edit view provide an almost wizard-style path to creating your automation.

Use these steps to create an automation:

1. **From the Automation Studio Overview screen, click the New Automation button, near the top right.**

2. **In the Create Automation window that appears, select one of the following, and then click OK:**

   - *Scheduled:* As the name implies, this automation will run on a recurring basis using a schedule you'll define. Or not; you'll want to select this option also if you need to create an automation that you'll start manually by using the Run Once function. You'll likely use this option frequently.

   - *File Drop:* This kind of automation starts when a file is added to a designated folder on your Enhanced FTP location. This is a great option if you need to bring in data from an external location that isn't being posted on a reliable schedule.

3. **For a file drop automation, click the Trigger Setup button on the Workflow tab.**

   Complete the Trigger Setup window that appears and click Save.

   This window is where you:

   - Indicate the location where adding a new file triggers the automation. You can specify a file-naming pattern so that only a new file that matches the pattern initiates the automation.

   - Have the option to Disable Queuing. If you select this check box and the automation is already running when another new file is dropped in the folder location, then Marketing Cloud stops the current instance of the automation and starts working on the new instance of the automation instead.

4. **On the Workflow tab, drag the kind of activity you want from the Activities pane on the left to the canvas.** The activity appears in Step 1. You can drag additional activities into Step 1 to instruct Marketing Cloud that it can work on both activities at the same time. You can drag activities into subsequent steps to indicate that Marketing Cloud needs to complete all the activities in the previous step before moving on to the next one.

   WARNING

   Activities that need to be run sequentially, such as a file extract and file transfer for the same data, should not be placed in the same step. All activities within a step are run at the same time, not in any sequence.

5. **Click the Choose button on the activity (Configure on the Send Email activity) to set up the specific information about that activity.** If you have created reusable activities, you can select the arrow next to this button and choose the activity you created. See the procedures for creating different types of activities in the previous section.

6. **For a scheduled automation, click on the Schedule tab and indicate when you want the automation to run.** You can choose the date and time and how often the automation repeats, if at all.

7. **Click Save.** If you have not given a name to the automation, the Save Automation window appears to prompt you to add a name, include an optional description, and choose the location in the folder structure where you want to store the automation.

TIP

If you're creating a complex automation, it is a good idea to incrementally save the workflow as you are constructing it. We have created workflows that contained 100 or more steps, and the last thing you want is to have to start over due to a time-out or connection problem.

Error Reporting

After you save an automation in Automation Studio, you have the option to go to the Activity tab and enter notification email addresses. You can enter a separate list of email addresses to receive notification if the automation fails or is skipped versus if the automation completes successfully.

The "set it and forget it" nature of some automations makes it particularly important for you to set up a notification email address; otherwise, you might never notice that the automation failed. The notification email tells you the step that was running when the error occurred. You can find more specific troubleshooting information by opening the automation in Automation Studio and reviewing the step mentioned in the notification email.

The successful completion email notifications are useful when running "one-time" ad hoc automations or for monitoring new or mission-critical automations.

4

Marketing Cloud Studios

Chapter **11**

Email Studio

The largest and, in our humble opinion, most important part of Salesforce Marketing Cloud is the email-marketing functionality. Email is where the Marketing Cloud began. Back in those days, the email application and the company that built it went by its original name: ExactTarget. Over time, ExactTarget added automation capabilities and social-messaging channels, and Salesforce acquired the company to become the powerful tool we know today.

Delivering your email-marketing campaigns via Marketing Cloud gives you access to features that other platforms just don't have. For example, data extensions (introduced in Chapter 6) afford you flexibility you simply can't find in other email-marketing software. As you continue to use Marketing Cloud, you will think of more and more creative ways to leverage data extensions to deliver highly customized content to your subscribers while also making your own life easier.

In this chapter, we show what email marketing in Marketing Cloud looks like and how you can use it to its potential. Your work is not done after you send an email, though, so we also cover reporting and tracking information that is available to you, as well as some advanced concepts for new email marketers.

Understanding Email Marketing in Salesforce Marketing Cloud

Email-marketing functionality in Salesforce Marketing Cloud allows you to deliver personalized email communications that make your subscribers feel like you're talking to them one-to-one. As subscribers receive and interact with your communications, Marketing Cloud collects important metrics that help you determine the success of your marketing efforts so you can fine-tune your campaigns.

The email channel in Salesforce Marketing Cloud

The email marketing functionality of Marketing Cloud resides mostly in the Email Studio category of apps, as shown in Figure 11-1.

FIGURE 11-1: Email Studio apps contain the tools you need for marketing through the email channel.

The Email app is where we begin to focus our attention. When you open the Email app, you see a toolbar of options (see Figure 11-2), an overview of recent emails that you have worked on, and some data briefly outlining the performance of the emails you most recently sent.

FIGURE 11-2: Email marketing power hides within this unassuming toolbar.

The following list describes each menu on the toolbar:

>> **Overview:** Click this menu from any other screen in the Email app to return to the dashboard that you see when you first open the app.

- » **Content:** Click this menu to open the Content Builder screen (discussed in Chapter 7) in the Email app. Here you can create, import, edit, or delete the words and images that you use in your email messages. This is also where you store your email definitions and templates.

- » **Subscribers:** Find many, many menu options here that let you maintain the subscriber data you use in your sends. For example, the Lists option on this menu enables you to create subscriber lists to send emails to.

- » **Interactions:** Create and manage the technical components that you need for your automations. The activities you create here appear in Automation Studio. See Chapter 10 for a full description of Automation Studio.

- » **A/B Testing:** Start a wizard-driven tool for doing simple A/B tests. You can find detailed information about this tool later in this chapter.

- » **Tracking:** Find the performance data for your email sends here, such as how many people open or click your emails and which links are most popular. Use these tracking tools when you want a snapshot of the performance of a particular campaign. For a more sophisticated analysis of your campaigns over time, see the analytics tools discussed in Chapter 9.

- » **Audience Builder:** Segment lists quickly using this optional, premium-priced add-on for Salesforce Marketing Cloud accounts. See Chapter 8 for a full discussion of Audience Builder.

- » **Admin:** Control specific administration functions that apply to the Email application only.

- » **Inbox Tools:** Understand how your emails place in terms of reaching your subscribers' inboxes, the reputation score of your sending domain, a live preview of your email in various email clients, and a report detailing the various email clients used to view your emails. Inbox Tools is an optional add-on for Salesforce Marketing Cloud accounts.

Benefits of email as a channel

The death of email marketing has been predicted several times in recent years. For reasons ranging from inbox overload to the latest and greatest social apps, pundits think that email can't survive against today's newest technology.

The truth, however, is that email remains the channel that consumers prefer for receiving messages from brands and businesses they like. Many businesses offer a variety of creative incentives for customers to become subscribers, and you can too. Of course, exclusive discounts are popular, but even just sending a notification when a hot item is back in stock can be a compelling reason for a person to join your email list.

The reasons people love to send and receive email are simple:

>> **Express interest:** If you're marketing properly, you're emailing only subscribers who have specifically opted in. This opt-in means they have expressly stated that they want to hear from you.

>> **Targeted communication:** You can target the content in an email more so than in any other medium, as long as you have the data about each subscriber to know which message he or she should receive. You can target messages to people who live in a specific ZIP code, who have purchased a specific item, or who have any other detail that you know about your subscribers.

>> **Testing capability:** Testing is easy and fast. With a little planning, you can create multiple versions of an email to send as tests and compare how they perform. After you declare a winner, you can send that version of the email to the remainder of your list to maximize your results.

>> **Detailed metrics:** Email marketing allows you to see the actions your subscribers take, down to the second they take them. Including web analytics code in the links in your emails makes it possible to build a data set that shows you ROI on your campaigns — a valuable metric for any business.

When to use email

Email is a great channel for your marketing efforts, but it shouldn't be the only channel and it shouldn't be used in every instance. The benefits outlined in the preceding section give a good explanation of *why* to use email marketing. The following list explains *when* you should use it:

>> **Sending semi-private messages:** Do you have an offer or information for a select group of people, or even just one person? Email is a good choice for this situation.

>> **Addressing an interested audience:** Do you have an offer you want to get out to your entire list of interested subscribers? Email is the easiest way to do that.

>> **Looking for immediate results:** When you need to see immediate results — either for a creative test or to sell something quickly — email is a great choice for getting the word out. Because your subscribers clearly indicated that they wanted to hear from you, they're ready to act when you ask them to.

>> **Automating communication:** Have you wanted to automate a series of messages to welcome a person to your business? Email marketing is a perfect vehicle for automation, allowing you to build a program that delivers different content based on the actions a person takes in each email you send.

>> **Sending regular communication:** Do you have a newsletter that you use to stay in regular communication with your customers? Sending it by email gives you great tracking information on how your subscribers are responding to your message.

Creating Email Content

For this section, we collaborated with Justine Jordan, email-marketing industry leader and vice president of marketing at Litmus. Litmus software helps you optimize your email marketing by providing email previews, comprehensive checklists, and advanced analytics. You can learn more about Litmus at `https://litmus.com`.

Subject-line best practices

The subject line is one of the first things that people look at when they're deciding whether to read your email. A lot of conflicting information about subject-line best practices exists. Unfortunately, there's no secret formula for the perfect subject line. The best subject line for you depends on factors such as the following:

>> The goal of your email

>> Your audience

>> How you measure success

>> How well the content of your email delivers — or doesn't — on the promise made in the subject line

Most marketers spend more time writing the headline in the body of the email than working on the subject line, but the subject line deserves more attention. Consider this: If your open rate is 15 percent, only 15 percent of your subscribers even have the chance to read the headline. Meanwhile, *all* your subscribers who received the message had the chance to see your subject line.

TIP

Do not neglect your from name either. Our research shows that your from name has a bigger effect than your subject line on whether a subscriber opens your email. Use A/B tests (see the "Advanced Tactics in Email" section, later in this chapter) to find the best from address for your audience.

Understand that the goal of your email's subject line isn't to get more opens. This probably goes against what you've read or heard elsewhere. The actual goal of a subject line is to *generate openers who are likely to convert.*

In general, the open rate is a poor measure of the success of your subject line. That's because the goal of most of your email campaigns is to drive metrics more closely tied to sales, such as email conversions.

TECHNICAL STUFF

You can use insert fields in your subject line that Marketing Cloud replaces with specific information about each subscriber. For example, if you include the field for first name, the system fills that field with the first name of each subscriber. You can also specify dynamic content rules in your subject line. See the "Advanced Tactics in Email" section, later in this chapter.

Avoiding the spam folder

A spam filter protects your subscriber's inbox. This filter searches emails before they arrive in the inbox and programmatically identifies patterns that indicate that the email is spam. Spam emails land in the spam folder instead of the inbox.

You might have heard that using certain words in your email or subject line automatically lands your email in the spam folder. This is a myth: A variety of things can trigger spam filters, but specific words alone are rarely the culprit. A spam filter is more sophisticated than that. Spam filters do assign point values to certain words. Each time one of those words appears in the subject line or body of an email, a point counter goes up. If the counter exceeds a certain threshold, the email goes to the spam folder.

These trigger words play only a part in the spam score, though. Your sender reputation and engagement metrics are much more important. You may need to test several tactics to see which one gets your email messages into the inbox the most reliably. Consider the following guidelines:

- » Set your subscribers' expectations and clearly state what's inside the email.
- » Don't write your subject lines like advertisements.
- » Keep your subject line straightforward.
- » Avoid using promotional phrases or anything you would think was spam if it arrived in your own inbox.
- » Know what interests your audience and use that in your subject lines.
- » All caps, the word *free,* and exclamation points are okay, but use them in moderation.

- » Make sure the subject line is relevant and valuable, and that the message is obvious to your subscribers.

- » Make it crystal clear to your subscribers who your email is from. You may want to mention your most recognizable brand product in your subject line.

- » Try to make your subject line stand out visually. Try brackets, variations on capitalization, phone numbers, and quotes.

- » If your subscribers need to act on the content of your email by a certain deadline, convey the urgency in the subject line. Timely topics, such as something in the news, can also inspire action.

- » People respond well when you ask them to do something.

- » Put the important information first in your subject line to make sure your subscribers see it. Mobile devices especially tend to cut off subject lines early.

- » If you include emojis, remember that they might look very different depending on the subscriber's device configuration. Some systems don't support emojis at all. Instead of a smiley face, the subscriber might see an empty box: □.

Preheader best practices

Technically, preheader text and preview text are slightly different concepts. *Preview text* is a snippet of copy from the body of your email that appears below the sender name and subject line in your subscriber's inbox. *Preheader text*, on the other hand, is any text that appears visually above the header in the body of your email.

People often use these terms interchangeably, probably because some email software uses the preheader text as the preview text automatically. In fact, in the Marketing Cloud software, the name of the field where you enter the preview text is actually Preheader Text.

Applications that subscribers use to view email messages usually display preview text on a separate line below the sender name and subject line. In most cases, two lines of preview text appear in the inbox; however, sometimes three lines appear.

Browser size, email app, and subject line length can all be factors in how much preview text appears in the inbox. For example, whereas the iOS Mail app can display approximately 90 characters of preview text, Windows Phone displays only about 40 characters.

Preheader text often contains instructions to "View this email in a web browser" or "Forward to a friend," which does not make a good impression on subscribers when included in the preview text. "Having trouble viewing this email?" in the preview is even worse, but not quite as bad as an unsubscribe link showing up front and center. To avoid spoiling your preview text, consider moving these administrative elements elsewhere in your email, or add a sentence or two of more compelling text before these elements.

Support for preview text varies. Even among email applications that display preview text, the appearance varies. Use these tips for creating great preview text:

>> Think of preview text as a second subject line and use similar strategies. Write preview text that is useful, is specific, and, if appropriate, has a sense of urgency.

>> Experiment with humor, symbols, or other tactics that aren't quite ready for subject line status.

>> Put keywords first to make sure subscribers see them before the email cuts off the preview.

>> Don't reuse your subject line or the headers from the email. Instead, play off the subject line and further encourage your subscribers to open the email message. For example, if your subject line is "50% off new arrivals," use preview text to explain what type of merchandise has arrived.

>> If you've had success using personalization fields in other parts of your campaigns, try personalizing preview text, too.

>> Include a call to action (CTA) or secondary CTA: Does your email ask the subscriber to do something? If that CTA pairs well with the subject line, consider showcasing it in your preview text.

>> Never try to trick your subscribers into opening your emails. The sender name, subject line, and preview text should work together so subscribers know what to expect when they open the email.

>> If you're sending a newsletter, highlight a featured article or two to encourage scrolling.

Rendering best practices

Rendering is how an email looks in different contexts: Different email applications, operating systems, screen sizes, and other factors affect how an email renders.

Because email messages use the same technologies as websites — HTML and CSS — many marketers assume that the same techniques for designing and coding websites work also for emails. Unfortunately, this is not the case. Email development requires using tables, HTML attributes, and inline styles in ways that are not best practices for websites.

Additionally, many email apps strip from emails code that could be a security threat or interfere with other functions of the app. Commonly stripped elements include JavaScript, object and embed tags, and Flash.

Starting with Outlook 2007, Microsoft stopped using the features of its web browser, Internet Explorer, to render emails in Outlook. Instead, Outlook users see emails as Microsoft Word would render them. Microsoft chose Word for this task because of its strengths in authoring and embedding other kinds of Microsoft content, such as spreadsheets and charts. Unfortunately, users also get one of Word's weaknesses: rendering HTML originally created outside Word.

Microsoft's choice to use Word as a rendering engine leads to other limitations as well, such as lack of support for animated GIFs. If your subscribers use Outlook and you include an animated GIF in your email, they see only the first frame of the animation. Make the first frame of an animated GIF count: Keep it simple and don't rely on the full, animated GIF to communicate your message.

Word (and therefore Outlook) doesn't support many common CSS properties that are used in websites, such as *float* and *clear*. To structure your emails for the best rendering across all devices, you must use tables to control where each element appears on the page.

Pressure for Microsoft to fix rendering in Outlook has grown over the years. In 2016, the company announced a partnership with Litmus to improve rendering in Outlook.

Style sheet best practices

Designers use CSS, or Cascading Style Sheets, to control things such as colors and fonts in web pages and emails. CSS lets you choose among three places to define your styles: in a separate CSS file (external stylesheet), at the top of your HTML file (embedded styles), or right next to each element in your document (inline style).

Web designers often favor the external style sheet approach because you can control the look and feel of an entire site in one centralized place. However, email doesn't support external style sheets. Most emails use a mix of inline and embedded styles.

If you've been around email marketing or email design for any length of time, you've probably heard the advice that you must always use inline styles rather than embedded styles.

The main structure and styling of emails are usually inline, because this is the most reliable way to achieve consistent rendering across email programs. For example, until September 2016, Gmail stripped embedded styles from emails. Inline styles were the email designer's only way to make an email render correctly in Gmail.

However, the technology is changing. To continue the Gmail example, in September 2016, Gmail began rolling out changes to support embedded styles rather than stripping them from emails.

If your testing shows that embedded styles can work, you can realize benefits from eliminating inline styles. Embedded styles mean smaller file sizes, shorter turnaround times, and less opportunity for inconsistency in the design of your email.

Choosing which CSS technique to use comes down to a few factors:

>> The skill set of the person or team building your emails.

>> The rendering capabilities of the email programs that your subscribers use.

>> Whether you intend to use responsive email — a kind of design that detects the size of the subscriber's screen and adjusts to match it. This advanced technique requires a media query, which is a special tool available only if you use embedded styles.

Creating an email

To create an email, use these steps:

1. **From the Content Builder app, navigate to the folder that you want to contain the email.**

   You can move the email later if you need to.

2. **Click the Create button (above the toolbar on the right side of the screen) and point to Email.**

   The Create an Email Wizard appears and steps you through the process.

3. **Complete the fields in the Define Properties step of the wizard.**

   Choose whether to create an email based on a template, from HTML, that's text only, or based on another email you already created. You'll populate other data depending on which you choose.

MORE LITMUS RESOURCES

Litmus maintains a freely available blog with lots of advice about creating excellent email content, including the following:

- 6 Shocking Myths about Subject Lines (https://litmus.com/blog/6-shocking-myths-about-subject-lines)

- Why Measuring Subject Line Success by Opens Is All Wrong (https://litmus.com/blog/why-measuring-subject-line-success-by-opens-is-all-wrong)

- How to Write the Perfect Subject Line [Infographic] (https://litmus.com/blog/how-to-write-the-perfect-subject-line-infographic)

- How to Write Captivating Email Subject Lines, Featuring Joanna Wiebe (https://litmus.com/blog/how-to-write-captivating-email-subject-lines)

- The Three Key Elements of Irresistible Email Subject Lines (http://www.copyblogger.com/email-subject-lines/)

- The Ultimate Guide to Preview Text Support (https://litmus.com/blog/the-ultimate-guide-to-preview-text-support)

- Update: Gmail Rolls Out Support for Responsive Design, Improved Font Styling + CSS for Accessibility (https://litmus.com/blog/gmail-to-support-responsive-email-design)

- Responsive Email Support in Gmail Is Coming (https://www.campaignmonitor.com/blog/email-marketing/2016/09/responsive-email-support-in-gmail-is-coming/)

- Understanding Gmail and CSS (https://litmus.com/blog/understanding-gmail-and-css-part-1)

- Mastering Outlook: A Look Back at Common Rendering Issues (https://litmus.com/blog/mastering-outlook-a-look-back-at-common-rendering-issues)

- Why Do Some Email Clients Show My Email Differently than Others? (https://litmus.com/help/email-clients/rendering-engines/)

- Scalable, Fluid or Responsive: Understanding Mobile Email Approaches (https://litmus.com/blog/defining-and-understanding-mobile-email-approaches)

- 10 Things You Didn't Know About Mobile Email (https://litmus.com/blog/10-things-you-didnt-know-about-mobile-email-google-hangout-with-litmus-hubspot)

- Understanding Responsive and Hybrid Email Design (https://litmus.com/blog/understanding-responsive-and-hybrid-email-design)

(continued)

(continued)

- Mobile Email Kit (`https://litmus.com/lp/mobile-email-kit`)

- Defining and Understanding Mobile Email Approaches (`https://litmus.com/blog/defining-and-understanding-mobile-email-approaches`)

- Understanding Responsive and Hybrid Email Design (`https://litmus.com/blog/understanding-responsive-and-hybrid-email-design`)

4. **Complete the fields in the Add Content step of the wizard.**

   Use the editor tool to create content. You can drag and drop images, content blocks, and code snippets into content areas or you can create content for a content area that is specific to this email.

5. **Complete the fields in the Preview and Test step, and then click Save.**

   Preview the email in various ways and then do a QA send (see the next section) to yourself and others in your company, just to make sure it looks right. The preview is powerful. It can show you things like the following:

   - The default, graphical view

   - The plain text view for subscribers who request text-only emails

   - The email as it looks on a computer and on a mobile device

   - The email as it looks to different subscribers, if you have personalization or dynamic content in any of the content blocks

Preparing an Email to Send

Now that you've created your email, you're ready to perform quality assurance tests with trusted people inside your company. Then you finally arrive at the monumental moment of clicking Send to deliver the email to your subscribers.

Previewing the email

Marketing Cloud includes a tool to see what you email will look like to different subscribers in your audience. When you reach the Previewing and Test step in the Create an Email Wizard, you choose a subscriber from your audience and the system displays your email with the personalization, dynamic content, and other automated content as it will appear for that person. You can scroll through all subscribers in the list or data extension to see what the email will look like for each subscriber.

The preview tool shows how you designed the email for each subscriber in the list, but the subscriber's email client might still render the email differently. Third-party tools, such as Litmus, are available to help you preview different renderings.

When you create an HTML email in Marketing Cloud, the system automatically creates a text-only version of the email. The text-only version mostly matches the email you created, except that all the text is the same size and color, and without the images. Both the HTML and the text-only version of the email are available for you to preview.

In some cases, subscribers request to receive the text-only version of the email. For example, subscribers with vision impairment who use screen-reader software probably prefer to receive only the text, because the software can't easily read images aloud.

In most cases, subscribers receive the multi-part MIME version of the email. Multi-part MIME emails include the HTML as well as the text-only version in case your beautifully designed HTML version can't render for any reason.

You should preview both the HTML and the text-only version of your email. The system updates the text-only version with your changes from the HTML version up until the moment you make changes to the text-only version. As soon as you make a change to the text-only version, the connection is broken; you can't count on further changes you make to the HTML version appearing in the text-only version.

You should wait until your HTML email is complete before making changes to the text-only version. After the HTML version is complete, though, you should remove any CSS or other code that doesn't make sense in the text-only version.

The system tends to move links to unexpected places in the text-only version of the email. Make sure the links make sense when you do your text-only preview.

Performing QA tests

For your quality assurance (QA) process, you should create an email list of a few internal people who have the time, interest, and attention to detail to do a thorough review. At a minimum, your testers should do the following:

>> Open the email on various devices and in different email clients to make sure it looks as you expected.

>> Review the grammar and spelling.

>> Click the links to make sure that they go to the right page.

The URL that the links in your email point to look different in the emails you send than they did when you entered them in the email editor. This is because the links need to first direct to Marketing Cloud and then redirect to the correct location so that the system can track who clicked.

As you continue to use Marketing Cloud, you'll develop a list of test items specific to your content. Your QA testers should perform the tests for both HTML and text-only versions of the email.

When you send an email for QA, choose the option to suppress the send from tracking. That way, the links your QA testers click won't alter the true count of links your subscribers click in tracking.

Choosing an audience

The content of an email is only half the story: You need subscribers to receive the message you've worked so hard on.

Marketing Cloud has several tools to put subscribers together for messaging, including the following. You may have even more subscriber-grouping tools if you've integrated your Marketing Cloud account with any other business tools you use, such as your CRM system.

>> **List:** The traditional tool for putting subscribers together to receive the same message. Marketers often name their lists after the kind of message it receives. For example, you might see lists named Newsletter or Daily_Deals.

>> **Group:** A subset of a list. You can create two kinds of groups. The first kind groups all subscribers who have the same value in an attribute, such as all subscribers in the list with the same birthday. The second kind groups a certain number of subscribers in the list at random. You create a group in the Email app by choosing Groups from the Subscribers menu and following a simple wizard.

>> **Data extension:** The relational-data model equivalent of a list. If you set up your account to use a relational data model, as described in Chapter 6, you use sendable data extensions instead of lists to contain the subscribers who receive an email.

>> **Audience:** The result of using Audience Builder. An audience is just a sendable data extension, but the Audience Builder app creates it to contain the results of your sophisticated segmentation. See Chapter 8 for complete information about Audience Builder.

>> **Data filter:** Like a group, but more powerful and compatible with data extensions as well as subscriber lists.

>> **Suppression list:** A list that you set up to prevent the subscribers on it from receiving a message. You might set up a suppression list to keep people who have complained about your emails from receiving further communication or to prevent subscribers who work for your competitors from getting your messages.

For the sake of simplicity, in this chapter we refer to all these options for grouping subscribers as *lists.* When you reach the Select Audience step of the Send Email Wizard, shown in Figure 11-3, you have more options than just choosing the list to which you want to send; you can also choose lists that should not receive the message.

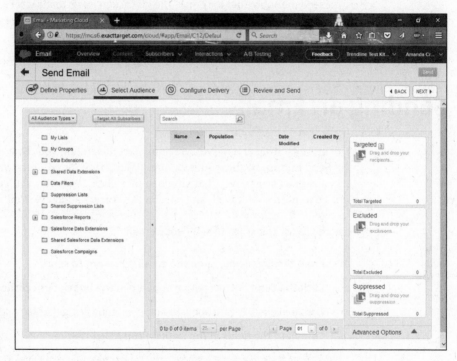

FIGURE 11-3: Select the audiences to send to and those to exclude from your send.

The Select Audience step includes the following categories of lists for you to specify for your send:

>> **Target:** The equivalent of the To field in your personal email client. The subscribers in this category are those whom you want to receive your email message.

>> **Exclude:** Lists of people whom you don't want to receive this particular message. When a subscriber exists on both a target list and an exclude list, Marketing Cloud does not send that subscriber the email.

You can use this list to make sure that you don't annoy members of a list by sending them too many messages. For example, if you sent a message to your Newsletter list an hour ago, you might exclude the Newsletter list from your send to the Daily_Deals list so that any subscribers on both lists don't receive messages too frequently.

You also might exclude a domain in which you are still going through the IP warming process (see Chapter 3) or are working through deliverability problems.

» **Suppress:** Lists of people whom you never want to receive a message. The mechanism for a suppression list works the same way as an exclusion list: If a subscriber appears on a target list and a suppress list, the system does not send the subscriber the email. The distinction exists to make it easier for you to maintain a list of subscribers whom you never want to receive your messages.

Sending an Email

The most exciting and nerve-wracking part of sending your first email is clicking the Send button. We have known many Marketing Cloud users who have experienced serious stress over that single mouse click. However, you've created excellent content, tested it well, and chosen the correct audience: You're ready.

Use the following steps to send your email:

1. **From the Email app, open the email you want to send.**

2. **Click the Send button, which appears in the upper-right corner.**

   The Send Email Wizard appears with the Define Properties tab open.

3. **Complete the fields in the Define Properties step.**

   - *Type the subject of the email in the Subject field and click Done.* The subject is usually the first thing the subscriber notices about an email in the inbox, so it makes the first impression for your message.

   - *Type 85-100 characters of a message preview in the Preheader field and click Done.* Some email clients — especially those on mobile devices — show the preheader as a short preview of the message in addition to the subject line.

   - *Choose the name that you want to appear as the sender of the email from the drop-down menu on the From Name tab.*

- *Choose the send classification, sender profile, and delivery profile that you want to use from the drop-down menus on the Saved Send Classifications tab.* Chapter 3 covers send classifications, sender profiles, and delivery profiles in detail.

4. **Complete the fields in the Select Audience step.**

   In the navigation pane on the left, navigate to the folder that contains your desired list. When you click the folder, the lists in that folder appear in the list pane in the middle of the screen. Drag a list from the list pane to the Targeted, Excluded, and Suppressed areas on the right side of the screen. You can find complete details about the targeted, excluded, and suppressed lists in the preceding section.

5. **Complete the fields in the Configure Delivery step.**

   - Choose whether to send the email immediately or schedule the send. If you schedule the send, choose the data and time.

   - Select the Track Clicks check box. We always leave this selected.

   - Select the Send Tracking Results to Sales Cloud. We always leave this selected. Even if you don't use Salesforce as your CRM, leaving this box selected won't hurt anything.

   - Select the Multipart MIME check box. We always leave this selected.

   - Select the Suppress from Send Reports check box *only* for test sends.

   - (Optional) Change the folder where you save the tracking data for this send by clicking Change under Tracking Destination Folder.

6. **Check all the information in the Review step, and then click Send.**

TIP

   The count of excluded subscribers that appears under Total Excluded includes the total number of subscribers in the list(s) that you excluded, without regard to whether those subscribers are included in the targeted audience. This is also true for the count of suppressed subscribers under Total Suppressed.

7. **Select the This Information Is Correct and This Email Is Ready to Send check box, and then click Send.**

Tracking Your Email

The Tracking menu in the Email app contains the traditional tracking and reporting tools that have existed in the product since its inception. Although more sophisticated analytics tools exist in the Marketing Cloud (see Chapter 9), the tracking tools in the Email app are still useful for a quick snapshot of the performance of an ongoing campaign.

The tracking results for an email change over time, especially in the first few days after you click Send. The sending process itself can play a role in this: Your email may take seconds to send if the content is simple and the audience is small, or it make take hours if you used a lot of code and personalized content and are sending to a very large list. During that time, only some of the subscribers have had the chance to open the email or click it.

Even when the email send process is complete, though, not all subscribers open an email right away. The number of opens and clicks will continue to increase over time as subscribers discover the email in their inboxes. Tracking usually settles down within two weeks of your send, but a subscriber could surprise you and open or click a link in an email months after you send it!

Accessing email tracking

You open email tracking from the Email app by choosing Sends from the Tracking menu on the toolbar. A tracking dashboard with a list of your sends appears, as shown in Figure 11-4.

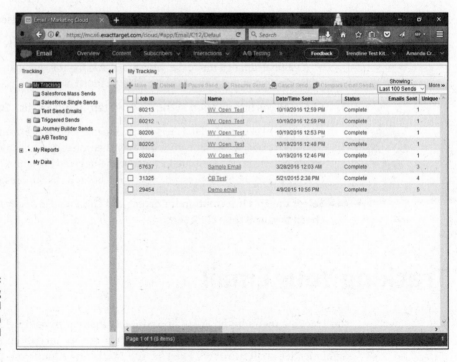

FIGURE 11-4:
The Tracking dashboard provides a snapshot of email performance.

By default, all sends appears in the My Tracking folder. If you selected a different folder for tracking on the Configure Delivery tab of the Send Email Wizard, you might need to navigate the folder hierarchy to find your particular send.

Navigating email tracking

You can click the name of a send to see its tracking details. The Tracking Details screen, shown in Figure 11-5, contains five tabs: Overview, Click Activity, Conversions, Surveys, and Job Links.

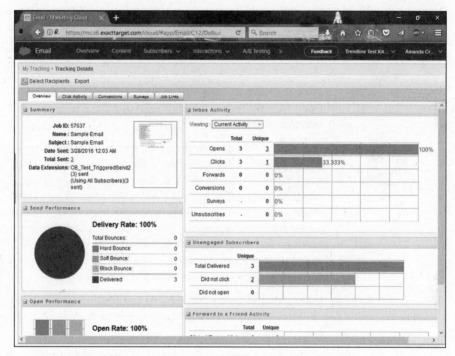

FIGURE 11-5:
Open Tracking Details to begin digging into the specifics of the email's performance.

Overview tab

The Overview tab offers a nice visual snapshot of the performance of the send. If you see an underlined number on this screen, you can click it to dig into the specific subscribers. For example, you can click the number next to *Did not click* to see the subscribers in the list who did not click any links in the email.

This screen contains sections for Summary, Send Performance, Open Performance, Inbox Activity, Unengaged Subscribers, and Forward to a Friend.

>> **Summary:** Contains the send properties, such as Job ID, email name, subject line, date sent, total messages in the send job, and the lists or data extensions to which you sent the message. If you sent to more than one audience, click the Select Recipients button in the toolbar and isolate one audience to see the tracking for that audience.

>> **Send Performance:** Shows how many emails bounced and categorizes those bounces into hard (a problem such as unknown email that is so serious that additional attempts to deliver the email are pointless), soft (a temporary problem such as a full inbox), and block (a subscriber who blocked your from address).

For each count, you can click the number and see the emails in each category, and you can export the list of bounces so you can use it to clean up your lists.

WARNING

The Summary box also lists the number delivered. However, Marketing Cloud calculates this value by subtracting the total bounces from the total sent. There is no way to verify that all these emails actually arrived in the inbox.

>> **Open Performance:** Contains the percentage of delivered emails that subscribers opened.

TIP

Open rate is not a good success metric because of the nature of the tracking pixel. Marketing Cloud includes a 1-pixel-by-1-pixel transparent image in each email. When a subscriber's email client requests that tracking pixel from the server, Marketing Cloud knows that the subscriber opened the email. However, you probably already realize that it's possible to open and read emails without displaying the images. You should use better metrics than opens and clicks to determine success. Consider your email marketing goals and think about metrics such as conversion percentage, downloads (of a white paper, for example), or dollars in sales.

>> **Inbox Activity:** Shows the following categories of subscriber interaction with the email. You can choose whether to see the numbers cumulatively or on a graph over time.

- *Opens:* The number of subscribers whose email clients requested the tracking pixel.

- *Clicks:* The number of times subscribers clicked links in the email.

- *Forwards:* The number of times subscribers forwarded the email using the Forward to a Friend tool. Because most subscribers use the Forward button in their email client to forward emails, this number doesn't necessarily capture all forwards.

- *Conversions:* The number of times subscribers made purchases after clicking a link in an email. Setting up this functionality requires a substantial configuration of your shopping cart and emails.

- *Surveys:* The number of subscribers who completed a survey. This number includes only surveys created with the Email app survey tool, which nowadays is rarely used, so this value will probably be zero.

- *Unsubscribes:* The number of subscribers who unsubscribed by clicking the unsubscribe link in the email.

>> **Unengaged Subscribers:** Shows how many subscribers haven't clicked a link in your email and how many haven't opened the email. These numbers may go down over time; don't forget that an email can have a tail of about two weeks. You'll see these numbers change a lot in the first two days, but you'll continue to see changes over the next few weeks in smaller increments.

>> **Forward to a Friend:** Contains counts of how many people clicked a forward to a friend (FTAF) link in your email, how many people they forwarded it to, and how many people subscribed to your list as a result. This box is useful only if you include a FTAF link in your emails and a subscriber uses it. Subscribers tend to use the Forward button in their email client instead of a FTAF link.

Click Activity tab

The Click Activity tab includes two options for seeing how many subscribers clicked links in the email: Email Overlay View and Link View.

The Email Overlay View shows you the email and overlays a percentage next to each link. This view is useful when you want to identify which physical locations in your emails are most popular to click.

REMEMBER

The Email Overlay View is not a heat map, which tries to measure which part of an email people *looked* at. This view shows you only where subscribers clicked.

The Link View simply lists the links and how many clicks they received.

Conversions tab

If you insert the right tracking code into your website and set up the links in your emails correctly, Marketing Cloud can keep track of which subscribers click the links and eventually make purchases on your website.

The link that the subscriber clicks in your email contains information about who the subscriber is and which link in which email he or she clicked. The website stores that information and associates it with data about any purchases the subscriber makes. Then the website passes that information back to Marketing Cloud so that you can view it in the Conversions tab of the Tracking Details screen.

Here you can see how subscribers become customers and evaluate how much revenue different parts of your email campaigns generated.

Surveys tab

The Surveys tab is useful only if you include Marketing Cloud surveys in your emails. The large majority of Marketing Cloud users do not use surveys.

Job Links tab

Unlike the other tabs, which show you a reflection of what subscribers do, the Job Links tab lets you correct incorrect links in an email. If you accidentally put the wrong URL in an email, you can use this screen to redirect it to the correct location. This new feature is a nice one because previously you had to contact Marketing Cloud support to redirect a link in an email you already sent.

Comparing tracking for multiple emails

In addition to viewing detailed tracking for an individual email send, you can select the check boxes next to multiple emails on the dashboard and click the Compare button. A high-level summary of how the email performed appears in a list so you can do a side-by-side comparison. See an example in Figure 11-6.

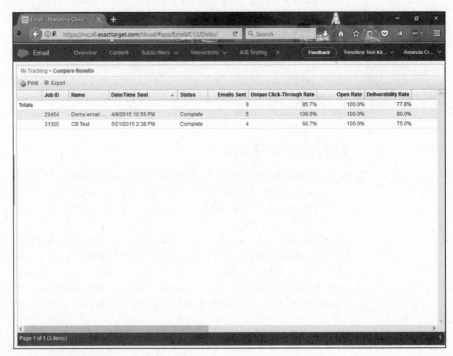

FIGURE 11-6: Comparing tracking helps evaluate the success of an email send in the context of another send.

Pausing or canceling a send

If you click Send on an email and immediately regret it, you might be able to pause or cancel the send before it finishes. Pause Send and Cancel Send buttons appear on the toolbar of the Tracking dashboard, as you can see in Figure 11-7. Select the check box next to the email send you want to pause or cancel and click the button.

FIGURE 11-7:
Prevent a scheduled send or stop an in-progress send, if you're fast enough!

In this case, the quick performance of Marketing Cloud is a double-edged sword. Even sending 50,000 emails might take as little as ten seconds! The likelihood that you can pause or cancel a send job already in progress is low, so make sure you do your email preparation work thoroughly.

On the other hand, you can use these buttons to prevent a scheduled send from starting, if you want to send the email at a future time instead of immediately.

Advanced Tactics in Email

After you become comfortable with the standard functionality in Marketing Cloud, you might want to begin using some of the more advanced tactics that email marketing experts leverage. In this section, we talk about A/B testing, dynamic content, and AMPscript.

A/B testing

Marketing Cloud offers a built-in tool that you can use to compare the performance of parts of two emails, such as subject lines, from names, and sections of email. You send two variations to small audiences to see which performs better. When you declare a winner, you send it to the larger list.

TIP

As you set up your A/B tests, always keep your goals in mind. Are you interested in driving up conversions? Clicks? Dollars? Testing should always, always, always relate to the goal. Think intelligently about possible changes to reach your goal.

Subject line and preheaders

When testing subject lines and preheaders, you want to discover what is most effective at getting subscribers to open the email. Testing a subject line and preheader makes sense with newsletters, for example, because they have so much useful content inside that all you need to do is convince the subscriber to open. After that, the content keeps the subscriber engaged.

Content area

When testing a content area, you want to discover what is most effective in getting subscribers to click. For example, you might test which color background results in more clicks.

From name

When testing a from name, again you want to discover what convinces subscribers to open the email. You might test your company name against your CEO's name, for example. A/B tests of from names are more common among B2B companies, where the subscriber might know someone at the company personally.

Send date/time

When testing send date and time, you want to discover when most of your subscribers are available to open your emails. Send date and time tests are common and may inform many of your future sends.

Dynamic content

Dynamic content, which we introduce in Chapter 7, is a content area in an email in which several different pieces of content might appear, depending on the attributes of the subscriber.

For example, you could create a dynamic content area in an email that shows the following:

>> A map of the closest store location to the subscriber, based on the subscriber's ZIP code

>> The subscriber's reward point balance

>> How many nights a subscriber has stayed in qualifying hotels and how many more the subscriber needs to spend to become a gold member

Consider using dynamic content to change the imagery in the email based on the subscriber's tier in the reward program. For example, create a gold header for gold-level members, a silver header for silver-level members, and a bronze header for bronze-level members.

Another example is to show just a few subscribers a special image. You could show a sports-related image to subscribers in the ZIP codes of the teams in the championship, but show a default image to the subscribers who aren't in those ZIP codes.

AMPscript

AMPscript is a scripting language that Marketing Cloud created to use in Marketing Cloud emails. Many people have become skilled with using AMPscript to personalize the content of HTML emails, text emails, landing pages, SMS and MMS messages, and push notifications through MobilePush (see Chapter 12).

You include AMPscript in these kinds of messages when you define them in your Marketing Cloud account. For example, when you're typing the content of an email in the email editor, you can also type AMPscript alongside the other text. When you preview or send the message, the system processes the AMPscript and renders the result of the code.

Some uses of AMPscript follow:

» Getting relational data from several different data extensions to use in the email. We introduce relational data and data extensions in Chapter 6.

» Choosing different content to show to different subscribers, based on information you know about the subscriber. For example, you could write an AMPscript to include different stories in a newsletter based on a subscriber's hobbies.

» Formatting data from your data extensions so the data looks the way you want.

» Defining regions in your email to track to evaluate their effectiveness.

AMPscript has flexible and powerful customization capabilities. However, AMPscript is an advanced topic in Salesforce Marketing Cloud, and its syntax and functions are outside the scope of this book.

Chapter **12**

Mobile Studio

obile marketing is about extending your digital marketing to reach your subscribers even when they are on the go. The technology that powers your mobile campaigns offers a lot of power and flexibility.

You can create mobile campaigns that are as simple as sending a text message to make an announcement. On the other end of the spectrum, you can set up sophisticated monitoring to notice when one of your subscribers comes close to your store and send him or her a personalized message at that moment.

The mobile marketing apps in Salesforce Marketing Cloud reside in the category called Mobile Studio. Mobile Studio contains three apps to cover three kinds of use cases:

» **MobilePush:** Integrate notifications and alerts into your mobile apps and create location-based beacons to trigger messages in your own mobile app when a user enters a designated area.

» **GroupConnect:** Send messages, stickers, emojis, and other rich content to narrowly segmented users. This Marketing Cloud app requires the use of the Line messaging app, which is already widely available in Japan and gaining popularity worldwide.

» **MobileConnect:** Send ad-hoc or automated mobile messages.

Deciding Whether You're Ready for Mobile Marketing

Mobile marketing gets you closer to achieving that ideal of delivering right time, right place messages to your customers. By integrating mobile marketing alongside your other messaging tools, you can broaden your reach and even enhance the effectiveness of other digital channels.

However, the effort of setting up and maintaining mobile marketing is not for the faint of heart. Consider the following challenges you will face when starting a mobile messaging program:

>> **The heavy lifting of setting up:** The apps in Mobile Studio can require substantial effort to enable, and the process can be expensive. For example, just leasing a private short code — the six-digit code that your customers use to text you — alone can cost $500 to $1,000 per month. More sophisticated location-based messaging requires you to set up beacons in the places where you want to send in-app push messages to subscribers. That means purchasing and installing equipment in your physical stores, plus developing a mobile app if you don't already have one and integrating it with Marketing Cloud. The effort, time, and cost to get up and running can be substantial.

>> **Designing for the medium:** Putting together a 160-character SMS message might seem easier than building an entire email message. However, composing an effective call-to-action that drives customer engagement within the constraints of an SMS/MMS message requires careful planning and efficient composition.

>> **Staying legal:** Regulatory and industry requirements around SMS/MMS programs are more complicated than the requirements for email. Getting access to legal assistance in drafting terms and conditions for your program is a must.

A clear vision for a mobile messaging program and the ability to deliver on the promise presented to subscribers are important. You need to make sure that you have a plan in place and the means to carry it out before diving in.

Understanding Mobile Terminology

If you're new to mobile technology, you might find the lingo a bit confusing. The following sections describe some of the terms you'll need to know as you get started.

SMS and MMS

You may have heard text messages referred to as *SMS messages.* SMS stands for Short Message Service. SMS messages must be text only and are limited to 160 characters, though many mobile devices will automatically divide longer SMS messages that you draft into multiple messages and send them in rapid succession.

More recently, MMS messages hit the scene. MMS stands for Multimedia Messaging Service. *MMS messages* can include multimedia, such as images, sound, and video. The 160-character limit on SMS messages does not apply to MMS messages. If a subscriber's mobile device supports MSS, rich media can appear in text messages; a separate app to create and read MMS messages is not required. From the subscriber's point of view, SMS and MMS are the same thing — text messages.

WARNING

By design, SMS/MMS messages interrupt your subscribers' lives. Unlike email, which sits quietly in the inbox until the subscriber decides to read it, a mobile message alerts the subscriber urgently, wherever the subscriber may be. To keep the trust of your subscribers and delight them with your mobile campaigns, you need to adhere strictly to the relevant regulations and industry-mandated best practices.

The CTIA (Cellular Telephone Industries Association) sets the guidelines for SMS/MMS messages. The CTIA is a wireless carrier industry organization that regularly performs audits of SMS/MMS marketing programs. Failure to comply with CTIA guidelines can result in cellular carriers suspending your SMS/MMS program. The Mobile Marketing Association (MMA) also provides best-practice guidelines.

SMS/MMS marketing falls under the federal Telephone Consumer Protection Act (TCPA). The TCPA requires things such as getting consent before sending mobile messages, providing easy options to opt-out of your mobile campaigns, and sending messages only during daytime hours. Your legal department should review the TCPA requirements. Failure to comply with TCPA can result in hefty fines.

Short codes

When you send text messages to your family and friends, you send them to their phone numbers. However, have you noticed that when businesses ask you to text them, they offer a shorter sequence (usually six digits or letters) to which to send your message?

Short code is the name for that short sequence of characters. SMS/MMS messages use short codes to communicate messages between businesses and individuals. When you decide to start mobile marketing, you'll need a short code.

You can save money by sharing a short code with other companies, but most companies that do mobile marketing eventually lease a private short code. You can lease a random series of numbers, or for an additional charge, you can choose the characters and create a vanity short code.

Mobile-originated campaigns

In a *mobile-originated campaign,* you put a keyword out into the wild — by printing it on billboards or in direct mail, for example — and see who signs up to interact with your brand. As the name implies, the campaign really begins when someone sends you a message from a mobile device.

Mobile-terminated campaigns

A mobile-terminated campaign is the other side of the mobile campaign coin. Whereas in a mobile-originated campaign the conversation starts when a subscriber sends you a message from a mobile device, in a *mobile-terminated campaign* you start the conversation by sending a message to the mobile device.

Any outbound message, including alerts and responses to inbound messages, is a mobile-terminated message.

Configuring Your Account for Mobile

You can purchase the mobile apps — MobilePush, MobileConnect, and GroupConnect — individually or together. Even if you purchase two or three of the apps together, you must configure each app individually. For MobileConnect you must also purchase additional support time from Salesforce to set up the app. Talk to your Salesforce account executive for details.

That said, some tasks, such as those described in the following sections, could help you prepare for mobile messaging in general.

Setting up your data for use with mobile

If you're accustomed to email marketing, you need to make some changes to your data mindset as you get ready for mobile.

Lists and data extensions

The same lists and data extensions that you use to send email messages also work for sending outbound SMS/MMS messages. The only difference is that for SMS/MMS messages, you need a mobile phone number instead of an email address to send your messages.

If you're using subscriber lists, you need to create a subscriber attribute to contain the mobile phone number. If you're using data extensions, you need to create a field for the phone number. See Chapter 6 for details on subscriber lists, data extensions, and how to create space for your subscribers' mobile phone numbers.

TIP

MobileConnect requires the use of lists rather than data extensions for sending. If you've stored your mobile records in data extensions, you must import them into a mobile list for sending.

You will also need to begin capturing your subscribers' mobile phone numbers. You can just publicize your short code and wait for subscribers to contact you, but you don't have to be limited to that approach. See Chapter 5 for ideas on drumming up good subscriber data.

Mobile campaigns

The campaign tool that you use for email marketing works also for your mobile campaigns. The main difference between email and mobile campaigns is their design more than the technology to manage them.

One big differentiating factor between email campaigns and mobile campaigns is immediacy. Because a large portion of the population has a mobile device within arm's reach at any time and tends to react quickly to incoming texts, the chances of your mobile message being seen right away are far greater than when your email lands in the subscriber's inbox.

MobileConnect

MobileConnect offers the traditional back-and-forth SMS/MMS communication with customers that probably comes to mind when you think of mobile marketing.

Typical kinds of mobile-originated campaigns that you might send with Mobile-Connect include the following:

>> **Email opt-in:** Subscribers can join your email list by sending a keyword and their email address to your short code. This is usually a one-time text-message interaction: After you have the subscriber's email address, you send him or her email messages rather than SMS/MMS messages.

>> **Info capture:** This kind of campaign is similar to an email opt-in campaign, but you can use it to capture any piece of data, not just email addresses. For example, you use this kind of campaign for "progressive profiling," where, once you have the subscriber's email address, you ask for the person's name. Once you have the name, you ask for the ZIP code. Once you have that, you ask for the birthday, and so on.

>> **Text/media response:** A subscriber triggers an automated response using a keyword — for example, replying with *MORE* to receive another message with more information. You can use media to get subscribers involved with something fun. We've seen a brand encourage subscribers in a stadium to reply with selfies holding its product. The brand gave a prize to the best image and meanwhile received a wealth of action shots with its product.

>> **Vote/survey:** This kind of campaign uses a specific message template to send an invitation to the subscriber to answer true/false, yes/no, or multiple-choice questions.

The mobile-terminating messages that you create in MobileConnect can be highly personalized. Some Marketing Cloud users make extensive use of AMPscript, Marketing Cloud's proprietary scripting language (see Chapter 11), to send messages at relevant times for the individual subscriber and to include subscriber information stored in data extensions (see Chapter 6) in Marketing Cloud.

You send mobile messages to a data extension, just as you can do with email messages. The data extension must have a field for the mobile number of the subscriber to be a valid target list for a mobile message. Any data that you set up your AMPscript to include in the message also needs space in the data extension.

MobileConnect overview screen

You get to MobileConnect by selecting MobileConnect from the Mobile Studio category on the app switcher. When you open the app, you see the Overview screen, shown in Figure 12-1.

From the Overview screen, you can take several actions in the MobileConnect app, such as creating a new mobile message.

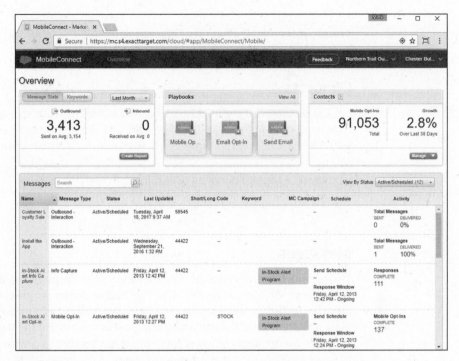

FIGURE 12-1:
The Overview screen is a dashboard of your mobile marketing efforts.

Message Stats/Keywords

The Message Stats/Keywords box, in the upper left of the Overview screen, shows message or keyword statistics. Message statistics relate to your outbound messages, whereas keyword statistics relate to the inbound messages you receive with a particular keyword.

In either case, you can see the number of messages over a length of time. Use the drop-down menu at the top of the box to change the time period to any of the following values:

>> Last 24 hours

>> Last 7 days

>> Last month

Click the Create Report button to generate a report of this information so that you can have access to the data outside of Marketing Cloud.

Playbooks

The Playbooks box, in the top middle of the Overview screen, is a link to playbooks. As we mention in Chapter 4, the use of Playbooks may be phased out soon in favor of Journey Builder (see Chapters 11, 16, and 17), so we will not discuss this box in any further detail.

Contacts

The Contacts box, in the upper-right corner of the Overview screen, contains your total number of mobile opt-in subscribers and the percentage growth of that list over the last 30 days. You can perform the following activities from this box:

» Click the Manage button to open Contact Builder.

» Click the Add Contacts button to import lists of mobile contacts.

Messages

The bottom three-quarters of the Overview screen displays the list of messages you've sent via MobileConnect. You can find a particular message by scrolling through the list (to move to the next page, you might need to use the pagination tools at the bottom of the box) or by using the Search field at the top of the box. You can limit the messages you see in the Messages box to those with a certain status by using the View By Status drop-down menu, in the upper-right corner of the box.

Setting up keywords

A *keyword* is the word that a subscriber texts to your short code to, for example, sign up for your program, get help, and opt-out. You have to set up keywords in Marketing Cloud so that the system knows how to respond when it receives a message from a subscriber that contains this word.

You set up your keywords in the Admin section of MobileConnect. To be compliant with industry regulations, you must set up a keyword that your subscribers can use to opt-out of the program and a keyword to get help.

Use the following steps to set up a keyword:

1. **From the MobileConnect app, click Administration in the gray toolbar at the top of the screen.**

   The Administration screen appears with an overview of the mobile-related settings in your account. The Short/Long Code section of the screen contains a list of all your short codes, and each is a hyperlink.

2. **Click the short code for which you want to create the keyword.**

   A screen appears with a list of all the keywords associated with that short code.

3. **Enter your keyword in the Create Keyword field that appears in the toolbar of the Keyword Management section on this screen.**

   Figure 12-2 shows where to find this field.

4. **Click the Create button.**

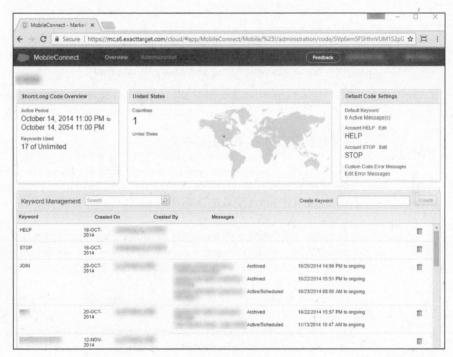

FIGURE 12-2:
The field where you define your keywords is tucked into the middle of this screen.

After you complete this procedure to define a keyword, you instruct the system on how to respond to the keyword as part of your message setup. See the "Creating a message" section, after the next section.

Setting your blackout window

The Federal Telephone Consumer Protection Act (TCPA) limits the hours of the day during which you can send text messages to your subscribers, and you might want to limit the sending window even further. After you've decided when you will *not* send text messages, you can set up a blackout window in the MobileConnect to prevent any sends.

Use the following steps to set up your blackout window:

1. **From the MobileConnect app, click Administration in the top toolbar.**

   The Administration screen appears.

2. **In the Send Blackout box on the right side of the screen, click the Set Blackout Window link.**

   The Set Blackout Window screen appears.

3. **Click the Enabled status to instruct the system to prevent the sending of text messages during this blackout window.**

4. **Select the start and end times of the blackout window, and then click Save.**

Creating a message

The steps to create an outbound (mobile-terminated) mobile message depend on the type of message you send and the way you send it. The following steps are for an outbound message sent by an automation.

For inbound (mobile-originated) messages, choose a keyword that you defined previously (see the procedure on setting up keywords earlier in this chapter) and then indicate the text of the message to send in response to a keyword.

Use the following steps to create an outbound mobile message in MobileConnect:

1. **From the MobileConnect Overview screen, click the Create Message button (on the right side of the toolbar).**

   The Create New Message Wizard appears, open to the Select Template step.

2. **Choose the template you want to use for your mobile message.**

   You can choose from the following options:

   - *Outbound:* A simple SMS message from your business to your mobile subscribers. For this example, we're choosing this template.

   - *Text Response:* An SMS message that the system is ready to send in response when a subscriber sends a keyword.

   - *Vote/Survey:* A message to invite your mobile subscribers to participate in a poll that you create as part of the message.

   - *Mobile Opt-In:* A message to invite people to become subscribers to your mobile messages.

- *Info Capture:* A message to ask your subscriber for information, such as his or her name or email address. You can store the response you receive as a contact attribute.

- *Outbound Media:* Similar to the outbound message, except this message uses MMS technology so it can include more rich media.

- *Media Response:* Similar to the text response, except with MMS.

- *Media Share:* A message to invite mobile subscribers to send you media, for example, photos of themselves using your product. You set up this type of message also to store the media so you can find it later.

- *Email Opt-In:* Invite mobile subscribers to subscribe to your email messages.

- *Send Email:* A message to invite subscribers to receive an automated email from your business.

3. **Click Next.**

   The Define Content step of the wizard appears. The files in this step may vary, depending on the message type you chose in Step 2.

4. **In the Message Name field, enter a name for the message.**

   You use this name to identify the message in tracking or when you want to edit the message definition later.

5. **In the Short/Long Code drop-down menu, choose the short or long code from which you want to send the message.**

6. **Choose the Send Method:**

   - *Schedule:* Choose a date and time when you want to send the message. This is the most common option.

   - *API Trigger:* API code that you write triggers the send of the message.

   - *Automation:* An automation in Automation Studio sends the message. See Chapter 10 for details about Automation Studio.

7. **Enter the text of the message in the Outbound Message field and then click OK.**

   When you start typing in this field, a preview appears to help you visualize what your message will look like on a mobile device. Tools also appear in this field to help you insert personalization strings, shorten URLs, and convert commonly abbreviated words to their abbreviations.

8. **(Optional) If you want to associate the message with a campaign in the Campaigns tools (see Chapter 4), click Add Campaign and choose the campaign.**

   If the campaign doesn't exist yet, click the Create Campaign button to create one.

9. **Click the Activate button to make the message available for the automation to send.**

MobilePush

The MobilePush app lets you send messages through your existing mobile app. Many consumer-facing businesses already have mobile apps even if they don't have a larger-scale mobile marketing plan. A mobile app can be almost as simple as your corporate website, offering information as basic as your store's location and hours of operation.

Mobile app development is relatively simple and straightforward these days. After you design the functionality of your mobile app, you can probably find a firm to develop it for you in short order.

Figure 12-3 shows the MobilePush interface.

General messages

Once you integrate your mobile app with MobilePush, subscribers who get the app will accept conditions during the installation process, such as the following:

>> "This app would like to send you notifications"

>> "This app would like to send you badges"

By giving your app these permissions, subscribers agree to let you push them messages through the app. For example, a newspaper app on your phone might use MobilePush to alert you to a breaking news story by sending you a synopsis of the story.

TECHNICAL STUFF

You integrate your app with MobilePush by using a tool called a Software Development Kit (SDK). The SDK is a group of files that make it easier for developers to integrate the systems. You can have your development organization download the SDK from the Salesforce developer site at this location:

```
https://developer.salesforce.com/docs/atlas.en-us.mc-sdks.meta/mc-
sdks/mobile-push-sdk.htm
```

FIGURE 12-3:
Create a message in the MobilePush interface to send to customers via your mobile app.

Your company's app has to have slightly different flavors for iPhones versus Android phones, and the integrations between these apps and MobilePush are also slightly different. Separate SDKs are available from the preceding URL for iOS and Android.

Location-specific messages

MobilePush supports location-based messages as well. You define the borders of your location, and when a mobile device with your app enters a border, you send a message.

One technique for sending location-specific messages is geofencing. *Geofencing* uses the same kinds of satellites your navigation or mapping device might use. However, that kind of location technology is probably not specific enough for your in-store needs. Satellites are better at knowing which city block users are on than which kiosk they are near. In addition, users often disable this functionality on their phones because it drains the battery faster.

The technique you're more likely to want to use is a beacon. A *beacon* is a special piece of hardware that uses Bluetooth technology to detect when a mobile device is nearby.

When a subscriber comes close, you can send a greeting or an exclusive offer. With beacon technology, you might even be able to send department-specific messages. For example, when users approach sporting goods, you could alert them to a sale on treadmills.

TIP

Location-based messages can backfire if you don't craft them carefully and warn your customers in advance. When customers realize that you know exactly where they are in the store, they might find it more creepy than cool.

GroupConnect

The GroupConnect app lets you send rich content to narrowly segmented users who also use the Line messaging app. Line is a popular social-networking tool in Japan that is gaining popularity in other parts of the world.

Figure 12-4 shows an example of the GroupConnect interface.

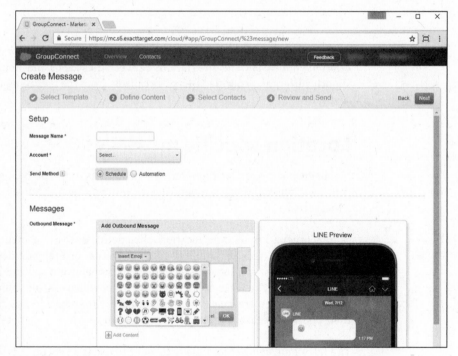

FIGURE 12-4: GroupConnect makes it easy for you to compose messages to your users on the Line social network.

If your customers use Line, this is certainly an app you want to evaluate. However, a discussion of its use is outside the scope of this book.

Respectful Mobile Marketing Checklist

No matter what tool you use, you want your subscribers to look forward to receiving your mobile marketing messages. To create a mobile marketing campaign that delights subscribers, provide useful, valuable content in a respectful way. The following checklist helps you make sure you're respecting the needs and privacy of your subscribers:

» **Always have opt-in permission.** For a program where you send recurring messages, you generally obtain permission by asking a customer to text a specific keyword to your short code to subscribe. You can also set up a form on your website where people can sign up to become SMS/MMS subscribers.

   To comply with CTIA standards, people signing up using your web form require an additional step, known as a double opt-in. You send an SMS/MMS message to the phone number on the form asking subscribers to confirm that they want to join your list. When the subscriber replies to the message to confirm, you add the subscriber to your list. This step makes sure that you have the correct number and that the person in possession of the phone intended to subscribe.

» **Set rules and expectations.** For recurring programs, your initial message should

   - Describe the program ("Thx for joining Flash Sale alerts").

   - Set expectations about frequency of messages ("receive up to 4 msgs/month").

   - Explain that the charges that the subscribers pay for any SMS/MMS messages apply also to your messages ("msg & data rates may apply").

   - Offer a link to detailed terms and conditions ("see example.com/terms").

   - Say how to stop the messages and how to get help ("STOP to stop msgs; HELP for help").

» **Always include your business's name in your messages.** If the message is part of a specific program, such as "flash sales" or "upcoming events," include the name of the program in the message as well. This information builds trust with your subscribers and helps them remember that they requested the message.

» **Control when you're sending messages.** The TCPA limits automated communications to between 8 a.m. and 9 p.m. in your recipient's time zone.

» **Let them say no.** CTIA requires the use of a stop function (usually a reply keyword) for opting-out as well as help instructions. A way to opt-out should always be included in every message, not just the first one.

Chapter **13**

Social Media Studio

S ocial media is hot. People use applications such as Twitter, Instagram, and Pinterest to meet, socialize, and shop. Companies are rushing to create visibility in social media because so many of their customers and prospective customers are there.

All the excitement around social media might lead you to believe that marketing in this channel is a silver bullet for all your marketing problems. The reality, however, is far different. Social media marketing, despite its current hype, is much like the other channels online marketers can use, with its own benefits and drawbacks.

Although it seems new, social media marketing has been around for a long time, when you compare it to all flavors of online marketing. Social media marketing just has a lot more visibility recently, especially when influencers at all levels (up to the US president) are leveraging social channels to either extend their own brand or influence other people to think or act a certain way.

In this chapter, we talk about the Social Media Studio app, which you can use alongside your other online marketing apps in Salesforce Marketing Cloud.

Deciding to Go Social

If your target audience is inclined to be on social channels, you should be there too. Even if your company is a business-to-business entity, it can benefit from a social presence. Getting started is easy — tons of people do it every day. You just make a wall on Pinterest, start a page on Facebook, or post some pictures to Instagram.

Mind you, business use of social media is not the same as personal use. Just as you would with email marketing, your business should have a list of specific objectives for its social presence. Suitable examples follow:

>> Improving customer service

>> Raising brand awareness

>> Introducing new products

>> Promoting a cause

>> Generating leads

You need to think about the voice you're using and consider what kind of statement you're making as a company. Your social presence influences how people perceive your company. Consider the Instagram account of General Electric. When you think of GE, you might think of appliances, but after a trip through its Instagram account (www.instagram.com/generalelectric), your perception of the company will probably be quite different.

On this Instagram account, you see pictures of widely varied and interesting projects that GE works on — from aircraft engines to locomotives to industrial power generation. Social has become an important branding tool for GE and has helped increase its perceived coolness, not just among potential customers.

Thanks to social media efforts like this one, more tech-savvy job candidates are interested in the company and shareholders have a better understanding of the core business. Those benefits are above and beyond the traditional marketing outcomes that affect the bottom line.

Figuring out if you're ready

Because social media tools are so easy to use, you might think that marketing through them is just as intuitive. The hard work of social media marketing is not in figuring out how to put up a post, though. Consider these questions:

>> **Is your company ready to hear your customers' unvarnished feedback?** A company's first role in a social conversation is to listen, but hearing customers complain about the products, services, or policies you worked so hard on can sting. You need to have a procedure for responding to complaints and train your employees to avoid becoming defensive. Rising to the bait of a customer who just had your product fail is one of the worst things you can do for your corporate image.

>> **How can your social media campaign add value?** Adding real value to the ongoing conversation about your brand is important in all communication channels, but social media users have an especially high expectation of your contributions. People stop listening immediately if all you offer is publicizing your product.

>> **Are you committed to the ongoing work of producing content?** Part of the attraction of social media to its users is the freshness of the content they can find there. If you can't make the time or don't have the budget to produce new content on a regular schedule, your social media marketing efforts will fall flat.

Going for it

It's great to be prepared and have a sophisticated plan for your social marketing efforts, but it's possible to overthink it! In the grand scheme of things, all your business really needs to get started in social media is the willingness to listen. Stop talking and listen. You must give up your need to control the conversation and be willing to be a part of it. When it's your turn to talk, be authentic — celebrate your successes and own up to your failures. If you let people see how genuinely awesome you really are, the rest will take care of itself.

Social Studio Concepts

Social Studio is the app for social media marketing in Marketing Cloud. You use Social Studio to do the following:

>> **Listen** to what your customers are saying about your brand. You might use this information just to get a sense of how your brand is perceived, but ultimately you'll use the insights from this data to make business decisions.

>> **Respond** to your customers' posts yourself or assign them to another department for response, if appropriate.

>> **Create, approve, and publish content** on your social media accounts. You can also automate workflow activities to schedule future posts and route incoming messages according to keywords.

Before we describe how to set up and use the product, we discuss a few special terms you'll see in this chapter.

Inspector

An *inspector* is a window that overlays another window in Social Studio. Usually you see an inspector slide in from the side of the screen. It shows you details when you click an item. (Skip ahead to Figure 13-7 to see an example of an inspector.)

Other apps in Marketing Cloud have similar tools to let you dig into detail information about something you see on the screen, but only Social Studio calls this kind of tool an inspector. Look for the term in the app's documentation and training materials.

Topic profiles

A *topic profile* is a collection of keywords or phrases that interest you. When you configure a topic profile, the system returns all mentions of your keywords from any sources on the social web that Social Studio tracks. Social Studio tracks more than 100 million sources, including blogs, forums, video sites, and news sites.

You can set up groups of related keywords so that you can use the same groups in multiple topic profiles. Similarly, you can set up reusable groups of sources to include or exclude from your topic profiles.

Figure 13-1 shows a topic profile that is the basis of a dashboard in the Analyze module. It searches for two keyword groups: Brand and Camping.

You can use the results collected by a topic profile in an abstract way when you're analyzing your brand's perception online or as a practical to-do list when you're engaging with your customers on social media.

If your topic profile returns results in which your keywords appear too far from each other, you can use the *proximity* feature. For example, a post that mentions your product name in one sentence and then coincidentally mentions the word *support* in the next sentence is probably a false positive for your customer service listening. However, if you set up a keyword with your product name, the word *support,* and ~3 (tilde and 3), that tells the topic profile to return results only if your product name appears within three words of the word *support.*

FIGURE 13-1:
Topic profiles can be used as the basis of dashboards as well as in other places in the system.

TIP

You can also set up your topic profile to exclude posts that include particular words. When you're first setting up your social presence, though, you'll probably want to include all matches from your topic profiles just to make sure that you're catching everything. Until you're overwhelmed with data that is more than 80 percent noise, you can just scroll past the false positives.

You create topic profiles on the Admin screen. You can also create them in the Engage or Analyze modules, if you are at least a Full User in the workspace.

You can edit a topic profile in the Edit Topic Profile inspector, shown in Figure 13-2.

TIP

In our experience, a good way to start is to listen for these important topics as you design your first topic profiles:

» **Customer service:** Use keywords such as *support* and *service.* Remember also to listen for negative words that people might use when they're having a problem, such as *fail* and *sucks.*

» **Lead generation:** Use keywords such as *looking at* and *recommendations* in addition to your product name or the name of the product category.

» **Competitive insight:** Listening for information about what your competitors are up to is less about choosing keywords and more about pulling information from the sources that your competitors make available.

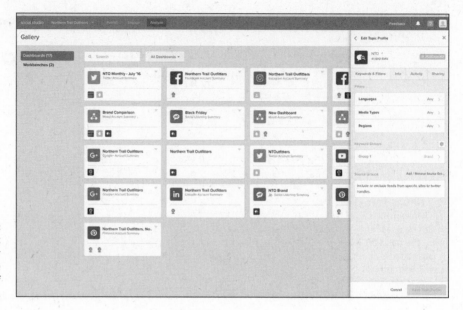

FIGURE 13-2:
Use the Edit Topic
Profile inspector
to update the
configuration of
your topic profile.

Marketing Cloud offers a spreadsheet of sample keywords for these and other topics. You might eventually create a lengthy list of words for each topic, so using a starter list can make your job of choosing keywords much easier.

Workspaces

The day-to-day work of social media marketing through Social Studio happens in a workspace. A *workspace* is a tool that limits user access to only certain accounts and makes sure they don't accidentally post to the wrong account. When you set up a workspace, you add users and social media accounts to it to control who has access to what.

Figure 13-3 shows a selection of workspaces set up in the account.

A workspace has the following features:

>> You add users to the workspace who will be working together. You can add a user to multiple workspaces.

>> You associate certain social accounts with the workspace so that workspace members can publish from there. You can associate a social account with multiple workspaces.

>> You associate certain topic profiles with the workspace, which gives members of that workspace access to only the content they should work on.

>> Each workspace offers a calendar that members of the workspace can use to schedule events.

You might set up a separate workspace for each product in your product line. Alternately, you might set up a separate workspace for each business unit in your company. Another possibility is a workspace based on a geographical area so that a team can collaborate on communicating with customers in a particular country. Any group of users in your account who work together and use the same calendars and social media accounts is a good candidate for a workspace.

To use a topic profile, you have to associate it with the appropriate workspaces. Use the following steps to add an existing topic profile to your workspace:

1. **From your workspace, click Add New.**

   The Add Topic Profiles window appears with a list of all topic profiles in your account.

2. **Select the topic profile whose results you want to import to the workspace.**

3. **To add the topic profile to the workspace, click Add Topic Profiles.**

   A message appears to tell you when the import is complete. The topic profiles you added then appear in the list.

Users and roles

In Social Studio, as in other Marketing Cloud apps, you assign roles to users to control what functionality they can access. However, Social Studio has a different approach to controlling user access than other Marketing Cloud apps: You can't override the role's permissions for a particular user. In addition, a user has two tiers of roles: User role and Workspace roles.

User roles control how much access a user has to see, add, and change content. The available User roles follow:

>> **Basic users** are the most restricted. They can see the content in their workspace, but can edit it only if they created it themselves or if the creator of the content shared it with them.

>> **Full users** are the default type of user. In addition to creating and editing content, they can also create workspaces, topic profiles, and social accounts.

>> **Super users** can do everything full users can. In addition, a super user can administer users, register social media accounts to use in the workspaces, create workflow approval rules, and more.

Workspace roles control the user's access to the tools in a workspace. A user can have different Workspace roles for each workspace, but the User role always stays the same. The available Workspace roles have the following names:

>> **Limited members** can

- Use the social media accounts for which the admin has given permission

- View content, the calendar, and analytics

- View the content they create themselves, plus anything shared with them

>> **Contributors** can

- Use all the social media accounts in the workspace

- View all the content in the workspace

>> **Admins** can

- Perform the same activities as a contributor

- Manage users, accounts in the workspace, and settings

- Create approval rules for content

Supported Social Media Networks

Social Studio interacts with your company's social media accounts to publish your posts and retrieve analytics. Before you can use Social Studio with your social media account, you (of course) need to create those social media accounts. Social Studio works with the following kinds of social media accounts:

- » Facebook
- » Twitter
- » Google+
- » Instagram
- » YouTube
- » LinkedIn
- » Pinterest

You are not limited to only one account in each social media network. For example, you could have three Facebook pages, six Twitter handles, and a LinkedIn page that you manage through Social Studio.

You might also find it useful to have a bitly account (go to `http://bitly.com`). Bitly is a URL-shortening tool: You enter a long URL into bitly, and it provides a short URL that you can use in your social media messaging. When readers click the short link, bitly forwards the user to your longer URL.

TIP

A short URL is particularly useful in social media channels that limit the length of your messages. Even when the social media network lets you use as many characters as you want, a shorter URL looks more polished. Plus, when you use Bitly to shorten a URL, you can log in to your Bitly account and use the analytics there to see, for example, how many clicks the link has received.

Getting Started with Social Studio

Social Studio originated as a separate application from Marketing Cloud, and it still requires separate credentials. Incidentally, Social Studio's functionality is also available outside Marketing Cloud, so you may come across documentation, training, or promotional materials that give instructions to log in directly to Social Studio. However, because this is a book is about Marketing Cloud, we assume that you're accessing Social Studio after logging in to Marketing Cloud first.

The Social Studio credentials come in an email when you license the app. Contact Salesforce Marketing Cloud if you didn't receive them. The first time you open the Social Studio app, you have to provide those credentials to connect your Marketing Cloud account to the correct Social Studio account. After that, though, Marketing Cloud stores the credentials so you shouldn't need to provide them again.

You access Social Studio from anywhere in Marketing Cloud by pausing your mouse pointer over Social Studio on the app switcher and clicking Social Studio in the list that appears.

A super user needs to go into Social Studio first and set up the tools that everyone else will be using. A super user needs to do the following to prepare the app:

>> **Set up users for Social Studio.** You can't add a user to a workspace until a super user has added the user to the app.

>> **Register social accounts in Social Studio.** After you've gone to each social media network and created the accounts that you'll use, a super user needs to register them — that is, set up Social Studio to use those particular accounts.

>> **Set up and configure workspaces for users to work in.**

At this point, someone other than a super user can get some work done in Social Studio. However, super users can still complete the following tasks as well:

>> **Create approval rules.** Using this feature, you can make sure that an appropriate approver gives the say-so to publish a post before the world sees it.

>> **Prepare publish labels for workspaces to use.** Publish labels are tags you can add to your posts. Later, you can segment analytics by the publish labels and see how all the social media efforts with a particular tag performed.

>> **Configure topic profiles.** Full users can also create topic profiles for the workspaces to which they belong.

Social Media Marketing in Social Studio

At last, you're ready to begin using the tools in Social Studio. It has taken a substantial setup — both inside Social Studio and with the social media networks themselves — to get to this point, but all your work is about to pay off.

Now when you log in to Social Studio, you see a list of available workspaces (refer to Figure 13-3). Full users can also create more workspaces and add users to a workspace.

The functionality of Social Studio functionality falls into three modules: Analyze, Engage, and Publish.

TIP

You might find that the different modules correspond to different people in your organization. For example, a marketing data analyst might mostly use the Analyze functionality, while a customer support agent mostly uses Engage.

Analyze

The Analyze module contains the tools that you use to review what social media is saying about your brand. Analyze can retrieve data about your own social media accounts: your own posts, and the comments, likes, and direct messages you receive. It can also let you dig into the results of a topic profile, which broadly listens for all mentions of the keywords that you configure it to look for.

Figure 13-4 shows the Analyze module when you first open it.

FIGURE 13-4:
The Analyze module defaults to the Dashboards tab so you can choose a dashboard to open.

The Analyze module has two tabs: Dashboards and Workbenches, described next.

Dashboards

Dashboards provide an at-a-glance performance summary over a specified time period. This tool is for business users, such as executives, whose job description doesn't include dedicating hours to digging into social data to identify market trends. This tool gives the casual viewer a quick overview of what's going on with the brand. Figure 13-5 shows a dashboard.

FIGURE 13-5:
Dashboards are pretty and functional, too.

Workbenches

Whereas the Dashboards tab gives the high-level executive view, the Workbenches tab offers the nitty-gritty analyst view. Somebody who is trying to discover the story of what is happening with the brand online will find ample material in the workbenches.

Each card on the workbench shows a count. The count represents either all the activity on one of your accounts or the results of a topic profile, depending on how you set up the card. In either case, you can click the filter icon on the card to open the Filter inspector. Here you can apply filters to reduce the count and make it more manageable.

You can segment your filtered data set by clicking any data you see on one of the cards and choosing how you want to segment it. For example, Figure 13-6 displays two parallel rows, each of which represents a separate segmentation of the original data.

In the top row, the analyst segmented the original dataset by hashtag. The resulting bar graph shows a bar for each hashtag that appears in the data. The analyst then clicked the #nto bar to further segment the data by sentiment. Finally, the analyst clicked the red section of the circle graph to segment the negative posts by the words that appear within them.

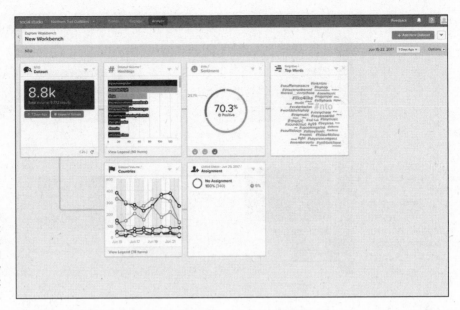

FIGURE 13-6:
Workbenches let data enthusiasts filter and thoroughly segment the data.

In the second row, the analyst took the same initial data set and segmented it by country. The analyst then segmented the data from the United States to see whether the posts appear on the work queue of anyone in the company.

Engage

The second aspect of social marketing to cover is engaging with the people you find by paying attention to the social networks. You may have people on your team whose entire job is spending the day in the Engage module of the application, participating in the online community to establish trust and help create brand advocates among your customers. Customer service organizations often make use of this module.

You use topic profiles in Engage to display all the activity directed at your accounts. You review the posts and determine whether they require a response. Figure 13-7 shows the Engage module populated with social marketing activity. Engage updates the information from the accounts every 30 seconds.

You can click an entry in one of the columns to open the Post inspector. In the Post inspector, you can view the post and do work on it, such as reply or forward it to someone else.

FIGURE 13-7:
The Engage
module includes
a column for each
account or topic
profile.

In addition to just the text of the post, the Engage module shows useful information that you can consider as you choose how to respond. For example:

» **Twitter Author Influencer Score:** A number between 0 and 100 that shows how much influence the commenter has on Twitter. This score appears for Twitter posts only.

» **Sentiment indicator:** A smiley or frowny face to indicate, at a glance, whether the tone of the post is positive or negative.

» **Author labels:** A classification of the intent of the post. For example, a post in which the author is looking for help using your product receives the Support Seeker label.

The Engage screen contains a panel of quick action icons from which you can perform actions such as replying, liking, and direct messaging in response to a post. In addition, you can set up macros that complete multiple common actions with a single button click. For example, you could set up a macro that sets the priority of a post to high and assigns a reply to a particular user in your customer support organization. Whenever you find a post that needs these two things, you can activate the macro with a single click.

Publish

When you first open a workspace, the Publish tab is what you see by default. However, we waited to discuss it until the end of the chapter because, conceptually, you should do this part last. Just as you wouldn't barge into an ongoing conversation at a dinner party and just start talking, you shouldn't jump into contributing to the social conversation until you've spent some time getting the feel for the room.

Now that we've discussed listening and engaging with people who are already talking about you, we're ready to address the idea of putting your own posts out there. The Publish module is where the people who create your outbound social communication do their work. Figure 13-8 shows what you see when you open the Publish module in a workspace.

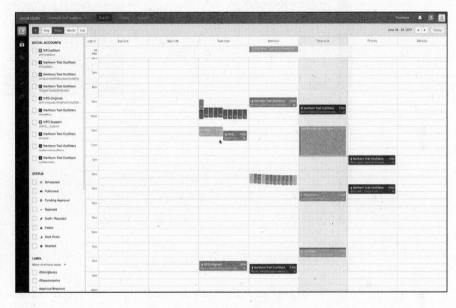

FIGURE 13-8:
The calendar shows the outbound social communications scheduled during the days visible on the calendar.

Along the left side of the screen, note the following tabs (represented with icons):

>> Create

>> Calendar

>> Drafts

>> Performance

>> Tasks

>> Shared Content

Create

The Create tab, shown in Figure 13-9, is where you create content. The options for controlling the post may vary slightly, depending on the social network to which you're publishing.

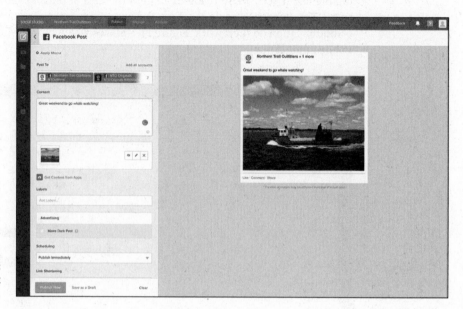

FIGURE 13-9:
The new post
editor.

Use the following steps to create a post:

1. **From any tab in the Publish module, click the Create Content button.**

   If you want to schedule a post for the future, you can instead start from the calendar and click the date on the when you want to publish the post.

2. **Select the social media channel in which you want to post.**

   The editor window appears.

3. **In the Post To field, choose which account or accounts you want to publish the post to.**

4. **In the Content field, compose the post.**

   You can use the buttons below the field to add images, video, and other media besides just text. The buttons available vary depending on which social media network you chose in Step 2. A preview of the post appears on the right side of the screen for you to review.

5. **In the Label field, enter labels.**

   Later, you can aggregate analytics data based on the values you enter in this field.

6. **In the Scheduling field, choose whether to publish the post immediately or schedule it for the future.**

7. **(Optional) Complete any other fields that you want to use in the inspector.**

   The other fields vary depending on the social media network.

8. **Click Publish Now (if you chose to publish the post immediately in Step 6), Schedule (if you chose to schedule the post in Step 6), or Save as Draft.**

TIP

If you chose a publish date in Step 6 but then click the Save as Draft button in this step, the system will not publish your post until you reopen the draft and click the Schedule button.

Calendar

When you schedule a message to publish, it appears on the calendar on the date you scheduled, as shown in Figure 13-10. The color-coding on calendar items indicates the social account that will publish the message. You can use the buttons in the upper-left corner of the window to see the day, week, or month view on the calendar. You can also choose to see the items in a list instead of on a calendar.

If you click a post, the Post Details inspector appears, overlaying the calendar on the right. The inspector includes the body of the post as well as details about its status and schedule. Figure 13-10 shows an example of a Post Details inspector for a post scheduled to appear on Twitter.

Drafts

When you create the content for a post, you can publish it right away or you can schedule it to publish later. You can also save a post in progress as a draft so that you can finish it later. The Drafts tab is where you find your drafts.

Performance

After you've published some posts from your workspace, you can see performance information in the Performance tab, shown in Figure 13-11. This tab gives you a high-level view of how many posts you've published on each account, how much interaction those posts have received, and more. You can also export some reports from this tab. Of course, you can get even more analytical information in the Analyze section of the app.

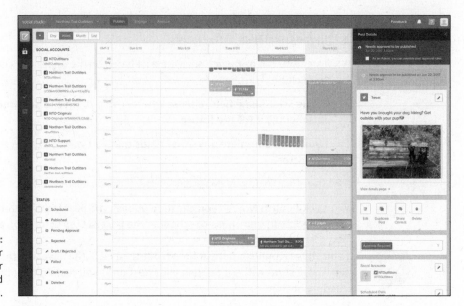

FIGURE 13-10:
The calendar
shows your
scheduled
messages.

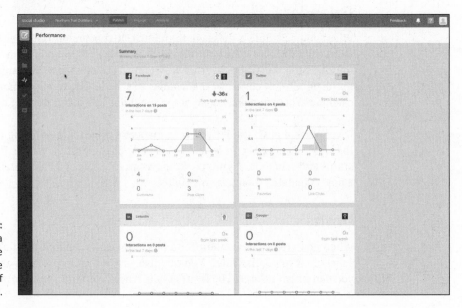

FIGURE 13-11:
Performance data
for the workspace
is available in the
Publish section of
the app.

Tasks

If you have set up an approval workflow, the Tasks tab is where you find your queue of tasks to approve posts.

Shared content

Other users and workspaces can share content with you; if they do, you find it on the Shared Content tab. Shared content can be a valuable resource for increasing engagement with tried-and-true posts. Figure 13-12 shows the Shared Content tab.

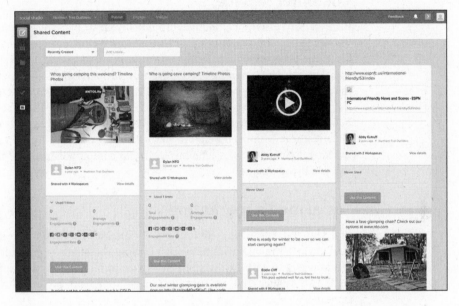

FIGURE 13-12:
If a piece of shared content was previously published, you can see how it performed.

Each piece of content on this tab tells you how many times the post has been published and how much engagement the content inspired from the social network. By leveraging successful posts in multiple channels, you can get the most out of your content.

Social Media Best Practices

For this section, we collaborated with Tom Hasselman, social media marketing thought leader and Product Manager at Salesforce Marketing Cloud. Some content in this section is adapted from Marketing Cloud's 50 Social Media Best Practices, available at `https://www.salesforce.com/form/marketingcloud/conf/50-social-media-best-practices-2017.jsp`.

Use cases

Although companies find many creative uses for their social media accounts, we mostly see two kinds of use-cases: customer service and social media marketing.

Customer service

Back in 2007, many companies did not invest in offering customer support via social media. The situation has changed significantly since then, but we do still see some companies that haven't invested in this channel and are ignoring the social phone. Not listening to your users on social media is akin to just not answering some of your support calls or replying to only a few of your email messages.

Some of your customers will send your company support requests directly, but not all customers who need help are so forthcoming. You will need to get creative in tracking down your users who misspell your company name, use abbreviations, or call you by nickname.

Social media marketing

Creating and publishing content via social channels is not the same as placing paid advertising on social networks. Placing social ads is possible, but it's a different use case with its own best practices. In fact, social media marketing, done well, can reduce the amount you need to spend on advertising to acquire customers.

An important tip for social media marketing is to develop a unique voice for each channel over which you engage you community. Users who follow your company across multiple channels should hear a coherent message but not just a copy-and-paste of the same message over and over again.

Other use cases

Maybe it's not surprising, but we've been seeing growth of public relations activity over social media. Public relations professionals use the channels to determine where messages are resonating and who is talking about the brand. Social media listening plays a pivotal role in managing and monitoring crises, which inevitably gain traction on social media. Public relations professionals need to understand how many people are talking about the crisis and on which social networks. They want to monitor the public perception and sentiment and get involved when appropriate.

Social selling is the other up-and-coming arena of social activity. For example, if a social user asks for recommendations on things to do while on a trip to New York, attractions in the area can chime in with links to special events or offers.

Businesses that sell products and services to other businesses (B2B companies) need not feel left out of the social sphere. Regardless of whether you're selling to an individual or a business, you're always selling to a person, so social media channels can offer a powerful opportunity to connect. Large B2B brands such as Salesforce, DocuSign, and Bombardier are blazing a trail as active social participants.

Listening and analytics

Regardless of your use case, you want to make sure to listen before you engage. These ten tips offer ideas for improving your listening plan:

>> **Research where on social media people are talking about you.** You probably already thought of places such as Facebook and Twitter, but don't forget about Snapchat, TripAdvisor, and Yelp. The nature of your business will heavily influence where you find people talking about you.

>> **Identify industry influencers.** If you can't find anyone talking about your brand, you might need to find the influencers in your industry and invite them to comment on your brand. You can find trusted influencers creating content related to even the most specific topics.

>> **Listen for social selling opportunities.** Be on the lookout for people who are looking for recommendations or even people who are displeased with your main competitor. You don't want to miss a chance to send your sales team an opportunity.

>> **Keep an eye out for nondirect brand mentions.** People might be talking about you even if you don't see your company's name in the post. Look out for misspellings, abbreviations, or general talk about the industry that doesn't include you by name.

>> **Connect social to the broader business.** The best businesses break down silos and have all parts of the company working together. Social media does truly affect your entire organization, so get different departments involved in using social media for support, selling, and growing a community.

>> **Create categories to organize mentions.** Over time, the number of keywords you track and, we hope, the number of discussions about your brand will grow. You need to categorize the information coming in through your social listening program so that you can act on it appropriately.

>> **Draft analytics reports to help shape future marketing endeavors.** As we just mentioned, your successful foray into social media can soon have you drowning in data. Reports and other automation can take some of the heavy lifting so that you and the other humans on your team can focus on making decisions based on the data.

- » **Be customer focused, not channel focused.** You're using Twitter and Instagram instead of a phone, but you're still talking to a person. Use your social engagement to get to know your customers, their needs, and their relationship to your company in a genuine way.

- » **Automate what you can, but keep the human element.** The tools available through the Social Studio can help you manage the flood of data coming in from across the Internet, but you never want your customers to feel like they're talking to a machine.

- » **Draw meaningful conclusions about your customers from sentiment analysis.** Sentiment analysis is a tool that automatically judges the customer's attitude about your brand from the kind of words used in the message. Although sentiment analysis is sophisticated nowadays, it's not perfect. Sarcasm, for example, is difficult for the tools to detect. Make sure to check a sample of the messages to make sure you're getting good information from your sentiment analysis.

Engaging your community

When you're ready to join the conversation, use these ten tips to improve your social engagement:

- » **Empower employees to be social brand advocates.** Your staff is knowledgeable about your product and enthusiastic about its success. Encourage your co-workers to represent your brand on social networks and make it easy for them to do so. Keep a list of fresh links and short messages that employees can customize and post to their own circle of friends.

- » **Put Share buttons in strategic places.** A few years back you couldn't miss seeing social icons everywhere you turned. Now, companies are becoming more selective about when they advertise their social presence. You might show off a social network icon to announce that you've just joined. Always tell users the benefit of connecting with you, for example, if you accept support requests or offer special deals through a particular channel.

- » **Humanize the brand.** Own up to mistakes, give a behind-the-scenes glimpse, and show your personality. In an increasingly social world, people expect to have a much more intimate view into the companies they work with. Let them see that your company consists of people who care about helping them succeed.

- » **Grow your audience the right way.** Having a big number of fans looks good on the surface, but it doesn't tell the entire story. You want fans who are engaged and looking forward to interacting with your brand. Provide useful content on a regular basis, have respect for your customers, and respond to comments in a timely manner. It might sound old-fashioned, but it works.

>> **Be mindful of oversharing.** You want to stay on top of recent developments in your field and in the world around you, but posting too much can be a real annoyance to your fans. Test your campaigns to see what frequency works best and then create a publishing calendar that your whole team uses.

>> **Don't feel compelled to always jump in.** A well-timed comment on the news of the day may delight your social media followers, but your company probably doesn't need to register an opinion on every celebrity faux pas. Even when the topic is your own company, you sometimes may be better off to let your community of online advocates speak up on your behalf.

>> **Aim for transparency.** Especially on social media, customers want to feel as though they are involved in the real-life happenings in your company. Authentic communications, such as your CEO soliciting feedback online, can go a long way.

>> **Help customers become experts.** People like to be seen as an authoritative source of knowledge, and if you can help your social media followers to become experts on your company, you will have built brand advocates. Answer questions and offer resources to help your interested followers.

>> **Engage intelligently with positive feedback.** Always thank those who say nice things about you, and look for opportunities to elevate their status in return. For example, you could promote their latest blog post or offer to feature them in a case study. Social media users — and people in general — care about their friends' opinions. It's worth your while to cultivate positive reviews.

>> **Deal with negative feedback swiftly and skillfully.** Also thank those who say bad things about you, and make sure to ignore any name-calling so you can stay focused on the issues. Don't delete complaints, even if the social network allows it: Deleting negative comments can make your company look like it has something to hide.

Chapter **14**

Advertising Studio

The growth of social media networks and other online ad networks has given rise to a new marketing channel. As existing and potential customers began spending more and more time online to socialize, relax, and shop, online marketers quickly recognized the new opportunity that these online arenas presented for placing advertising messages.

The depth of information available about people online makes targeting ads with online advertising easier than it ever could be with older channels. When you can target your message to exactly the right people, you can spend less money on placing ads and get a more positive response from the people who do see them.

The Advertising Studio app is the online marketing tool in Salesforce Marketing Cloud. It helps you take advantage of the contact information that you already have about your subscribers, such as email addresses and phone numbers, to find those same subscribers on Facebook, Instagram, Twitter, YouTube, and other ad networks. Advertising Studio users have had impressive success using online ads to reengage audiences who have become unengaged with email marketing campaigns.

Advertising Studio also helps you find new customers by way of *lookalike audiences*, a group of social media users similar to existing customers. Because social media networks collect information about all their users — including your subscribers — and make that data available to you as a marketer, you can find other social media users who have key characteristics in common with your subscribers. Members of a lookalike audience may be more inclined to become your customer because they're similar to the customers you already have.

Advertising Studio Editions

Advertising Studio offers three different editions. The lowest edition comes free with your Marketing Cloud account. You can choose to license more functionality for an additional fee:

>> **Lead Capture:** This edition of Advertising Studio is included automatically with your Marketing Cloud account. It lets you pull data from Facebook into data extensions. (See Chapter 6 for more information about data extensions.) You can use this data to augment the data you already have about your subscribers and identify new potential customers.

>> **Professional:** For a fee, you can access the Professional edition. You should spring for the Professional edition if you want to place targeted ads in front of your existing subscribers while they're using websites or social networks.

>> **Enterprise:** For a higher fee, you can sign up for the top-tier Enterprise edition. You can use this edition to connect Salesforce CRM data to social and ad networks for lead generation campaigns. This edition requires substantial implementation and a thorough knowledge of your Salesforce CRM system, so its functionality is outside the scope of this book.

Lead Capture Edition

The lowest-level edition of Advertising Studio is the Lead Capture edition, which is the one that comes automatically with your Marketing Cloud account. To access Lead Capture, you select Lead Capture from the Advertising Studio category on the app switcher, as shown in Figure 14-1.

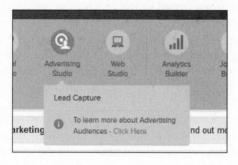

FIGURE 14-1: Lead Capture appears in the Advertising Studio category even if you haven't paid to license anything related to Advertising Studio.

You use Lead Capture with the lead capture forms in Facebook specifically. When you open the Lead Capture app, you create lead capture tasks and specify a corresponding Facebook lead capture form that you want to use to capture data into a data extension in your Marketing Cloud account.

The result of using Lead Capture is a data extension of contact information for Facebook users who are interested in your offer. The app does not currently provide any analytics.

You can also use Lead Capture to create Facebook lookalike audiences. Currently, Lead Capture can create lookalike audiences of Facebook users only.

TIP

Other social media platforms, such as Google and Twitter, let you generate lookalike audiences using their own proprietary tools.

When you open the Lead Capture app, an overview of your Facebook lead capture tasks appears, as shown in Figure 14-2. The overview lets you quickly see the status of each lead capture task in your account. From this overview, you can also create a new lead capture task.

FIGURE 14-2:
The Lead Capture dashboard offers a quick summary of your lead capture tasks.

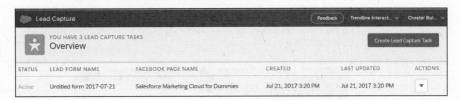

Before you can create the lead capture task, though, you need to create the lead capture form in Facebook that will generate the user information.

Facebook lead capture forms

You use a Facebook lead capture form to let Facebook users tell you they want to receive information from you. Usually you offer something, such as a discount or a newsletter, to entice users to sign up. Interested users go to the form and fill in their contact information so that you can send them whatever you offered. Figure 14-3 shows a sample Facebook lead capture form.

TIP

The Facebook lead capture form depends on you also placing an ad on Facebook to make users aware of your offer and drive them to your form. Figure 14-4 is a sample Facebook ad that drives use to the lead generation form.

FIGURE 14-3:
Fields on the Facebook lead capture form will eventually contribute subscriber data to your Marketing Cloud account.

FIGURE 14-4:
Sample Facebook ad that would lead subscribers to the capture form.

Knowing that its users are likely to be accessing the site via a smartphone, Facebook designed the forms to work well on mobile devices and require as little typing as possible. The form fields automatically prepopulate with whatever information the user has provided to Facebook in the past. Fewer empty fields are faster and easier for Facebook users, which makes it that much more likely that the user will complete your form.

You can find instructions on how to create a lead capture form at `www.facebook.com/business/a/lead-ads`.

Creating a lead capture task

After you set up your Facebook lead capture form (including the Facebook ad to drive users to the form), you can create the lead capture task.

WARNING

At this time, you cannot delete a lead capture task from Advertising Studio once you set one up. You can stop capturing leads through it by discontinuing the lead capture form on Facebook.

Use the following steps to create a lead capture task in Advertising Studio:

1. **From the app switcher, select Lead Capture from the Advertising Studio category.**

2. **Click the Create Lead Capture Task button that appears near the top right of the screen.**

   The Create a New Lead Capture Task Wizard appears on the first step: Select Facebook Page.

3. **Log in to the Facebook account that contains the lead capture form that you want to use.**

   You might need to grant the app permission to access information in your Facebook account as part of this step.

4. **Select the correct Facebook page, and then click View Lead Forms.**

   The wizard moves to the Choose Lead Forms step.

5. **Select the lead form you want to use, and then click Confirm Selection & Continue.**

   The wizard moves to the Define Data Extensions step.

6. **Review the configuration of the data extension to contain the lead information, click OK, and then click Continue.**

   The Define Data Extensions step in the wizard defaults to naming the data extension with the same name as the lead capture form. The data extension contains a field to correspond to each field in your lead capture form.

7. **Review the alert telling you that the system will create the data extension, and then click Submit Lead Capture Task.**

When Facebook users complete the lead capture form, Advertising Studio pulls the data into the data extension. Use the information in the data extension to deliver on the offer you made in your ad. Then you can also add the contact information that you gathered to your other marketing efforts.

Sample lead data extension

Figure 14-5 shows a sample data extension definition that Advertising Studio might create as the result of a lead capture task.

Fields					Edit Fields
Name	Data Type	Length	Primary Key	Nullable	Default Value
Lead ID	Text	64	☑	☐	
Lead Gen Form ID	Text	64	☐	☑	
Facebook Page ID	Text	64	☐	☑	
Facebook Ad ID	Text	64	☐	☑	
Date Collected	Date		☐	☑	
company_name	Text	1024	☐	☑	
email	EmailAddress	254	☐	☑	
full_name	Text	1024	☐	☑	

FIGURE 14-5: You define the fields in the data extension when you define it.

This data extension contains the following fields:

>> **Lead ID:** A unique identifier for the Facebook user. This field is meaningful only within this table.

>> **Lead Gen Form ID:** A unique identifier of the Facebook lead generation form that collected the data. You might use this information to evaluate the success of one form against another, or just to find out how a particular Facebook user got in to your system.

>> **Facebook Page ID:** A unique identifier of the Facebook page that contains the lead generation form. Again, you might use this information to evaluate how successful your Facebook pages are relative to each other.

>> **Facebook Ad ID:** A unique identifier of the Facebook ad that drives users to the lead generation form.

>> **Date Collected:** The date when the Facebook user completed the lead generation form.

>> **company_name:** The company name of the Facebook user who completed the form. This could be useful for identifying corporate users who may have a need for your service or would fit in your target demographics.

» **email:** The email address of the Facebook user who completed the form. This field appears in the data extension because there was a field for an email address on the lead generation form. You could add this kind of contact information to you email-marketing efforts.

» **full_name:** The first and last name of the Facebook user who completed the form. Even if you already had the email address for this subscriber, you could add the subscriber's full name to your records for use in your email-marketing and other online-marketing efforts.

Creating a lookalike audience

Using Advertising Studio, you can create lookalike audiences only in Facebook. However, other social networks, such as Google and Twitter, also allow you to target lookalike audiences in their own, native tools.

Your first step in creating a Facebook lookalike audience is to create a data extension of your best customers. See Chapter 6 for more information about data extensions. You can use the Email app (see Chapter 11) or the Contact Builder app (see Chapter 8) to get the subscriber information into the data extension.

You'll use the information in this data extension to tell Facebook about the kinds of users who are your ideal customers. The current customers that you include in your data extension are the ones that you want your new prospects from Facebook to "look like."

Of course, you'll also need to have a Facebook account for your company and have it mapped in your Marketing Cloud account to complete this process. After the data extension and the Facebook account are ready, use the following steps to create a Facebook lookalike audience:

1. **In Advertising Studio, click the Create Audience button.**

   The Create New Audience window appears.

2. **Enter the name of the lookalike audience and, optionally, the description.**

3. **Choose Facebook as the destination and then choose the Facebook account that you want to use. Click the Configure button.**

   The Configuration tab appears for your new audience, as shown in Figure 14-6.

4. **In the column of options on the left, select List or Data Extension, and then select the Data Extension radio button on the right.**

FIGURE 14-6:
The Configuration
tab with its initial
set of fields.

5. **Select the data extension that you previously created with your top customers.**

   When you select the data extension, the screen updates with new fields on the tab, as shown in Figure 14-7.

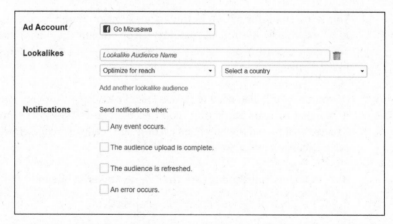

FIGURE 14-7:
The Configuration
tab with different
fields.

6. **Click the Add a Lookalike Audience hyperlink.**

7. **Select whether you want to optimize the list for reach or for similarity.**

   If you choose reach, you'll receive the 5 percent of Facebook users in the country you choose in the next drop-down list who are the most similar to the subscribers in your data extension. If you choose similarity, the lookalike audience will include only the 1 percent of Facebook users who are the most similar.

TIP

It's a best practice to make both a reach audience and a similarity audience, send to both, and see what works better for your particular situation. Just remember to suppress the similarity group from the reach group when you do your sends so that top 1 percent doesn't get the same message twice and mess up the veracity of the test.

8. **In the Select a country drop-down list, select the country where you want to find new customers.**

9. **Click Activate.**

   The Activate Audience window appears, where you can set up the lookalike audience to refresh at a time interval of your choosing.

If you choose to refresh your lookalike audience, Marketing Cloud will automatically resend the data extension to Facebook at the time interval you selected. It will bring back the resulting lookalike audience anew. You can change the subscribers in the data extension before it refreshes, but you don't have to. The audience you receive from Facebook will contain many new prospects either way because of how frequently Facebook users join or change their preferences.

Professional Edition

The mid-level edition of Advertising Studio is the Professional edition. Advertising Studio Professional requires a license at an additional fee above and beyond your Marketing Cloud account.

This edition lets you upload a list of your subscribers' email addresses or phone numbers to a social or ad network. The network then tries to find those people from that information and present your ads to them.

This edition lets you target online ads to particular audiences. For example, if you wanted to test whether subscribers who have become unengaged with your email marketing campaigns respond better to seeing your advertising messages in their social networks, you could create a list of your unengaged email subscribers and target those people as Facebook users.

It is possible to accomplish this same functionality manually without using Advertising Studio. However, Advertising Studio makes the process a lot easier and a lot more secure. You don't have to worry about having your subscribers' information stolen with this process like you might have to if you were to download the contact information from your CRM and upload it to the social or ad network site.

If you've purchased Advertising Studio Professional, you can access it by selecting Advertising Audiences from the Advertising Studio category on the app switcher, as shown in Figure 14-8.

FIGURE 14-8:
If you've licensed the Professional edition, it appears in the Advertising Studio category alongside Lead Capture.

The Professional edition is an app more for connecting data than creating it: You create your audiences in other Marketing Cloud apps and use Professional to connect them with social or ad networks. The social or ad networks show your ads to those users.

Advertising Studio Professional does not include performance reporting, but the social or ad studio that you use probably does. Advertising Studio Professional does show you how many subscribers from your audience the social or ad network was able to find among its own users, which correlates to the size of the audience who may see your ad.

When you choose the Professional app from the app switcher, an overview screen appears showing all your audiences. After you create an audience, statistics from the social or ad network start to appear in the audience overview screen.

Figure 14-9 shows an example of the overview screen.

Before you can begin using Professional, you need to set up some prerequisites:

>> License the professional edition of Advertising Studio.

>> Create a data extension or list that contains the audience you want to target. See Chapter 6 for more information about data extensions and lists.

TIP

You can use the Email app (see Chapter 11) or the Contact Builder app (see Chapter 8) to do the technical work of creating the data extension or list, but the hard work of this step comes before that. You need to be thoughtful about which subscribers to include in your targeted audience so you can achieve your business goals. Don't skimp on the planning step when deciding whom to include on your list.

FIGURE 14-9: The Professional dashboard offers an overview of the performance of the audiences you've created.

>> Create accounts with whatever social or ad networks you want to use to place ads, and have your credentials near at hand when you begin using Advertising Studio Professional.

When you log in to your social or ad network in one browser tab and then open Advertising Studio in another tab of the same browser window, Advertising Studio will notice the account and ask for permission to interact with it.

When someone else owns the ad network accounts

In many companies, the person in charge of using Advertising Studio in Marketing Cloud is the same person who sets up the company's social account and purchases the company's online ads. However, as the online marketing team grows larger, you might find yourself needing to coordinate with someone else who takes responsibility for the company's social or online advertising presence.

Even if you don't have access to the account credentials, though, you do have some other options for getting Advertising Studio connected with the social and ad networks that you need:

>> Use screen-sharing technology to let the person who owns the ad accounts log in remotely. Make sure the account owner stays in the screen share long enough to approve Marketing Cloud's permission to communicate with the ad network.

>> Create a Marketing Cloud login for the ad account owner and have that person associate the accounts to your Advertising Studio Professional account.

>> Have the ad account owner grant you admin rights so you can access the ad account from Marketing Cloud.

Supported social and ad networks

Advertising Studio uses the attributes of your subscribers to look up profiles on social networks. The social networks that Advertising Studio works with follow:

>> Facebook and Instagram can accept email address and phone number of your subscribers to find matches.

>> Twitter can also accept the Twitter user ID in addition to email address and phone number.

>> Google and YouTube can accept only email.

Facebook acquired Instagram in 2012 and joined their destinies. Similarly, Google acquired YouTube in 2006 and brought it under the Google umbrella.

Neither Google nor YouTube is exactly a social network; nevertheless, Google works with Advertising Studio as well. For example, you can target the ads that appear when a subscriber uses Gmail (or YouTube, of course). You can also target the ads that appear alongside Google search results.

If you've ever sold advertising space on a website, you know that you rarely negotiate with the sponsor directly. Instead, you offer a space on your website to an advertising network. The advertising network acts as a go-between, negotiating with the sponsors and choosing the perfect ads to insert into the space you provided.

The advertising networks have a surprisingly large amount of data about each person viewing the page. As the ad buyer, you can use the advertising networks' knowledge to target subscribers even when they access websites other than social networks.

The following ad networks work with Advertising Studio. This list also includes the attributes that each accepts for looking up users:

>> **Krux:** Email address and phone number

>> **LiveRamp:** Email address only

>> **LiveIntent:** Email address only

>> **Neustar:** Email address and phone number

>> **Viant:** Email address only

This is not an exhaustive list, nor is it a limit on what you can do to target your online ads. As new social and advertising networks gain prominence, Salesforce Marketing Cloud is likely to expand the functionality of Advertising Studio to support them.

Creating an audience

After your ad network accounts are set up, you can use the following steps to create an audience:

1. **From the app switcher, select Professional from the Advertising Studio category.**

2. **Click the Create Audience button that appears near the top right of the screen.**

3. **Enter a name for the audience and choose the social or ad network for which you are creating the audience.**

   A list of accounts for that network appears.

4. **Select the correct account and click Configure.**

   A new screen appears.

5. **Choose a source type that applies to your audience, and then click Select:**

   - *Template:* A template is a predefined definition of an audience based on common use cases. For example, all subscribers who clicked in the last 30 days might be a template.

   - *List or Data Extension:* You can use this option for subscribers in Marketing Cloud or for audiences you built from systems outside Marketing Cloud. For example, if you created an audience of recent purchasers in your POS system, you could include them in a data extension.

   - *Contacts:* Audiences from Contact Builder.

6. **Select the attributes that you want the system to use to find profiles that match the subscriber data in your audience.**

   Select more than one attribute to increase the chance of finding a match.

7. **Indicate whether you want to receive an alert when an audience is ready for use, and then click Activate.**

   We recommend that you receive the alert; this step can take a while and, without an alert, you'll just have to keep checking whether your audience is there to know for sure.

8. **Indicate whether you want to refresh the audience manually or on a scheduled basis.**

   It's more common to schedule audience refreshes because data sources change regularly as part of other schedules. Scheduling the refreshes makes sure that you are always targeting the audience you intend without having to remember to update it manually.

An audience refresh takes quite a while, depending on factors such as the size of the audience and especially which network you're using. The following list gives a general range of how long you can expect each network to take to refresh the audience:

>> Facebook: 2 hours

>> Google: 7 hours

>> Twitter: 24 hours

>> Krux: 2-7 days

>> LiveIntent: 24 hours

>> LiveRamp: 5-7 days

>> Neustar: 3-5 days

>> Viant: 1 hour

Chapter **15**

Web Studio

Without a web presence, your business might as well not exist to the potential clients who are looking for your products or services online. The days when you could count on prospects walking past your door are long gone; nowadays, even prospects just down the street want to be able to find you virtually. Today, your corporate website is as essential as your yellow pages listing was a generation ago.

About 10 years ago, Salesforce Marketing Cloud (then ExactTarget) introduced *microsites* — its tool for publishing web pages — to help online marketers be more responsive. Back then, the processes for getting pages published required a lot of time and deep technical knowledge. Without the microsites feature, even creating a single page to promote a limited-time-only event might take months of planning to negotiate the policies that made sure that the text was right, the visual design was on-brand, and the site was secure.

Corporate policies have become simpler and processes have become faster since that time, but the demand for web content keeps increasing. Most companies want to have a presence on social media in addition to a corporate website, and even your mobile marketing may require you to create web content.

Web Studio is the name of the category of web content apps in Salesforce Marketing Cloud. It currently contains only one app: CloudPages. You use the CloudPages app to build content for the web, social media, or special pages you use with Mobile-Push, the Marketing Cloud app that you use to send customers messages in your business's mobile app. (See Chapter 12 for details on MobilePush.)

In this chapter, you learn how to use CloudPages to centralize and control the publishing of web pages, Facebook pages, and MobilePush pages. You also discover how to review analytics on how the content performs so you can make informed decisions about future publishing.

Supported Online Content

CloudPages provides the power of sophisticated website programming techniques through tools that non-programmers find intuitive and easy-to-use. You can use the tools in CloudPages to assemble, publish, and evaluate three kinds of content: web pages, social pages, and mobile pages.

Web content

The web content you create in CloudPages comprises landing pages, microsites, preference centers, and Google Ads. The following descriptions outline each type of content you can create in more detail:

>> **Landing page:** Technically, you could consider any web page to be a landing page as long as users can land on it somehow, such as by clicking a link in an email, by typing a URL from a flier, or by a web search. Usually, though, marketers think of a landing page as being a web page with a special objective that stands apart from the rest of your corporate website. For example, a landing page might contain information about an event or have special content for users who found it through social media.

>> **Microsite:** If you create multiple related landing pages, you can connect them using a microsite. A microsite helps users by adding an easy-to-use navigation menu. A microsite can also help you by improving how high landing pages rank in search results and by aggregating analytics for all related landing pages for you to view in one place.

>> **Preference center:** A *preference center* is a form that you link to in your email marketing messages. Subscribers who follow the link see their personal preference center, where they can choose the kinds of messages to which

they want to subscribe. Marketing Cloud automatically sets up a preference center for each subscriber, but you can customize it using CloudPages. For more information about preference centers, see Chapter 5.

>> **Google Ads:** If you purchase display ads with Google, your ad appears near the top of the screen when someone searches for a keyword. For example, if your business sells handmade pottery, you could arrange for a photo of one of your pieces to appear when a person searches for *pottery.* You can use CloudPages to assemble the content of the ad that appears in Google.

When you publish the microsites and landing pages that you create in CloudPages, the system assigns each page a URL. By default, the URL is a Marketing Cloud URL, but you can set up your account to use your company's domain in the landing page URLs.

If you plan to include links to the landing pages in the emails, SMS, or other messages you send to individual subscribers, you can also set up your account to use *personalized URLs,* or *PURLs.* A PURL (pronounced "pearl") includes a variable that the system replaces with a value specific to the particular subscriber so that when the subscriber clicks the link, the system knows whose particular content to populate in the page.

For example, you could use PURLs to include a link to a landing page with information about the subscriber's number of points in your rewards system. When the subscriber clicked the link, the system would go to a version of the landing page with the rewards information of that specific subscriber.

WARNING

If the subscriber forwards an email containing a PURL, the recipient of the forwarded message can click the link and see the subscriber's personalized information. To protect your subscribers from accidentally breaching their own security when they forward your emails, always be careful not to include data that is too sensitive in your landing pages.

Setting up the system to use your company's private domain or PURLs requires advanced setup. Contact Marketing Cloud support for help.

As an example, Figure 15-1 shows a landing page created in CloudPages. The landing page contains a form where site visitors can enter to win a drawing.

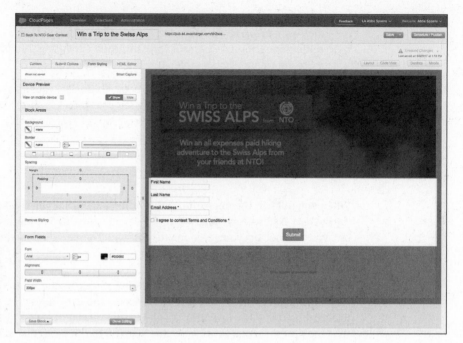

FIGURE 15-1:
Unlike general-purpose pages on your corporate website, landing pages contain content relevant for a specific audience or period.

Social content

You can create Facebook tabs, Facebook ads, Twitter posts, and LinkedIn blog entries in CloudPages. This is only one way that you can use Marketing Cloud for social media marketing, though. Read about the Social Studio app in Chapter 13.

The following list describes the kinds of social content you can create in CloudPages:

» **Facebook tab:** Your company's Facebook page has space for content that you publish in Facebook, such as your wall posts and photos, and space for content that you create in other applications. That third-party application content you create appears in a Facebook tab. Users on your company's Facebook page see the tab listed in the navigation near the top of the screen and can click it to see special information you've created there. Figure 15-2 illustrates a custom Facebook tab containing CloudPages content.

» **Facebook ad:** Even if a Facebook user isn't visiting your company's Facebook page, you can make your corporate presence felt, whatever the user is doing in Facebook. When you place Facebook ads, Facebook users see them in a sidebar alongside their wall.

>> **Twitter posts and LinkedIn blogs:** You can create the content that appears in a tweet you post on Twitter or a blog you post on LinkedIn by using CloudPages. Using CloudPages for this kind of content helps you keep all your social content creation centralized in Marketing Cloud.

Figure 15-2 shows an example of CloudPages social content in a Facebook tab.

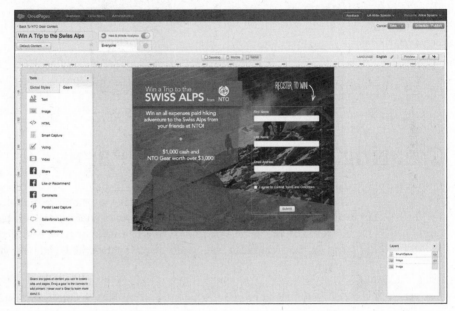

FIGURE 15-2:
Using CloudPages for your Facebook tab content centralizes your content creation processes.

Mobile content

In addition to a corporate website and a social media presence, many companies have a mobile app that customers can install on their mobile phones or other devices. The Marketing Cloud MobilePush app integrates with your mobile app to send messages to app users. You use CloudPages to assemble the messages that you send with MobilePush. See Chapter 12 for details about MobilePush.

Figure 15-3 shows what a MobilePush message might look like.

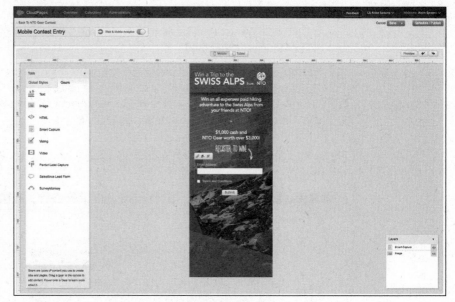

FIGURE 15-3:
CloudPages
works with
MobilePush and
your own
company's mobile
app so you can
craft an in-app
message
experience for
your users.

Creating Content in CloudPages

The CloudPages tools let you easily manage your online marketing by yourself, without needing to take the time and effort to coordinate with technical experts. However, if you're an HTML or AMPscript whiz or have easy access to someone who is, you can also use your own sophisticated code in your CloudPages content.

The content you create in CloudPages remains visible only inside your account until you publish it for the world to see. Then, when your content is ready, you can publish it right away or schedule the system to publish the content automatically at a certain date and time.

TIP

You might want to use a schedule to delay publishing a time-sensitive announcement until just the right moment.

To create any type of content in CloudPages, you start by defining a collection. A *collection* is just a wrapper that pulls all the words, images, and other content into a single place for you to manage. A collection is similar to a folder that you create on your computer's hard drive to contain related files.

After you have a collection, you choose the template type that you want to use. The templates that appear in your account depend on the functionality enabled in it. The list of possible template types follows:

>> Landing page

>> Code resource

>> Microsite

>> MobilePush page

>> Facebook tab

Figure 15-4 shows an example of a landing page template.

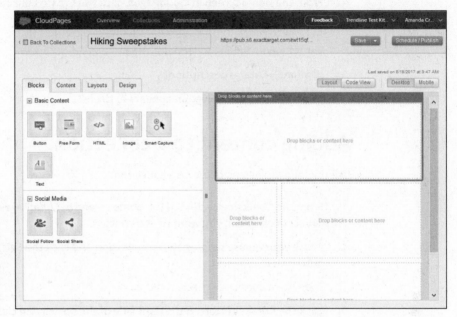

FIGURE 15-4:
A landing page template has spaces where you can drag all component parts of your web page.

When you have chosen and named the template you want to use, you can just drag content to the boxes on the template. Examples of the kinds of content you might add to a collection include the following:

>> Coupons

>> Email sign-up form

>> Sweepstakes entry form

>> Ads

>> Product showcase

>> Lead generation form

The images and text that you create in Content Builder (see Chapter 7) are available to drag to your template. As described in the following sections, you can also create content directly in CloudPages by using the embedded Content Builder content editor.

Creating a collection

Use the following steps to create a collection:

1. **From the home screen in CloudPages, click the Create Collection button.**

   The Create Collection window appears.

2. **Enter a name for the collection.**

3. **(Optional) Enter a description.**

4. **Click Save and the collection appears in the list.**

Adding content to a collection

Use the following steps to create a collection:

1. **From the Collection section of the home screen in CloudPages, locate the collection to which you want to add content.**

2. **Pause your mouse pointer on the collection and click the Edit Content button that appears there.**

   The system opens the collection canvas.

3. **Click the Create button on the right side of the screen and choose one of the following options:**

   - Landing Page
   - Code Resource
   - Microsite
   - MobilePush Page
   - Facebook Tab

4. **Add content as described in the following sections.**

Landing page

Use these steps if you choose to add a landing page to your collection:

1. **In the Create a Landing Page window that appeared when you chose Landing Page, enter the name and description of your landing page.**

2. **If you want to require that only visitors with secure connections visit this site, select the HTTPS Connections Only check box.**

3. **Click Next.**

TIP

4. **If you have the option, select Content Builder as the Editor.**

   At the time of this writing, a classic editor was still available, but Marketing Cloud was planning to remove it from the application.

5. **From the Select Layout step in the wizard, choose the icon that best represents how you want your landing page to look, and then click Create.**

   The Content Builder editor appears for you to create your landing page with the template you chose. See Chapter 7 for full information about using Content Builder.

Code resource

The content editor is not your only option for creating content. If you have programmatic content, you can add it as a code resource. This option lets you store web programming code that you created outside Marketing Cloud in a file that you can link to from CloudPages.

Later, when you're using the editor to edit content in your pages, you can insert a link and navigate to the code resource to which you want to link.

Use the following steps to add a code resource to your collection:

1. **In the Create Code Resource window that appeared when you chose Code Resource, enter the name and description.**

2. **Select one of the following content types:**

   - JavaScript
   - CSS
   - JSON
   - Text files
   - RSS Feed
   - XML

3. **Click Next.**

   A simple text editor window appears.

4. **Type or paste your code.**

5. **Click Save.**

Microsite

When you create a microsite, you design a site map that organizes landing pages. CloudPages uses the page hierarchy that you set up as the basis for a navigation menu that website visitors can use to move around the site. You can also control the look and feel of the site navigation here. Figure 15-5 shows what the microsites editor looks like.

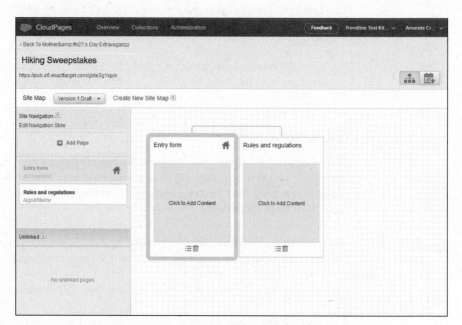

FIGURE 15-5: The microsite workspace.

Use the following steps to add a microsite to your collection:

1. **In the Create a Microsite window that appeared when you chose Microsite, enter the name and description of your landing page.**

2. **If you want to require that only visitors with secure connections visit this site, select the HTTPS Connections Only check box.**

3. **Click Create.**

   An editor workspace appears.

4. **Click the Add Page button in the left panel.**

The Add New Page window appears.

5. **Type the name of the landing page, and then click Create.**

A card appears on the workspace to represent the landing page.

6. **Pause your mouse pointer on the card and click the Add Content button that appears.**

The Create Content window appears.

7. **Select the method you want to use to create landing page content.**

Valid values follow:

- *Create New Content, Design View:* Launch the Content Builder editor.

- *Create New Content, Code View:* Open an editor window where you can type or paste HTML and other web programming code.

- *Start from Existing Content:* Open a copy of a landing page that you created previously. Choose from the list of landing pages that appears.

8. **Click Next.**

9. **Create or edit the landing pages in the microsite.**

For complete information on using Content Editor, see Chapter 7.

10. **Click the Back to the *microsite name* link at the top left to return to the microsite editor.**

11. **Repeat Steps 6 through 10 to add the remaining landing pages to the microsite.**

Each landing page you add to the microsite appears as a box in the left panel. Drag the boxes to change the order of the pages in the microsite navigation. To make a page a child of another page, position the child just under the parent and then drag it to the right.

12. **To preview and edit the site navigation, click the Edit Navigation link.**

The Navigation Editor appears and you can change the visuals aspects of the navigation bar, such as the background color, the font of the menu items, and whether arrows appear next to menu names to indicate that the user can click the name.

13. **Make your changes and then click Done.**

MobilePush page

Use the following steps to add a MobilePush page to your collection:

1. **In the window that appeared when you chose MobilePush page, enter the name and description of your page.**

2. **Click Create and a window appears.**

3. **Select the method you want to use to create landing page content.**

   Valid values follow:

   - *Create New Content, Design View:* Launch the Content Builder editor.

   - *Create New Content, Code View:* Open an editor window where you can type or paste HTML and other web programming code.

   - *Start from Existing Content:* Open a copy of a landing page that you created previously. Choose from the list of landing pages that appears.

4. **Click Next.**

5. **Create or edit your MobilePush page.**

   For more information about creating MobilePush pages, see Chapter 12.

Facebook tab

Use the following steps to add a Facebook tab to your collection:

1. **In the Create Facebook Tab window that appears when you click the Facebook tab, complete the following fields.**

   - *Name:* Type the name of the Facebook tab.

   - *Description:* Optionally, add a description of the Facebook tab.

   - *Start from existing SocialPages content:* Select this check box if you want to make a copy of content you created previously in SocialPages (see Chapter 13). If you select this checkbox, you need to check the content that you want to start from.

   - *Destinations:* Optionally, select the Facebook page where you want this tab to appear.

2. **Click Create.**

   The Create Content window appears.

3. **Select the method you want to use to create landing page content.**

   Valid values follow:

- *Create New Content, Design View:* Launch the Content Builder editor.

- *Create New Content, Code View:* Open an editor window where you can type or paste HTML and other web programming code.

- *Start from Existing Content:* Open a copy of a landing page that you created previously. Choose from the list of landing pages that appears.

4. **Click Next.**

5. **Create or edit your Facebook tab.**

   For more information about creating Facebook tabs, see Chapter 13.

Publishing Content

You can create content all day long, but until you publish it, no one outside your Marketing Cloud account can see what you've created. This is a good thing because you want the chance to make sure your content is ready before the world can see it.

When you are ready, you publish the content in your collection from the same screen where you created it. Simply click the Schedule/Publish button in the upper-right corner. Figure 15-6 shows the window that appears when you click the Schedule/Publish button.

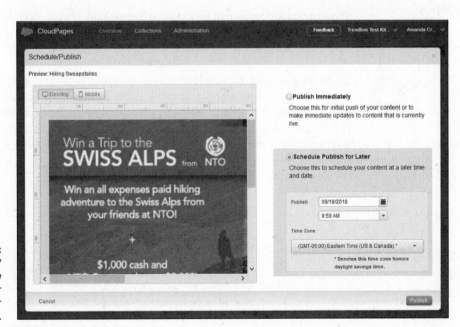

FIGURE 15-6:
The Schedule/ Publish window with fields for scheduling a later time to publish.

From this window, you can do one last preview of the content for each device. You can choose to publish immediately or in the future. If you schedule a future date to publish, you choose the date, time, and time zone when you want the content to become live.

You can tell whether content is published on the Page Details screen, as follows:

1. **From the CloudPages Overview screen, click Edit (pencil icon) on the card for the collection you want.**

   A list of items in the collection appears.

2. **Click Page Properties (bullet list icon) on the card for the content you want.**

   The Page Details appear on the left.

From this screen, you can also find the URL where the content is or will be available for people to find.

Unpublishing content

If you decide to take down content that you've already published, either because there's a problem with it or just because it's outlived its usefulness, you can unpublish it.

The Unpublish button can be a little tricky to find. On the Page Details page, look for an Unpublish button right next to the Published status. Figure 15-7 shows where you can find the Unpublish button.

TIP

If you created content with a deadline, consider replacing the page rather than unpublishing it. For example, if you created a content entry form that had to be completed by a certain time, you can schedule a new version of the page to publish at the time of the deadline. The new version of the page can thank the readers for their interest, inform the readers that the contest has ended, and suggest other pages that they might find interesting.

FIGURE 15-7:
The Unpublish
button appears
next to the
Published status
on the Page
Details screen.

Analyzing Content Performance

CloudPages keeps track of metrics that you can use to evaluate the success of the content you've published.

TIP

The content must be currently published or have been published in the past for analytics about it to be available.

For each piece of content that you publish, CloudPages keeps track of the following activity:

» How many people view the content

» How many people click a link in the content

» How many people complete and submit a SmartCapture form

This data is available on the Activity tab for the piece of content. Use the following steps to open the Activity tab:

1. **From the CloudPages Overview screen, click Edit (pencil icon) on the card for the collection you want.**

A list of items in the collection appears.

2. **Click Page Properties (bullet list icon) on the card for the content you want.**

   The content appears on the right in the Content tab, which is open by default.

3. **Click the Activity tab to view the metrics for the content.**

   You can change the time period that the graphs represent by using the Today, Last 7 Days, and Last 30 Days buttons.

Figure 15-8 shows the activity for a landing page.

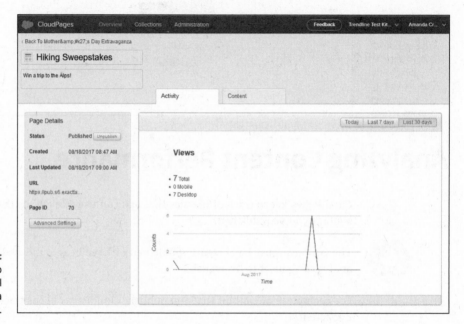

The very highest performing piece of content in each channel (web, social, and mobile) appears in the Stats section of the Overview screen.

TIP

Reports are available also in the Reporting feature. For details, see Chapter 9.

5
Mapping the Customer Journey

Think of each customer's interaction with your brand as a journey.

Envision what you want that journey to be like and map it out.

Learn how to use Marketing Cloud apps to make your vision a reality.

Chapter **16**

Designing a Customer Journey

When you've been marketing online for a while, you start to notice that you're dedicating a large part of your day to routine tasks. These tasks might not be straightforward enough to create a simple, linear program in Automation Studio (see Chapter 10), but they are predictable and based on logic.

For example, when a person signs up to receive your newsletter, you might send her an email asking her to confirm her email address and phone number. If the person responds within three days, you send a thank-you message with information about how to get to the website where she can control her subscription.

If the person doesn't respond in three days, though, you send her a reminder and start the three-day waiting period over again. If she replies, you send the thank-you message. If not, remind again. You don't want to send reminder emails every three days forever, of course. If the subscriber doesn't respond after two of them, you probably want to try something else.

When you write the logic like this, you can see how you aren't just talking about a series of emails. This process flow also has waiting periods, decision points, and different messages that subscribers might or might not receive, based on their behavior. Two subscribers who both enter this process flow could go down different branches in the logic, depending on their behavior, and end up having different experiences.

Salesforce Marketing Cloud calls this kind of process flow a *journey*, and Journey Builder is the Marketing Cloud app where you can assemble those actions, decision points, and waiting periods into process flows that automate your routine tasks and clear your schedule for more important things.

Journeys can be simple or sophisticated, but they all require forethought and planning. In this chapter, we discuss the concepts you need to understand before you start, as well as what you need to do to get ready to build a journey. In Chapter 17, we discuss how to use the Journey Builder app to implement the process flows that you design in this chapter.

Understanding Journeys

A *journey* is a process flow that controls how and when Marketing Cloud sends messages to your subscribers. All messages in a journey relate to each other because a journey describes how a subscriber moves through a process, such as becoming a new customer or celebrating an anniversary as part of your loyalty program.

The experience of going through a journey isn't necessarily the same for every subscriber who enters it. You intentionally define different branches of the process flow to create an appropriate experience for different subscribers. Even though each subscriber probably goes down only one branch and never sees what the other branches do, you design the entire journey — branches, waiting periods, messages — based on the logic you use to control your messaging.

Subscribers do not need to enter a journey at the same time. For example, if you were messaging subscribers manually to thank them for an order, you would probably wait to send the thank-you message at the end of the day so you could send just one message to the entire batch of customers who ordered that day. With a journey, though, you can set it up so that customers enter the journey at any time and progress through it at their own pace. They could get their thank-you message right away without having to wait for others to get their orders in.

Subscribers also don't need to stay in the journey for the same amount of time. Depending on the journey steps, subscribers can exit the journey once they reach a decision point, if that's what makes sense according to your process logic.

For example, a common and simple kind of journey to create is a welcome series. In a welcome series, you send a few messages, each a few days apart. The messages welcome a new subscriber, such as someone who just joined your rewards program or your newsletter mailing list. In this example, you might create the following:

>> An initial email to welcome the new participant in your rewards program

>> A second email to invite the new participant to join other programs you offer

>> A third email to offer a discount

Figure 16-1 shows what a welcome series journey might look like in Journey Builder.

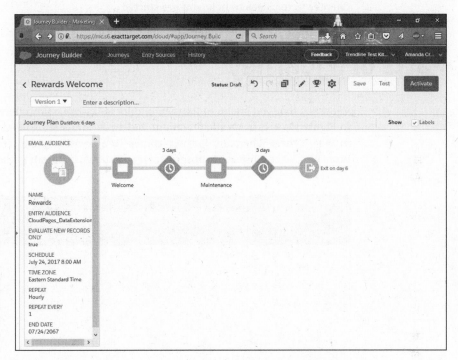

FIGURE 16-1:
A Journey Builder welcome series to welcome new members of the rewards program.

When you create this journey, you instruct the system to have subscribers enter the welcome series journey when they appear in the audience that contains the members of your rewards program. Then, you have the journey do the following:

>> Send the initial email immediately.

>> Wait three days.

>> Send the second email.

>> Wait another three days.

>> Send the third email.

After the system sends the three emails, the subscriber exits the journey. After a subscriber finishes the journey, you can have him enter another journey right away, but you don't have to. A subscriber who exits a journey can simply remain in your system, waiting until you decide to add him to another journey sometime in the future.

The kinds of journeys that you set up will depend on your company's marketing efforts. However, most online marketers set up several common journeys. See Chapter 18 for ideas to help you get started.

Parts of a Journey

A journey that you create in Journey Builder looks like a flowchart, as you can see in Figure 16-2. It has a starting point and arrows indicating what actions happen in what order. When the journey comes to a decision point, it can break into branches, where different subscribers can go down different paths.

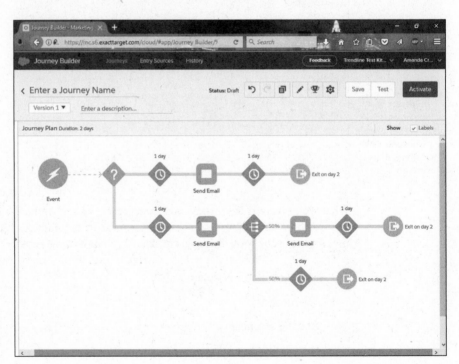

FIGURE 16-2:
A sample journey with different paths.

The journeys you create can include the following types of components:

>> Entry sources

>> Messages

>> Splits

>> Joins

>> Waits

>> Customer updates

We discuss each of these journey components in detail in the following sections.

If you also use Salesforce Sales and Services Cloud as your sales and service software tool, you can perform the following actions in the Sales and Services Cloud in the course of your journeys:

>> Create a task.

>> Create an opportunity.

>> Create a lead.

>> Create a contact.

>> Open a case.

>> Add a campaign member.

>> Add an account.

>> Create an object activity.

>> Convert a lead.

The integration with Salesforce Sales and Services Cloud is powerful, but it is outside the scope of this book. If you use both of these Salesforce tools together, check out the Marketing Cloud documentation for more information on how to use these activities.

Entry sources

The *entry source* feeds subscribers into the journey. Every journey must have an entry source; otherwise, no one will ever go through the process flow that you create. An entry source can be any of the following:

TIP

>> **Audience:** When the system adds a subscriber to an audience, that subscriber can also enter the journey.

The word *audience* in this context is different than in previous chapters. In those chapters, *audience* means a special kind of sendable data extension that comes from Audience Builder (see Chapter 8). Here, however, *audience* refers to any sendable data extension (see Chapter 6).

>> **API event:** You can use the Marketing Cloud API to create a bit of code that adds the subscriber to a journey. The API code you write can work from your website, your mobile app, or any other place where your subscribers interact with you online.

>> **CloudPages:** If you include a form on a web page or social media page that you create through CloudPages, you can set it up so that anyone who completes that form enters the journey. Figure 16-3 shows a web form that you could use as an entry source. See Chapter 15 for information about CloudPages.

FIGURE 16-3:
A sign-up form on your website is a great way to get people started on a journey.

>> **Salesforce data:** If you also use Salesforce Sales and Services Cloud, you can pull information you already have about subscribers in Salesforce to select subscribers to enter your journey.

>> **Event:** A particular date adds a subscriber to the journey. For example, you can use the event entry source to create a Happy Birthday journey that subscribers enter on their birthday.

Messages

Messages in a journey are email messages, just like any email message you might design, send, and track in Marketing Cloud. See Chapter 11 for information about email marketing.

A message isn't technically required for a journey. It would be possible to set up a journey that never sent a message to subscribers, especially if you are using Salesforce Sales and Services Cloud and using the events to create, say, cases and leads. However, the purpose of the vast majority of journeys is to control sending messages to subscribers, so your journey is likely to contain multiple email messages.

For example, in the scenario described at the beginning of this chapter, you would need to create the following separate email messages:

>> The initial email message to welcome the subscribers to the newsletter subscription and ask them to verify their information

>> The first follow-up message

>> Possibly the second follow-up message, though you might be able to write the first follow-up message in such a way that it serves both purposes

Depending on what action you decide to take for subscribers who never reply to any of the reminder messages, you might need yet another message in addition to these.

Splits

A *split* is a decision point. When a subscriber reaches the split in the journey, the system determines along which branch the subscriber should continue. You can split your journey according to three different types of information:

>> **Decision split:** This kind of split looks at a piece of information you have collected about the subscriber and chooses the correct path from there. For example, you could create different paths for subscribers who live on each continent. Each time a subscriber reached that split in the journey, the system would look at the field that contains the subscriber's continent. The subscriber would proceed along the appropriate branch according to that data.

>> **Random split:** When you set up a random split, you indicate the percentage of the audience that you want to proceed along each branch. When a subscriber reaches this kind of split, the system chooses a branch based on the percentages you indicated.

>> **Engagement split:** An engagement split considers whether the subscriber has engaged with a particular message. Subscribers who clicked a link in your newsletter, for example, could go down one branch, while those who did not would go down the other branch.

TIP

You can create complex queries that use data from more than one data extension (database table; see Chapter 6) to determine which subscribers enter the journey or as the decision split criteria. To make the fields from multiple data extensions available to use this way, you need to map the data extensions to the contact model in Contact Builder (see Chapter 8) as part of an attribute group, as shown in Figure 16-4.

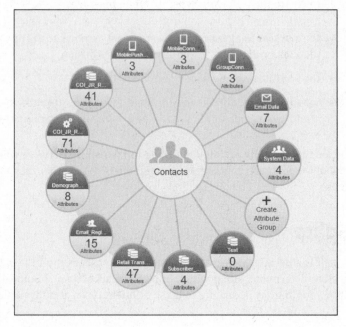

FIGURE 16-4:
View of attribute groups in Contact Builder.

Although this kind of data manipulation might be beyond the scope of your first few journeys, knowing the importance of using Contact Builder when you set up your data model might make later journeys easier to build.

Joins

A *join* merges the branches of your journey. After you split your journey for different parts of the audience and sent whatever messages are appropriate for each group, you might want to bring them back together to proceed together through some of the activities in your journey.

For example, in the scenario at the beginning of the chapter, an engagement split would have sent subscribers who replied to the initial email down a separate path from those who did not. Only those who did not respond would receive the first reminder, but the subscribers who responded to the first reminder could rejoin the original group for the remainder of the journey.

Waits

A *wait* is a period of time with no activity. This might be a few days when a subscriber has an opportunity to take action, or it might be just a pause between messages to avoid annoying your subscribers with too many messages all at once.

Customer updates

You can update the information you have about a subscriber in Marketing Cloud by using an Update Contact activity, which appears in the Customer Updates category.

For example, imagine you created an attribute on your subscriber record to hold the date of the most recent email message you sent to that subscriber. You could add the Update Contact activity to the journey immediately after a message send to set the value of that field to the current date.

Considerations before Starting

The Journey Builder app makes setting up sophisticated automation easy, but you still have to do the hard work of designing the automations. After you have an idea for a journey you want to create, you'll want to think about the following topics and prepare before you get into the Journey Builder app to start building.

Choosing the right tool

Journey Builder isn't the only tool that you can use to create marketing automation in Marketing Cloud. Automation Studio is an obvious candidate for building automations, but other apps, even those not focused on automation, might offer simple automation solutions for certain common tasks.

The first question you should consider before you dive into using Journey Builder is whether you need all the power it offers. Look at the path you're considering for your journey and ask yourself the following:

>> Does the process contain multiple decision points?

>> Does the process contain multiple messages?

>> Do the decision points reference data that might have changed between the time the subscriber entered the journey and the time the subscriber reaches that decision point?

If the answer to all these questions is no, using Automation Studio might be a quicker way to get going. See Chapter 10 for more information on Automation Studio.

Data extension prerequisite

Journey Builder uses data extensions for data management and sending. If you absolutely must use Journey Builder but haven't implemented data extensions for your subscriber data, you have some work to do.

Data extensions are required by several apps, not just Journey Builder. To get the full power of Marketing Cloud, you need to implement data extensions, which requires some work and planning. See Chapters 5 and 6 for a full discussion of setting up your data model and using data extensions.

Contact Builder prerequisite

Using Contact Builder isn't technically required for creating your first journeys. However, when you get ready to start using complex logic that requires data from multiple data extensions, you need to be using Contact Builder to make that data available to Journey Builder. See Chapter 8 for more information about Contact Builder.

Data powers the journey

The entry source can use data to select who enters the journey. The splits you set up may refer to subscriber data to choose a path. The messages you send may require data to generate the content. You might even update subscriber data in your system as a part of the journey.

Knowing what data the journey requires is an important part of planning the journey. If you don't have all the data you need, you can plan strategies to find that data. See Chapter 5 for ideas on how to deal with a data shortfall (when you don't have all the data you need).

Knowing what data the journey will update is another important step. You want to create the subscriber attributes and data extensions that you need before you begin to set up the journey. Doing so will save you the frustration and annoyance of stopping your journey design midway so that you can create what you need.

Message content

When you think through all the possible branches of your journey, you may be surprised by how many different messages you need to create. Stepping through the logic ahead of time to list what messages you need will make the process of creating the journey easier.

TIP

Creating messages for the journey may turn out to be an iterative process: You can create the messages first, but then as you design the journey you might realize that you need to enhance the messages. Keep a "parking lot" list of changes you notice you need while you're building so you don't forget to come back to them later.

Beginning to Map a Customer Journey

A visual map of how subscribers will flow through a journey can be a useful tool. It helps you to visualize all the different branches involved and determine the data you need.

For a simple journey, just laying out the messages, splits, and waits in a numbered or bulleted list might be enough. When the journey is short and straightforward, a simple list can help you understand how you'll translate your journey to the canvas.

If your journey contains several branches, joins, and different exits, though, you'll probably want to create a map. A paper sketch or a whiteboard is the preferred tool for artistic types who like to put pen to paper. These tools are perfectly acceptable, especially if you're the only one who needs to review the journey map.

If you're the kind of person who prefers a computer mouse to a dry erase marker, or if you need to email the flowchart to people throughout your company, you might want to use flowchart software. Microsoft Visio is a powerful flowchart tool, and your company might already have it under license. If not, check out, Lucid Chart, an online tool that is free to use, as long as you stick to the basic version. Figure 16-5 shows a journey mapped out in Lucid Chart.

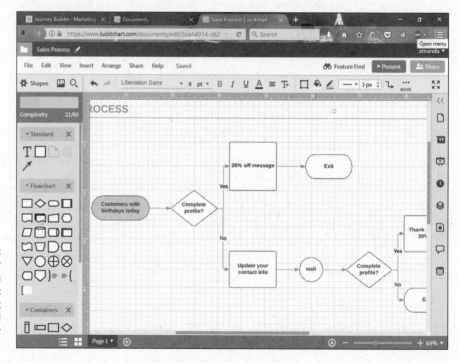

FIGURE 16-5: Mapping your journey in a flowchart software tool first helps you find holes in your logic.

Whether you're working on a hard copy or an electronic copy of the map, you should draw all the message sends, splits, joints, waits, and customer updates. From this flowchart, you can identify all the items you need for your journey checklist.

Journey Preparation Checklist

Every good journey starts with preparation. You wouldn't start a hike through the forest without making sure you had everything first; it would be a hassle to have to stop and go back for your water, camera, or favorite trail mix. In the same way, you want to make sure you have all the components ready before you start the work to build your journey. That way, you won't have to stop in the middle and lose momentum.

Use the following checklist as starting point. Add your own items to the list as you create more journeys and uncover areas for which you need to remember to plan:

» Create the messages you need to create, and update any existing messages that you plan to use in the journey, if needed.

» Populate the data that the journey needs. Decision splits use subscriber data fields, and messages can also include subscriber data. Your entry sources could also require certain data.

» Create the data extensions that the journey will use. See Chapter 6 for instruction on creating data extensions.

» If you want to tie data from more than a single data extension together to use as part of a journey, remember to configure it in Contact Builder. See Chapter 8 for more information about Contact Builder.

After you've thought through your journey, created all the components you need, and assembled the data that the journey will use, creating the journey in Journey Builder will be simple. In the next chapter, we go through the tools in Journey Builder that turn your plans into automation reality.

» **Splitting the journey at decision points**

» **Assembling components into a journey**

Chapter **17**

Creating Your Customer Journeys

I n Chapter 16, you identify an opportunity to automate a series of email messages (or SMS messages or ads), figure out what data the system needs to run
the automation, and build the component parts. After you complete that preparation work, you need to put it all together in Salesforce Marketing Cloud so that
it can start saving you time and bringing value to your subscribers.

Journey Builder is the app in Marketing Cloud for automating communications. In
this chapter, we talk about how you can use the tools in Journey Builder to create
dynamic and sophisticated paths along which subscribers can travel. The system
determines which path a subscriber takes based on how you configure the journey
and may send different messages to different subscribers depending on which
path they're following.

The strength of Journey Builder comes from its capability to use filter logic to split
the journey into different branches. The branches are parallel paths that segments
of your audience follow so that each subscriber receives the most relevant
messages.

Revisiting the Basics of a Customer Journey

As you learn in Chapter 16, a *customer journey* consists of an audience of subscribers who move through a series of activities. You define entry sources that start subscribers on the journey: audiences, API events (code on your website or mobile app), or a form on a landing page you create in CloudPages. (See Chapter 15 for more information about CloudPages.)

TIP

We're playing fast and loose with the term *audience* here. Strictly speaking, an audience is a special kind of sendable data extension that comes from Audience Builder (see Chapter 8). However, in the context of journeys, the common vernacular is to use *audience* to refer to any sendable data extension (see Chapter 6).

When the subscribers reach a decision point, or a *split*, the system uses your configuration logic to choose a correct branch of the journey for each subscriber. You can define the split based on the following:

>> A piece of data that you have about the subscriber, such as the state where the subscriber lives

>> Whether the subscriber engaged with a particular message, for example, whether the subscriber clicked a link in your newsletter

>> Random chance, such as when you set up your split to choose branch A for 40 percent of the subscribers and branch B for the remaining 60 percent

After a subscriber is following a particular branch, the activities of that branch may include sending email messages, updating your customer data, or just waiting. A subscriber can exit the journey if he or she meets the exit criteria that you configured.

The Journey Builder Dashboard

You open Journey Builder by pausing your mouse pointer on the Journey Builder category on the app switcher and then clicking Journey Builder on the menu that appears. When the app appears, the dashboard shown in Figure 17-1 is the first screen that you see.

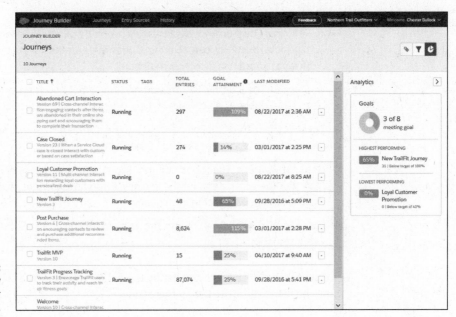

FIGURE 17-1:
The Journey
Builder
dashboard.

TIP

You can get back to this screen by clicking Journeys in the gray toolbar at the top of the screen. That toolbar also contains Entry Sources and History options. The Entry Sources option is a legacy feature; you don't need to click that option. The History option, on the other hand, is particularly useful considering some of Marketing Cloud's most recent changes. We discuss the History screen later in this chapter.

Journeys menu option

On the left side of the dashboard is an overview of the status of all your journeys and their performance. You see the following columns of information about each journey:

» **Title:** The first column contains the name of the journey, the current version number, and the description if you added one when you made the journey. Click the name to open the journey.

» **Status:** The second column shows whether the current version of the journey is available for subscribers to enter. Valid values in this field follow:

   • *Running:* The journey is available for subscribers to enter.

   • *Draft:* The journey is still available for you to edit. Subscribers can't enter a journey with this status.

- *Finishing:* The journey was previously running but now is no longer available for subscribers to enter. Subscribers already in the journey are flowing through to activity completion.

- *Stopped:* The journey was previously running but now is no longer available to subscribers. The activities in the journey have stopped.

>> **Total Entries:** The third column displays the number of contact records that have entered the current version of the journey.

>> **Goal Attainment:** The fourth column displays the percentage of contacts that have met the goal criteria for the journey, if you have a target goal set. (We discuss target goals later in this chapter.)

>> **Last Modified:** The final column shows the date and time that the journey was last modified.

You can sort the journeys in the list by the values in any of the columns. Click the column header to sort the list by that value.

On the right side of the screen is the Analytics panel and the following three buttons:

>> **Tag:** Use this button to associate your journey with an existing campaign or add new keyword descriptors. See Chapter 4 for more information about campaigns and campaign tags. You must select the check box next to one or more journey names before you can click this button.

>> **Filter:** By default, the right side of the dashboard is the Analytics section. You can click the funnel icon that appears above the Analytics section to change it to the Filters section, as shown in Figure 17-2. On this part of the screen, you can search for a particular journey by name, filter the list of journeys by status, or filter them by tags.

>> Click the pie chart icon above the Filters section to return to the Analytics section. This part of the screen shows which journeys are achieving their goals. It also lists which journeys are the highest and lowest performing against their goal targets. Refer to Figure 17-1 for an example of this part of the screen.

History menu option

The Journey Builder History menu maintains all the journey-related activity for the last 30 days. Every time a subscriber completes a step, receives an email, or exits a journey, a row appears in the History menu. Because the History menu records every step in every journey for every subscriber, the history can contain an exceptional amount of data. Your history might have millions or tens of millions of actions.

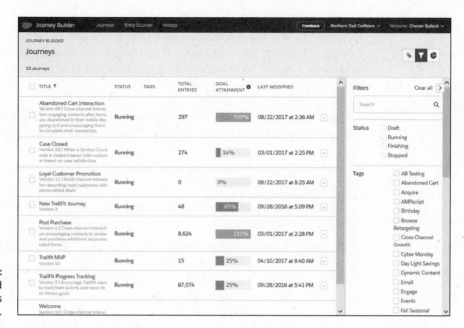

FIGURE 17-2:
The dashboard
with the Filters
panel enabled.

To view the history, click History in the top navigation bar. The records in the history appear, as shown in Figure 17-3. Note the panel on the right side of the screen, where you can search for the records for a particular subscriber or filter the records based on other criteria.

FIGURE 17-3:
The Journey
Builder History
menu, with the
search/filter
panel on the
right.

The first field of the search/filter panel lets you search by contact key, which is an email address for most accounts. If you search for a particular email address in this field, you can see exactly where the subscriber is in a journey and what steps he or she has completed in the last 30 days.

Regardless of whether you search for a particular email address, you can also use this panel to filter the results. You can filter the results to show only those

>> **For a particular journey:** If you choose this option, you can further filter by the versions of the journey.

>> **Related to a particular kind of activity:** Examples include wait step, decision split, or email send.

>> **Within a particular date range:** You can choose 12 hours, 24 hours, 7 days, 30 days, or a custom range within the last 30 days.

Figure 17-4 shows the search/filter panel.

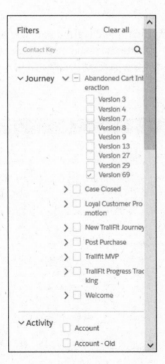

FIGURE 17-4: Search by email address and configure filters to limit the results.

Journey Builder does not include a feature to export history data. However, we have had success highlighting the rows on the History screen and then copying and pasting them in a spreadsheet program, such as Microsoft Excel.

Journey Canvas

To create a journey, click the New Journey button on the right side of the screen. The journey canvas appears, as you see in Figure 17-5. Enter the journey name and optional description at the top of this screen.

FIGURE 17-5: The journey canvas where you create a new journey.

The primary action you take on the journey canvas is dragging entry sources or activities from the Builder on the left side of the screen to where you want them to appear in the flow of the journey on the right side of the screen. After you have the entry source in the place you want, you click the entry source or the activity on the right side of the screen to configure it.

We discuss the parts of the journey canvas next, in the following sections:

» Version

» Undo, redo, copy, and delete icon buttons

» Goals

» Settings

» Save, Test, and Activate buttons

» Tags

» Builder

Version

Near the top of the screen, between the name and description, is a version indicator. If a journey has multiple versions, you can click the down arrow next to the version number and choose which version you want to view.

Journey Builder freezes a version of the journey when it becomes active — because you clicked the Activate button or because the scheduled activation time has arrived. When you create a journey, the version indicator says Version 1. After Version 1 is active, you can't change the decision points, wait times, or other activities of the journey without creating another version.

TIP

You can update email send activities to, for example, swap in different images or update the subject lines without having to publish a new version of the journey.

The option to create a new draft appears on active journeys. Click this option to create a copy of the journey as Version 2. You can make changes to this draft version, and then activate the new version or schedule it to become active later.

After the new version becomes active, all new contacts entering the journey would start Version 2. Version 1 continues running for the contacts who had already begun the journey. Version 1 appears with the status of Finishing. When you're sure that all contacts in Version 1 have exited the journey, you can stop it.

The next time you want to make updates to the journey, you create another draft (Version 3) and continue to iterate in this fashion.

WARNING

It's possible to stop the current version of a journey without having a new draft version activated or to stop all versions of a journey at the same time. We don't recommend doing this unless it's an emergency. In both cases, all contacts in the journey would immediately exit, which could result in a poor experience for your customers.

Undo, redo, copy, and delete buttons

Above the canvas appear three useful icons buttons: undo, redo, and copy. You're probably familiar with buttons like these from other applications, but just in case, here's what they do:

>> **Undo button:** Undo the most recent action you performed. For example, click this button to retrieve an activity that you accidentally deleted.

>> **Redo button:** Redo the action that you undid with the undo button. You can't click this button until you've clicked the undo button at least once.

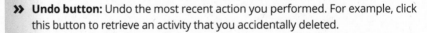

>> **Copy button:** Create a draft copy of the entire journey. If you click this button, a window appears where you type a new name and description for the copy of the journey. *Note:* You might expect this button to create a copy of an individual activity, but it creates a copy of the entire journey.

>> **Delete button (trash can):** Delete the journey or the version of the journey. Like the copy button, the delete button doesn't delete individual activities.

TIP

If you want to delete the entry source or an activity from the journey, pause your mouse pointer over the thing you want to delete. A window appears that contains a trash can icon. Click that icon to delete the item.

Goals

Goals provide a quick, visual way to see whether the subscribers who are passing through a journey are meeting your marketing objective for the journey. You set a goal for a journey by clicking the trophy button above the canvas (and shown in the margin).

When you set up a goal, you choose a data extension field and set the value that you want that field to contain. As Journey Builder finds subscribers whose data extension field matches the value you set, it updates the percentage of the whole that has met the goal.

For example, you could create a goal of 50 percent of people who abandon their carts then going on to make a purchase, as shown in Figure 17-6. Journey Builder will update the statistics to show the goal as met. (For this example to work, you would need to set up some code to update a field in a data extension to record whether this subscriber completed the purchase.)

Setting a goal is optional. If you set a goal, you can also configure the journey so that subscribers exit the journey as soon as they meet the goal.

WARNING

You can choose a data extension field as your goal field only if you have defined the data extension as a contact data type of data extension. To do this, include it in an attribute group defined in the Contact Builder app (see Chapter 8). If you haven't included the data extension that you want to use in an attribute group, you won't be able to choose the fields from that data extension from the drop-down menu when you define the goal criteria.

After you choose the data extension, field, and field value, you set the number of people or percentage of people that you want to meet that goal. Journey Builder uses this information to determine which journeys are the most successful.

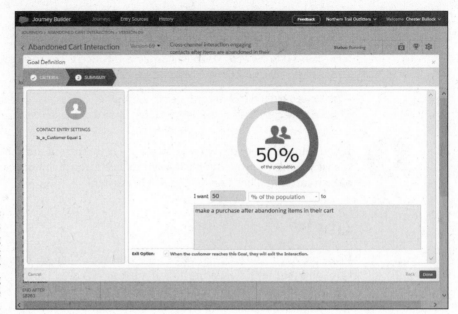

FIGURE 17-6:
This journey has a goal of getting people who left items in their online shopping cart to finish the transaction.

The system checks whether a subscriber has met the goal at the following times:

>> When the subscriber enters the journey

>> When a subscriber gets to the end of a wait activity

>> Each day at midnight, Central Standard Time

Settings

The next button above the canvas has the gear icon. Click this button to open the journey settings.

The first setting you can manage is Contact Entry. This setting controls whether a subscriber can enter a journey more than once. Valid values follow:

>> **No re-entry:** Choose this value if a subscriber can enter this journey only once.

>> **Re-entry anytime:** Choose this value if a subscriber can enter this journey multiple times, even if he or she hasn't exited it.

>> **Re-entry only after existing:** Choose this value if a subscriber can re-enter the journey, but only after the subscriber has finished it.

The other setting you can manage is Default Channel Addresses. As of the time of this writing, this setting was slated to be deprecated; if you still see it, you should probably just leave it set to the default value.

When you've finished managing the settings for the journey, click the Done button to return to the journey canvas.

Save, Test, and Activate buttons

The last items on the toolbar are the Save, Test, and Activate buttons.

WARNING

>> **Save button:** Save the draft version of the journey that you're working on.

Journey Builder does *not* automatically save as you make changes, so make sure to save often, especially if you are building a complex journey.

>> **Test button:** Verify that all paths in the journey are set up correctly. The system checks that you have configured the filters for all split activities and associated all message activities with messages.

>> **Activate button:** Set the current draft version of the journey to active, meaning that all new contacts entering the journey will flow into that active version of the journey.

TIP

We strongly recommend that you perform a begin-to-end test with the journey set to active to verify that sends are working as expected. You should set up special testing contacts and email addresses for this purpose. If necessary to facilitate testing, you can reduce the wait periods to minutes instead of hours or days. After you've completed the testing and verified that it's working as you expected, you could create a new draft version with the correct wait times. Make sure to set that version to active before allowing your audience to begin to flow into the journey.

Builder

Builder is the panel on the left side of the screen that contains the components of your journey. You click an item in Builder and drag it to the workspace on the right. You can choose the following categories of items:

>> Entry sources

>> Activities

We discuss the types of entry sources and activities in the following sections.

Journey Entry Sources

The first step in configuring a customer journey is to define where the subscribers who go through the journey come from. Journey Builder offers the following methods to get subscribers into your journey:

>> The most commonly used method is an audience (read: sendable data extension). You can refresh your memory of sendable data extensions in Chapter 6.

>> Another relatively straightforward way to get subscribers into your journey is to use a Smart Capture form that you set up on a CloudPages site. You can read all about CloudPages and Smart Capture in Chapter 15.

>> Using the API is a powerful and flexible way to start subscribers in a journey. However, it does require you to write code to use the Marketing Cloud API and incorporate that code into your website or mobile applications. Because of the complexity and advanced technical knowledge required to use it, the API is out of the scope of this book.

>> If you use the Salesforce Sales and Services Cloud and have integrated it with Marketing Cloud, you can also bring in subscribers from the Sales and Services Cloud to your journey.

In this chapter, we assume that you're using an audience as your journey's entry source. Not only is it the easiest entry method, but it's also the method that Salesforce recommends. Several Marketing Cloud apps can produce audiences. In this section, we discuss the audiences that come from Email Studio, Automation Studio, and Mobile Studio.

Depending on the nature of the journey, the audience that you use might already have all the subscribers in it when you start the journey. You can configure the journey to start only new subscribers in the journey to avoid starting the same subscribers over when you run the same journey again in the future.

On the other hand, you could also import new subscribers into the audience even while the journey is running. You can set up the journey to check the audience periodically for new records.

TIP

Another entry source — events — is available for adding subscribers to a journey. An event entry source is a date, such as the subscriber's birthdate. Journey Builder looks for subscribers in a list whose birthdate is the current day and adds those subscribers to the journey. At the time of this writing, Marketing Cloud announced plans to deprecate this feature.

The event entry source was previously the most common method and is the most heavily documented. Even after the feature is gone, you might find references to the event entry source. Fortunately, you can achieve the same functionality using the audience method.

Email Studio audiences

Email Studio can send email messages to subscribers who are on a list or on a sendable data extension (refer to Chapter 11). You can configure Email Studio to evaluate and insert records from a sendable data extension into the journey at the time you activate the journey or on a schedule. If you set up a schedule, you can indicate whether to evaluate all records in the data extension or only those that are new to the data extension since the last time you did the evaluation.

Starting a journey with an Email Studio audience

Use the following steps to start a journey with an Email Studio audience:

1. **From the journey canvas in Journey Builder, click the Audience icon in the Entry Sources panel on the left and drag it to the Start with an Entry Source area on the canvas.**

   The Start with an Entry Source icon is replaced with an Audience icon.

2. **Pause your mouse pointer on the Audience icon and click the Configure button that appears.**

   The Select Audience window appears.

3. **Select Email Studio Audience, and then click Next.**

   The Select Audience Wizard appears open to the first step: Properties.

4. **On the Properties step, enter a name for the audience.**

5. **(Optional) Add a description and select a different icon to represent the audience.**

6. **Click Next to move to the Select Audience step.**

7. **In the Folders pane on the left, navigate to the location of the Email Studio audience, and select the audience from the list on the right.**

8. **Click Next to move to the Contact Filter step.**

   If you select a data extension that no other journeys are using, a green banner appears. But if you choose a data extension that another journey is using, a warning appears. Journey Builder will let you proceed, but you should try to keep separate data extensions for each journey entry point.

TIP

9. (Optional) Click an attribute from the Attributes pane on the left and drag it to the canvas on the right.

The attribute appears on a line where you can set a value as a criterion. You use this step to determine a subscriber's eligibility to enter a journey based on attribute data.

10. Click Next to proceed to the Entry Schedule step.

11. Select one of the following values:

- *Run Once When the Journey Is Activated:* The journey gets the subscribers out of the audience when you activate the journey. Any subscribers that you add to the audience after that time will not enter the journey unless you run the journey again.

- *Run Using the Following Schedule:* You must indicate when you want the journey to retrieve the subscribers from the audience. Optionally, you can configure the journey to repeat the subscriber retrieval periodically. In that case, you must also indicate whether to evaluate the entire audience or only new subscribers. See the note at the end of this procedure for more information.

12. Click Next to move to the Summary step.

13. Review the summary details on this screen and then click Done.

Special note about the Entry Schedule step: You can feel as if you're going down a rabbit hole when you reach the Entry Schedule step of this wizard. If you choose Run Once When the Journey Is Activated, you simply select a single radio button and get on with the wizard. If you go the more common route of choosing Run Using the Following Schedule, however, it's a different story. Figure 17-7 shows the Entry Schedule step as it looks when you first reach it.

When you click this second option, the following additional fields appear:

>> Start date

>> Start time

>> Time zone

>> Repeat

The Repeat field is where you can choose how frequently the system should run the process to retrieve subscribers from the audience and start them in the journey. The default value is None (Run Once), and if you leave it set that way, no more fields appear on this screen and you can move on. Running the retrieval only once on a scheduled date is basically the same as choosing Run Once When the Journey Is Activated; the only difference is that you're choosing a different time to retrieve the subscribers from the audience.

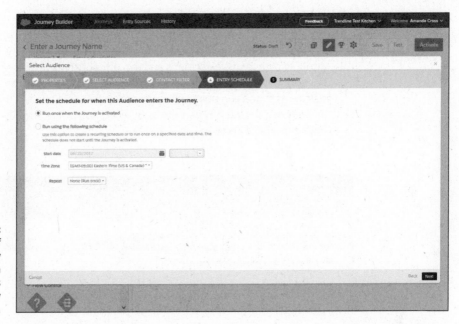

FIGURE 17-7:
The initial view of
the Entry
Schedule step in
the wizard is
deceptively
simple.

When you choose a different value in the Repeat field, things start getting complicated. For example, if you choose Hourly in that field, another field appears where you indicate how many hours between retrievals and yet another field appears where you indicate when the recurrence should end.

In addition, a gray box appears and you have to indicate how the system should evaluate the records when the scheduled retrieval runs. The options are as follows:

>> **Evaluate new records only:** This option is faster because the system considers only the subscribers who have joined the audience since the last scheduled run. You should use this method when you expect to add new subscribers to the audience while the journey is running and you want to make sure that you don't miss adding those new subscribers to the journey.

If you choose this option, you're telling the system to look at only new subscribers. However, because you're still creating the journey, the definition of what is a new subscriber could be confusing when you first activate the journey and the system does the initial retrieval of the subscribers.

That's why this gray box also requires you to make yet another selection to indicate how you want the system to deal with the initial run. The Entry Schedule step in the wizard, completely expanded to show the most possible fields, appears in Figure 17-8.

>> **Evaluate all records:** The second option is slower because the system looks at every subscriber in the audience every time it runs. If your journey uses attribute data to make decisions and that attribute data might change between the time you activate the journey and the time the subscriber reaches that decision point, this is the option for you. Choosing this value ensures that the journey gets the most recent subscriber attribute value before making a decision.

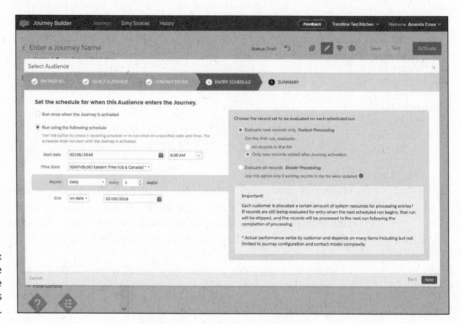

FIGURE 17-8:
As far down the
Entry Schedule
rabbit hole as
you can go.

Automation Studio audience

As we discuss in Chapter 10, you can use the Automation Studio app to automate simple, linear processes. Automation Studio does not offer the sophistication that Journey Builder does. For example, Journey Builder enables you to create parallel branches of a program, but Automation Studio doesn't.

However, Automation Studio is much simpler to use than Journey Builder, and many people — even people who know and use Journey Builder — prefer to use Automation Studio when its functionality suits the task they want to automate. To support people using both Automation Studio and Journey Builder, Marketing Cloud has made it possible to use an Automation Studio program to add subscribers to a journey.

Automation Studio programs can include activities that import subscriber data into a data extension, filter subscriber data already in a data extension, or query a data extension of subscriber data to return only subscribers who match certain criteria. A data extension that results from one of these activities can be the entry source for your journey.

For example, you might use Automation Studio to import a file of customer data into a master data extension. The data that you load might contain both new records that need to enter the journey as well as data updates for records that already exist. After the import runs, you would need to run a query to select the new records from that master data extension that would be entering the journey.

When you create your Automation Studio program to generate an audience, you set up the schedule for when it should run and when it should repeat. When you use that audience as the entry source for your journey, the journey just uses the same schedule that you set on the program, so you don't have to set all that information again.

Use the following steps to start a journey with an Automation Studio audience:

1. **From the journey canvas in Journey Builder, drag the Audience icon from the Entry Sources panel on the left to the Start with an Entry Source area on the canvas.**

   The Start with an Entry Source icon disappears and an Audience icon appears in its place.

2. **Pause your mouse pointer on the Audience icon and click the Configure button that appears.**

   The Select Audience window appears.

3. **Select Automation Studio Audience, and then click Next.**

   The Select Audience Wizard appears open to the first step: Properties.

4. **On the Properties step, enter a name for the audience.**

5. **(Optional) Add a description and select a different icon to represent the audience.**

6. **Click Next to move to the Select Automation step.**

7. **In the Folders pane on the left, navigate to the location of the Automation Studio automation. Choose the automation that contains an activity associated with the data extension you'll use for journey entry.**

8. **Click Next.**

   The Select Data Extension step of the wizard appears.

TIP

   You can see a list of all data extensions associated with the automation in the Associated Data Extensions column on the right side of the screen.

9. **Select the data extension that you want to use as your journey entry data extension, and then click Next.**

   The Summary step appears.

10. **Review your selections on the summary page, and then click Done.**

MobileConnect audience

Chapter 12 discusses mobile marketing and the MobileConnect app. The Mobile-Connect app lets you send and receive SMS/MMS messages with subscribers who have given you their mobile phone number.

A common kind of mobile campaign to set up is an email opt-in campaign. In this kind of campaign, you publish a keyword that people can text to you to join your email list. For example, you could print fliers that you hang up in your store to tell people to text DEALS and their email address to your short code to start receiving coupons by email.

MobileConnect collects the email addresses from an email opt-in campaign in a data extension that you can use as the entry source of your journey.

Use the following steps to start a journey with a MobileConnect audience:

1. **From the journey canvas in Journey Builder, drag the Audience icon from the Entry Sources panel on the left to the Start with an Entry Source area of the canvas.**

   The Start with an Entry Source icon is replaced with an Audience icon.

2. **Pause your mouse pointer on the Audience icon and click the Configure button that appears.**

   The Select Audience window appears.

3. **Select MobileConnect Audience, and then click Next.**

   The Select Audience Wizard appears open to the first step: Properties.

4. **On the Properties step, enter a name for the audience.**

5. **(Optional) Add a description and select a different icon to represent the audience.**

6. **Click Next to move to the Select List step.**

7. **Select a list from the options, and then click Next.**

You can use the Search field to find a particular list if you don't immediately see the one that you want. The Entry Schedule step appears.

8. **Select one of the following values:**

- *Run Once When the Journey Is Activated:* The journey gets subscribers out of the audience when you activate the journey. Any subscribers that you add to the audience after that time will not enter the journey unless you run the journey again.

- *Run Using the Following Schedule:* You must indicate when you want the journey to retrieve the subscribers from the audience. Optionally, you can configure the journey to repeat the subscriber retrieval periodically. In that case, you must also indicate whether to evaluate the entire audience or only the new subscribers.

9. **Click Next to move to the Summary step.**

10. **Review the summary details on this screen, and then click Done.**

Understanding Activities

Activities are the things that happen after a subscriber enters a journey and travels down its paths. When you're creating your journey in Journey Builder, a list of activities appears in Builder. You can click these activities and drag them to the canvas on the right.

As you can see in Figure 17-9, the Activities section of the left panel has four sections:

» **Messages:** Send messages, such as email or SMS.

» **Flow Control:** Split the journey into branches or join the branches back together. This is also the section where the wait activity appears.

» **Customer Updates:** Update your database of subscriber information with data you received as part of the journey.

» **Sales and Service Cloud:** If you use Salesforce Sales and Service Cloud and have integrated it with your Marketing Cloud account, you'll see this section in the Activities panel. The activities in this section let you update information in Sales and Service Cloud, and they open up lots of opportunities to use journeys in powerful ways. However, this section of the panel is outside the scope of this book.

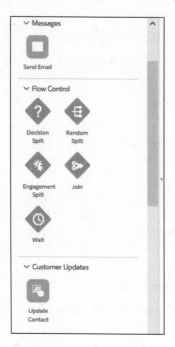

FIGURE 17-9:
Activities in the
Builder pane on
the left of the
screen.

Messages

To add a message to your journey, you simply click the message type from the left panel, drag it to the place in the journey where you want it, and then configure it. To configure the message, pause your mouse pointer over the icon and click the Configure button that appears, as you see in Figure 17-10.

FIGURE 17-10:
The Configure
button appears
when you pause
your mouse
pointer on the
message icon in
the journey.

For email messages, you see a wizard similar to other email send wizards in Marketing Cloud apps. You choose the email and then have the option to override properties, such as the subject line and the from name. Because you probably set these properties as you wanted them when you created the email, it's unlikely that you'll want to change them now.

For SMS messages, you must choose a message that you created in Mobile Studio using an Outbound template and configured to send as an interaction. See Chapter 12 for more information on Mobile Studio.

TIP

In this wizard, you choose a message that already exists, not to create one, so make sure you create all your messages before you begin assembling your journey.

Flow Controls

The Flow Controls section contains five activities that you can use to move your subscribers through their journey:

» **Decision Split:** Probably the most commonly used way to split paths along a journey, a decision split chooses the right path for a subscriber based on a piece of subscriber data you have in the data extension.

» **Random Split:** Random splits allow you to create up to ten branches, with a random selection of subscribers passing down each path. You can choose the percentage of subscribers that you want to proceed down each branch.

» **Engagement Split:** An engagement split allows you to create Yes or No paths based on whether the subscriber opened or clicked an email that you sent earlier in the journey.

WARNING

Engagement splits currently do not support links containing dynamically generated variables from AMPscript or query strings, which are commonly used for things such as analytics tagging. Therefore, if you include variables in your links for analytics purposes, it won't count as a click when a subscriber clicks it.

» **Join:** Inserting a join step after the last activity on a branch allows you to merge subscribers from that branch onto another branch in the journey.

» **Wait:** The wait activity holds subscribers on the current activity for the amount of time you specify before letting them proceed to the next activity in the journey. A wait can be as a little as a minute or as much as months. You might use a wait when you want to give the subscriber time to engage with an email before you use an engagement split. You might also use a wait to put some time between email messages in a series to prevent them all showing up in the subscriber's inbox at once.

TIP

Journey Builder automatically adds a one-day wait after most activity types when you drag them to the canvas. You can delete the wait, but we have found that it's better to leave it there. You can reduce the wait time if necessary.

Similar to messages, to add a flow control activity to your journey, you can click it from the panel on the left and drag it to the canvas on the right. Pause your mouse pointer on the activity icon and click the Configure button.

Decision split

When you configure a decision split, the Decision Split window appears, as shown in Figure 17-11.

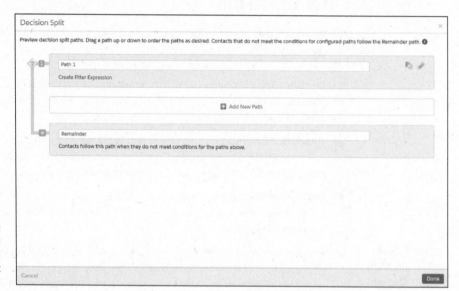

FIGURE 17-11:
Create and reorder paths in the Decision Split window.

The window defaults to containing two paths: The first is for subscribers who meet the criteria you configure, and the second is for everyone else. You can add more criteria-based paths by clicking the Add New Path button. Subscribers who don't meet the criteria for any of the paths will follow the Remainder path.

You can enter a name for the path, and then you click the Create Filter Expression link or the pencil icon to define the criteria. Figure 17-12 shows the Decision Split window that appears.

Navigate to the attribute upon which you want to base the criteria. Click the attribute from the panel on the left and drag it to the workspace on the right. Depending on the data type of the attribute you chose, fields appear where you define the attribute value that a subscriber must have to qualify for this path.

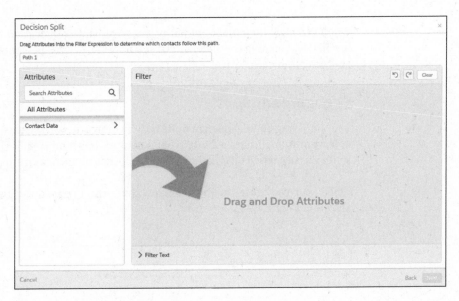

FIGURE 17-12:
Define the criteria
for this path.

The criteria that you use for your paths need not be mutually exclusive. For example, you could configure the first path to take everyone who lives in Indiana, but configure the next path to take subscribers who have birthdays in June. When a subscriber matches both criteria, how does the system decide which path to use?

This is where the order of steps in the workspace matters. The system evaluates the paths in order and sends the subscribers along the first one they match. You can change the order of paths in this workspace by dragging a path to the place in the order where you want it.

Random split

When you drag a Random Split activity on to the workspace, the Random Split window appears, as shown in Figure 17-13.

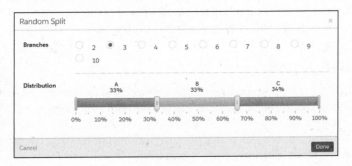

FIGURE 17-13:
Choose the
number of
branches and
what percentage
of subscribers
to send down
each path.

When you click the number of paths you want, sliders appear on the Distribution line below. You drag the sliders until you have the desired percentage of subscribers going into each path.

Engagement split

You can't drag an Engagement Split activity onto your workspace until you include at least one email send activity. That's because this kind of split chooses the subscriber's path based on whether he or she clicked or opened an email that you sent.

When you configure an Engagement Split, the Engagement Decision window shown in Figure 17-14 appears.

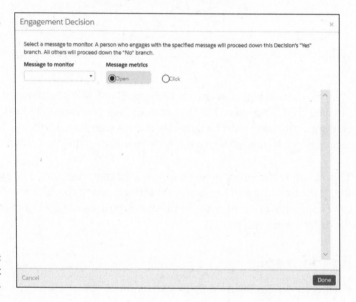

FIGURE 17-14:
The Engagement Decision window.

In the Message to Monitor drop-down menu, select the message that is the basis for the path decision. Then choose Open or Click to indicate what a subscriber must do with that message to qualify for the path.

Join

You must have at least two paths defined in your journey before you can use the Join activity. The Join activity brings two paths together.

When you drag a Join activity onto a path in your journey, two icons appear on the path: a Join icon and a Drag to Join icon.

Click the Drag to Join icon and drag it to the path with which you want to join. The paths of the journey appear connected after you join them as shown in Figure 17-15.

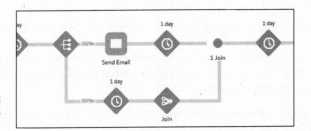

FIGURE 17-15:
Joining two paths
in your journey.

Wait

When you add a Wait activity to a path, the Wait window appears, as shown in Figure 17-16.

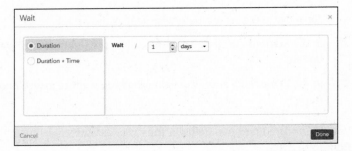

FIGURE 17-16:
Configuring the
Wait activity.

First, you choose whether you want the wait period to be a duration (for example, two days) or a particular hour of the day after a duration (for example, 8 a.m. after two days have passed).

Next, you enter the length of the wait duration. If you chose Duration + Time, you also enter the time of day when you want the wait to end.

Updating contacts

The third section is Customer Updates. This section contains the Update Contact activity, which updates your customer database with information about subscribers as they pass through this point in the journey.

You might use the Update Contact activity to make a note that the subscriber completed the previous activity. Later in your journey, you can set up a decision split to look at that note and choose a branch based on that information. You might also have a "journey completed" field in your data extension where you set a yes-or-no value based on whether the subscriber completed the journey.

Use the following steps to add and configure an Update Contact activity:

1. **Click the Update Contact activity in Builder on the left side of the screen and drag it to the position where you want it on a journey path on the right side of the screen.**

2. **Pause your mouse pointer over the Update Contact icon on the path, and click the Configure button that appears.**

   The Update Contact Wizard appears, open to the first step: Choose Data Extension.

3. **Choose the data extension that contains the field you want to update with this activity.**

4. **Click Next.**

   You move to the Set Attribute/Value step of the wizard.

5. **In the Attribute drop-down menu, select the field that you want to update.**

6. **In the Value field, enter the value that you want to insert, and then click Done.**

TIP

You can update up to five fields in the same data extension using a single Update Contact activity.

Real-time metrics

After you have completed your journey and activated it, Journey Builder begins to collect metrics about how the journey is performing.

As subscribers pass through activities, an on-screen mouse-over on the canvas increments the total number of subscribers that have passed through that point. For example, pause your mouse pointer over an email activity to display sent, open, and click counts and rates for the message. If applicable, these metrics also show the percentage of a goal achieved.

Figure 17-17 shows the real-time metrics for an activity.

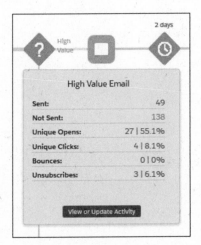

FIGURE 17-17:
Watch your success unfold with real-time metrics.

Journey Builder reporting

Reporting for emails sent from Journey Builder can be found in the Tracking menu in the Email Studio app. Look for a folder labeled Journey Builder Sends. A new subfolder is automatically generated for each version of a journey. More comprehensive reporting for Journey Builder can be generated through the Reports app by selecting the Journey Builder Email Send Summary or Journey Builder Email Send Summary By Day reports (see Chapter 9 for more information on using reports).

6

The Part of Tens

Find ideas for where to get started in a product with seemingly limitless options.

Discover suggestions for getting your Marketing Cloud initiative off on the right foot.

Learn from the mistakes of others.

Chapter **18**

Ten Customer Journeys for Beginners

In Chapter 16, you learn about how to plan a customer journey and what information you need to prepare. In Chapter 17, we talk about how to use Journey Builder to set up the customer journeys that you designed in Chapter 16. Of course, knowing *how* to do something only goes so far if you don't have an idea of *what* to start building! The sheer range of things you can do with customer journeys can be so overwhelming that it's hard to know where to begin.

In this chapter, we describe ten relatively simple customer journeys. Setting up these customer journeys not only offers quick value to your subscribers but also helps you to become familiar with the tools. As you continue, you'll customize these customer journeys for your needs and probably think of new customer journeys that are perfect for your audience.

Welcome Series

The welcome series is so common that it made an easy example to visit repeatedly in the last two chapters. A *welcome series* is just what it sounds like: a series of emails that you send to a new subscriber or customer. The emails reinforce the prospect's positive perception of your brand by talking up the value of the communication for which the new recipient signed up.

We see success from a welcome series when we intend to convert a prospect to a purchaser. Obviously, the prospects are interested because they subscribed, and the welcome series is a great opportunity to get prospects to make a purchase while our brand is still fresh in their minds.

Figure 18-1 shows an example welcome series design.

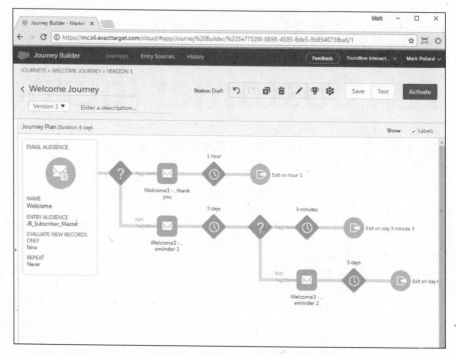

FIGURE 18-1:
The welcome journey sends messages to engage new subscribers.

In addition to welcoming a new subscriber, this journey checks to see whether a user has completed a website registration. It sends messages as reminders to those subscribers who haven't yet registered.

Abandoned Cart

Unlike in a bricks-and-mortar store, customers shopping in an online store might forget that they were shopping at all if they get distracted in the middle of the experience. Items that the subscriber had already added to the cart may go unpurchased simply because the prospective customer suddenly had to take a phone call and then got busy doing other things.

An *abandoned cart* customer journey reminds customers that they were shopping and shows them what is still sitting in their cart. If your customers tend to abandon shopping carts because they're shopping around (rather than just getting distracted), you might want to include a discount offer in your abandoned cart messages.

Figure 18-2 shows an abandoned cart journey design.

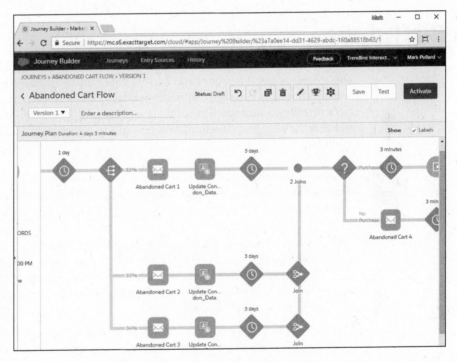

FIGURE 18-2:
The abandoned cart journey tries to entice customers to complete their purchase.

In this journey, we set up a three-way random split to test offers in the email content. After each send, we update the contact to record which version the contact received. Then we add a decision split three days after the message sends. This split checks a data extension to see whether the customer completed the purchase. If not, we send another email.

The key to this journey is getting the cart abandonment data from your online store into Marketing Cloud. If you're using Marketing Cloud's Web Analytics, you might already have this data in a data extension. If not, you'll need to come up with a different solution to get the data.

A common solution is to have you online store periodically post a file of abandoned cart data to the Marketing Cloud FTP site. That way, you create an import activity in Automation Studio (see Chapter 10 for details on Automation Studio) to bring the data into Marketing Cloud that you can then access as an Automation Studio audience in your journey's entry source. By using an Automation Studio audience, you can run the process to add customers to this journey on a schedule that meets your needs.

Another possible solution is to add some API code to your online store that would add the data to a data extension.

Birthday

Regardless of whether a person is excited to be having another birthday, receiving a happy birthday message can make the day brighter. Companies that sell products directly to individual consumers can enjoy a high level of engagement by sending an offer for a discount or a free gift in a message to customers on their birthday.

TIP

As always, you want to avoid creepiness in your email marketing campaigns. Make sure you send birthday messages only to customers who meet both of the following criteria:

>> *You have an existing relationship with the customers.* Even though you could potentially purchase all kinds of information about a great number of people, those people don't necessarily want to hear from you about their special day. Receiving a birthday email from a company from which you've never made a purchase seems pretty creepy.

>> *The customers have told you their birthday themselves.* Some people are sensitive about their age, so let subscribers volunteer information about their birthday before you make a big deal out of it.

Figure 18-3 shows a birthday journey design.

A birthday email is not typically a problem you use a journey to solve. Usually, you use different tools — triggered sends or Automation Studio automations — to send birthday emails.

However, journeys do provide benefits over the other tools. In this example, we use a date-based entry event to select records where the contact's birthday is seven days after the current date, and where contacts reenter the journey every year. This type of entry makes setup quick.

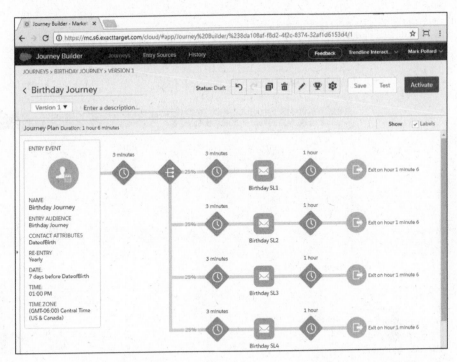

FIGURE 18-3:
Birthday journeys
send an email on
a particular date.

Additionally, we're using the random split control to test the performance of four different subject lines. Again, this test and other kinds of testing are easy to set up in Journey Builder.

Browse Retargeting

Increasingly, people who spend a lot of time online don't mind the fact that the websites they visit seem to know a lot about them. Therefore, your customers probably wouldn't be too surprised to receive an email from you that says, "We noticed you were looking at product X and we thought you might also be interested in product Y."

That's what a *browse retargeting* journey does. You use the data you have from customers' app or website viewing sessions to send an email suggesting related content. Browse retargeting doesn't need to be limited to products. You could also suggest articles similar to an article a person was reading, songs similar to a song a person was listening to, or whatever piece of web content you want to drive more subscribers to look at.

Figure 18-4 shows a browse retargeting journey design.

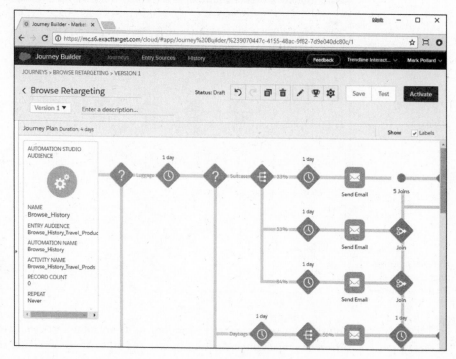

FIGURE 18-4:
Browse
retargeting
journeys send
contacts more of
the kinds of
things you
already know
they like.

As with the abandoned cart journey we discuss earlier in this chapter, your biggest hurdle to setting up this journey is probably going to be getting the browse history for a contact from your website into Marketing Cloud.

If you're using Marketing Cloud's Web Analytics, the data might already be available in a data extension in your account. If not, you'll probably start your journey with an Automation Studio audience, after Automation Studio imports a file with the browsing history.

In this journey example, we begin with an Automation Studio audience as the entry point. We segment the browse history data to narrow it down to people who have browsed for travel products on a retail site.

We begin by using a decision split to break out the messaging by product category: luggage, accessories, gear, and so on. Then we further split into particular types of product. Finally, we use a random split to test different email designs before joining back to a single path for additional follow-up messaging.

Customer Anniversary

Whereas companies that sell directly to individuals might want to recognize their customers' birthdays, businesses that sell to other businesses don't have a single birthday to acknowledge. In this case, you can replace the customer's birthday with the anniversary of when the business first became a customer. This approach is especially effective if you have an ongoing service relationship with your customers.

Even for companies that do serve individuals, acknowledging the anniversary of the date when a customer joined your rewards program can be a nice touch that customers appreciate.

Figure 18-5 shows a customer anniversary journey design.

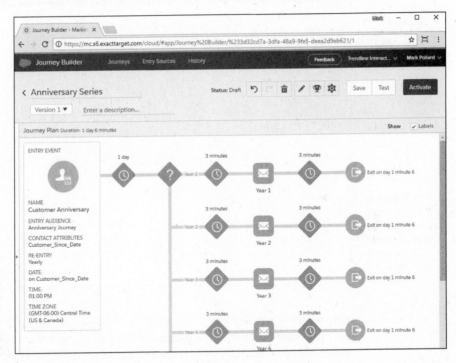

FIGURE 18-5: The customer anniversary journey acknowledges the day your contact became a client.

In this example, we create a separate path for each of the anniversary years for the customer's first five anniversary dates.

Just like sending birthday messages, acknowledging a customer's anniversary is not an obvious time to use Journey Builder. However, the date-based entry event, annual reentry, and decision split features of Journey Builder do make setup easy.

Loyalty Series

A *loyalty series* is similar to a welcome series, only instead of welcoming subscribers to your newsletter or other email updates, the series of emails welcomes them to your loyalty program.

Your loyalty series emails can highlight the benefits that members receive and get your new participants excited about earning points right away.

Figure 18-6 shows a loyalty series design.

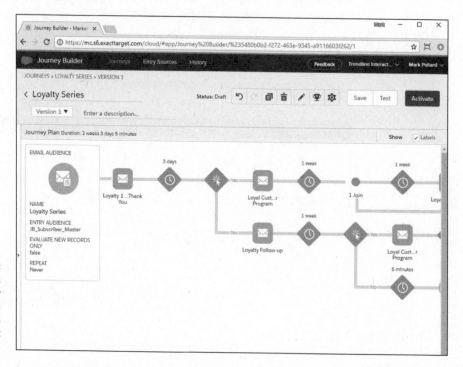

FIGURE 18-6: A loyalty series journey gets new loyalty program participants excited about rewards.

This example journey begins by sending a thank-you email to customers who have purchased more than two times in the past six months. It features engagement splits to send a reminder if the recipient does not open the initial thank-you email.

After the contact does open the initial email, the journey sends an invitation to participate in a customer rewards program. After joining the rewards program, subscribers receive a special promotional offer.

App Download

An *app download* journey sends a series of emails that encourages subscribers to download your company's mobile app and then use it for product research, purchases, or whatever your mobile app lets customers do.

Mobile apps are wonderful for collecting specific information about your customers' behavior. Because you control the entire app, you can report every action a customer takes in your app to your central database. That information can be available for you to use in the emails you send during this journey.

Figure 18-7 shows an app download journey design.

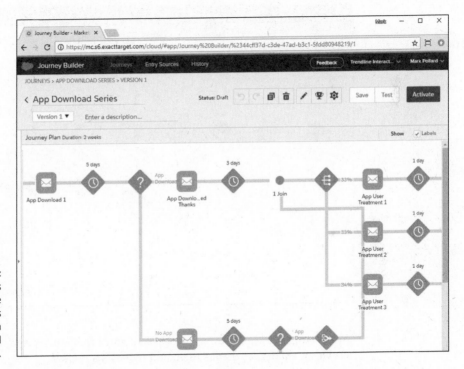

FIGURE 18-7: Raise awareness of your mobile app and its benefits with an app download journey.

This app download journey begins by identifying contacts who have not yet downloaded the app. The journey sends those contacts a message encouraging them to download. After a five-day wait period, the decision split checks to see who still hasn't downloaded the app and those who haven't receive another message. This wait, check, and remind process happens again in a few days. Contacts who still haven't downloaded receive a second reminder using a random split testing subject lines

Whenever contacts download the app, they join the branch of the journey that receives one of three random creative treatments.

Post-Purchase

A *post-purchase* customer journey encourages customers to provide feedback, leave customer review, or perform other activities after a purchase. Reviews play a big role in people's decision making when they compare products online, so reminding your customers to come back to your site and share their experience with other prospective customers can improve future sales.

Figure 18-8 shows a post-purchase journey design.

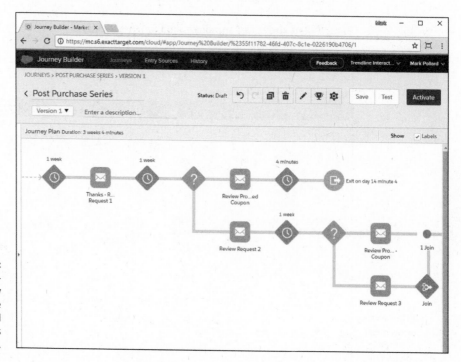

In this simple journey design, purchasers enter the journey and, one week later, receive an email that thanks them and requests a review.

After a one-week wait period, a decision split checks to see whether the customer provided a review. If yes, the customer receives a thank-you email with a coupon offer. If no, the customer receives a reminder message before ending another one-week wait period.

Re-engagement

Re-engagement journeys send messages to customers who haven't been in touch in a while. For example, you might use a re-engagement journey for subscribers who haven't been opening your emails, customers who haven't made any purchases recently, or users who haven't used your mobile app lately.

The re-engagement journey can be a single email or a series of emails to highlight the benefits that made the subscriber want to engage with you in the first place. If you use a series of emails and the subscriber continues not to engage, the last one you send can contain a link that the subscriber has to click to remain on the list. In addition to giving the subscriber incentive to engage, this approach can help you remove bad email addresses from your list.

Figure 18-9 shows a re-engagement journey design.

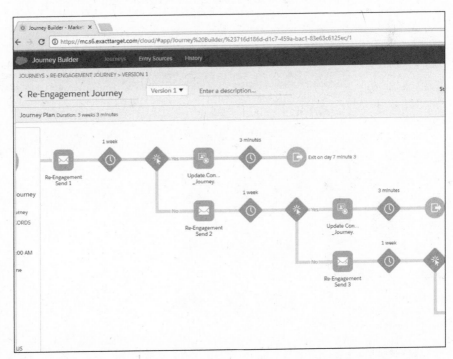

FIGURE 18-9: The re-engagement journey helps you stay top-of-mind with your contacts.

This sample re-engagement journey shows contacts entering who haven't opened a newsletter message in the past six months. Over a three-week period, the contacts receive up to three messages trying to get them to open.

After each message send, the journey waits a week and then an engagement split checks to see whether the contact has opened the previously sent message. If so, the contact exits the journey. If not, the journey sends the next message. We use the update contact activity to record the date that the contact exits the journey for future reference.

Newsletter Series

A *newsletter series* is a journey that sends your newsletter or any other ongoing series of information emails that you distribute. Sending a newsletter establishes you as a source of useful and authoritative information and offers value to the subscriber. Using a customer journey to send your newsletter automates the routine parts of the process, freeing you up to write the valuable content that subscribers are looking for.

Figure 18-10 shows a newsletter series design.

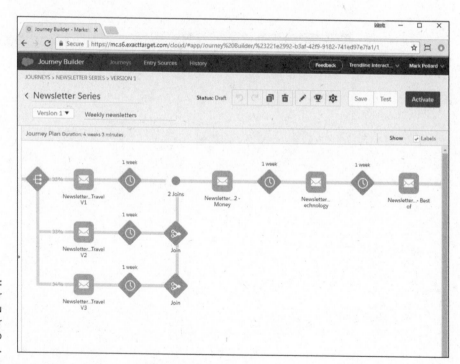

FIGURE 18-10:
A newsletter journey helps you develop your contacts into experts.

This sample journey begins with newsletter subscribers entering a four-week series of weekly newsletter sends. During the first week, a random split facilitates a three-way test of different email designs. After a wait period of one week, the three paths join and subscribers proceed to the next send in the series.

Chapter 19

Ten Secrets to a Successful Implementation

Now you know all the things that Salesforce Marketing Cloud can do. You've created your list of goals, and you've considered how you can use the tools to help you achieve them. Finally, it's time to implement.

There's time for just a few words of advice to help your implementation go smoothly. The following tips are based on the process we use at Trendline Interactive to onboard a client to Marketing Cloud.

Set Realistic Function Expectations

One of the nice things about software-as-a-service (SaaS) products is that you can easily add additional features when you need them. You don't have to buy every app you might ever consider using. Just purchase the apps that you're going to use at first and be ready to grow from there.

Cutting unnecessary features off your invoice will also help you as you manage the expectations of your team and your management. Communicate specific goals internally, explain how the features you're purchasing help you, and brag about your results early and often.

Set Realistic Time Expectations

The migrations that we at Trendline Interactive help our clients perform take two to three months on average. You can't — and shouldn't — rush the process. Cutting corners early on will just result in big problems later.

Design for the Data

As you have probably noticed by this point, data is absolutely essential to target your online marketing campaigns properly, so establishing your data model should be one of your first priorities. Use the information in Chapters 5 and 6 to figure out what information you want, what you have, and what you need. Don't forget to build in flexibility for future data you might need.

Purchase Support

If you're generally good with software, you might think you can get by without a support contract, but this one is worth the money. Higher tiered support contracts are especially useful if you're planning to use advanced features such as Audience Builder or Journey Builder. Moreover, the higher tiered support contract you buy, the faster response time you get from the Marketing Cloud support team.

Take Care with Your IP Warm

In Chapter 3, we discuss the process of getting IPs accustomed to you as a sender before blasting out a bunch of emails lest the IP flag you as a spammer. If you have small lists (under 50,000 subscribers), this process might not be strictly necessary. However, if your lists are over 50,000 and you'll be sending more than one email per month, a proper IP warm will make a huge difference in getting your email messages into your subscribers' inboxes.

Work Closely with Your Implementation Partner

If you're using an implementation partner, don't just hand the project over and wait for results. You need to understand as much as you can about what your partner did. Get your partner to walk you through the work and provide documentation for your future reference.

Establish Standards

At first, establishing file-naming conventions and standards for the hierarchical folder structure to contain your assets will seem like unnecessary overhead. However, believe us: After awhile, you'll be drowning in files. Your future self will thank you for giving those files a predictable name and storing them in the right place.

Document Everything

Time after time, we hear about clients who wish they could go back and write things down. Something that seems so obvious or so unforgettable can just evaporate from your memory when you need it months or years down the road. Specific areas to document include the following:

» The blueprint for your data model.

» The map of your internal data flows, before the data gets to Salesforce Marketing Cloud.

» A list of your API interactions. This should be a living document that you always keep current.

» App Center implementations for API calls. Your developers use App Center to integrate Marketing Cloud with your other business systems. The App Center establishes the credentials you need to connect the systems. You can find the App Center at http://appcenter-auth.s1.marketingcloudapps.com.

» Folder hierarchy for content and assets.

Inform All Key People

No one likes to feel out of control, especially when it comes to the tools you use at work every day. Avoid surprising the people on your team who will feel the effects of the implementation, especially the ones who could derail the success of the project! Don't forget to communicate with people from the following parts of your company:

>> Data team

>> Creative team

>> Call center personnel

>> Anyone who interacts with customers, especially people who accept customer complaints

Allow Time for Training

We each have nearly 10 years of experience in Salesforce Marketing Cloud, but we still find out new things about the platform all the time. The software is intuitive, but skipping the full training regimen can limit you to only the beginning features. You want to graduate to using the advanced features of the platform.

Beyond just learning how to use Marketing Cloud, keeping up with the latest advancement in email marketing is important. Continuing your marketing education makes you a more valuable contributor to your team.

Chapter **20**

Ten Bad Habits of Digital Marketers

t's been a long, fun journey through the world of digital marketing with Salesforce Marking Cloud. As we wrap up, we'd like to leave you with some words of caution. This chapter lists mistakes that impede — or even sink — digital marketing efforts time and time again. If you can learn from the mistakes of others and avoid these bad habits, you'll be well on the path to success!

Not Testing Enough

In digital marketing, theory doesn't always translate smoothly into action. You might have a clear concept of how your campaign should run, but you can't be sure that you've covered everything until you build and test the campaign.

You might have forgotten to add personalization, inserted the wrong image for one of your dynamic content conditions, left out a link, or any of a million other things. You try to get everything right from the beginning, of course, but nothing can replace a thorough review of your complete messages.

At Trendline, we always make sure to test at least the following areas:

>> Message's appearance in a variety of devices

>> Grammar and spelling (for English emails)

>> All links to make sure that they work *and* go to the right location

>> Proper placement of links within the email

>> Correct From name and address for this message

>> Correct send classification for this message

>> Correct audience for this message

Over time, develop a checklist of items that are important for your testing. (You can use this list as a starter and add or modify items as experience indicates.) Although testing can be time consuming, for us it has resulted in a 98 percent error-free rate during the last six years.

Testing Too Many Variables

We just said that testing is a vital component to ongoing success, but here we're talking about a different kind of testing. You almost can't do too much of QA-type testing (short of finding yourself in analysis paralysis and unable to make yourself click Send). However, you can easily bite off more than you can chew when you're doing the kind of testing in which you compare the performance of message content, such as images, subject lines, and send time.

You must be patient and deliberate when you design and execute performance comparison testing, or A/B testing. For example, if you try to measure too many things at once — such as testing an image and a subject line in the same message — you can receive misleading results.

If you like to dive deep into statistics, you can investigate Taguchi methods of multivariate testing in your email, but it is probably easier to test just one thing at a time!

Assuming That Flashy Features Equal Better Results

While reading this book, you've probably discovered at least one cool feature of Marketing Cloud that you can't wait to try. Using an innovative capability is tempting because trying out new things is fun. Everyone wants to be on the cutting edge of technology.

However, the purpose of a marketing message should always dictate the technology you use, not the other way around. Cramming a new technology into a campaign where it doesn't fit introduces risks, such as the following:

>> Slowing down your deployment

>> Increasing opportunities for errors

>> Creating annoyed subscribers

>> Making you look silly

For example, you don't have to use dynamic content in every email. If you understand the interests that all your subscribers have in common, you can construct a message that appeals to all of them.

Hyper-Targeting

We've worked on campaigns for clients in which we put a lot of time into identifying the right subscriber criteria to define the perfect target audience for the message. Then, after we filtered through the subscriber list to see who would satisfy the criteria and receive the message, we ended up with a handful of people.

A hyper-targeted campaign performs very well of course, but at what cost? When it takes more to create the campaign than you could possibly get in return, you've gone too far in customizing your message.

Forsaking Proven Channels

From time to time, an expert declares the email channel to be dead. Text message marketing, or social media marketing, or some other new channel marketing is the new, most important place to put your marketing dollars, they say.

These so-called expert proclamations have been happening for more than a decade. Such a statement grabs headlines but fails to offer good advice to digital marketers. We've seen budgets shift toward a new channel but then shift back when it doesn't prove to be a magic bullet.

As with most things in life, getting a good reward means expending some effort, and email marketing has consistently proven to be worth that effort.

Buying the "It Just Works" Myth

Over the last several years, a myth that has made its way around digital marketing conferences is that the latest tool, gadget, or suite of products will make your digital marketing effort "just work."

Sadly, a product that "just works" on its own doesn't exist. Integrated marketing takes planning, resources, and effort. For example, data issues are the number one problem our clients encounter with their digital marketing. Buying a new tool with flashy features isn't going to heal the problems in their data.

Over-Messaging

This one should go without saying, but it's still an issue we see, especially with new people entering the ranks of digital marketing: Yes, it is possible to send too many messages. When you over-share with your customers or potential customers, you run the risk of changing their opinion of you from "trusted brand sending valuable information" to "spammer."

The threshold of how-much-is-too-much differs for every business. The nature of your product and the content of your messages matter, of course, but so do the expectations you set in your sign-up process and ongoing communications. Keep an eye on your key indicators and the open and unsubscribe rates. You'll see changes in these measures if you're wearing out your audience.

Forgetting That Content Is King

After you get a taste of success in email marketing, you may be tempted to use the relationship you've grown with your audience to share each and every thing about your company that makes you proud. However, subscribers are more mercenary:

They joined your list because they think they'll get something good out of it. Over time, using email to send what you want to say — instead of what subscribers want to hear — can have a dramatic effect on performance.

Content will always be king, and you need to remember to always add value for the recipient of your message, regardless of the channel. If you do not consistently deliver some kind of value, subscribers will stop responding.

Not Staying Current

We've each been in the digital marketing space for 20 years. During that time, we've seen staggering changes in the business. The amount of personnel turnover we've seen in that time is just as striking, and a lot more frightening. People who don't put in the effort to keep up with changes don't last.

Continuing education is vital to a long career in digital marketing. Of course, digital marketers are also busy, which makes it hard to find the time at work to learn. Making the effort is worthwhile, however, lest you find yourself replaced by someone with the latest knowledge.

If you can't make time to stay current at the office, consider making it your hobby at home. Although your current employer will benefit from your ongoing education in the immediate term, you'll benefit from it even more over the long run. Invest in yourself; your career is worth it.

Not Asking for Help

When we started in this field, companies expected a digital marketer to be a jack-of-all-trades. The same person would

>> Create the website.

>> Optimize search engine positioning.

>> Handle customer feedback.

>> Address anything else that touched marketing on the Internet.

As each new channel emerged (email, social, virtual reality, and so on), that same person was supposed to immediately become an expert. In some cases, companies expected the same person to do all this *and* write code!

These expectations were a challenge then but are simply unfair now. You have to be able to get help, perhaps by hiring an agency or adding personnel. You can't do it by yourself without hurting your performance and burning out.

For your own sanity, never be afraid to ask for help!

Index

A

A/B testing, 167, 185–186
A/B Testing menu (Email Studio), 165
abandoned cart customer journey, 306–308
accessing
  apps, 29–31
  business units, 27–29
  Calendar tool, 50
  Content Builder app, 94
  email tracking, 180–181
  Journey Builder, 276
  Marketing Cloud, 21
  MobileConnect, 194
  Personalization Builder, 144
  Professional edition (Advertising Studio), 238
  Social Studio, 214
  Users page, 35
  Web & Mobile Analytics, 142
Account menu, 26
Account Send Summary report, 139–140
Activate button (journey canvas), 285
activities
  creating, 150–158
  testing, 150–151
Activities screen (Automation Studio), 150, 151
Activities section (Journey Builder), 293–294
ad hoc campaigns, 19–20
ad networks, supported, 240–241
adding
  associations to campaigns, 57–58
  content to collections, 250–255
  messages to customer journeys, 294–295
  Update Contact activities, 300
adjusting
  displays in Content Builder, 94–95
  reports, 133–134

Admin menu (Email Studio), 165
administration
  about, 33
  delivery profiles, 44–47
  managing users, 34–37
  providing access for use, 37–41
  security, 41–44
  send classifications, 44–47
  sender profiles, 44–47
  warming IPs, 47–48
Administrator role, 38
admins, in Social Studio, 212
Advertising Studio app
  about, 30, 229
  editions, 230
  Lead Capture edition, 230–237
  Professional edition, 237–242
All Contacts menu, 117
All Content option (Content tab), 96
AMPscript, 187
Analyst role, 38
analytics, tips for, 225–226
Analytics Builder app
  about, 30, 131
  Discover tool, 132–136
  standard reporting, 136–140
analytics reports, drafting, 225
Analyze module (Social Studio), 215–217
analyzing content performance, 257–258
AOL, 8
API event, as an entry source, 266
app download customer journey, 313
app switcher, 24, 26, 31
applying filters, 134
approval rules, creating in Social Studio, 214
approval workflows, 110, 111–113

evaluating records, 289–290

events (Calendar tool)

creating, 52–53

sources for, 51–52

events, as an entry source, 267

events view (Data Designer menu), 116

ExactTarget, 163, 164–167. *See also* Email Studio app

Exclude category, 177–178

Exclusions tab (Audience Builder), 124

expectations, setting, 317–318

exporting history data, 280

external style sheet, 171

F

Facebook

about, 213

adding tabs to collections, 254–255

audience refresh, 242

creating lookalike audiences, 231

lead capture forms, 231–232

as a supported network, 240

Facebook ad, 246–247

Facebook Ad ID field, 234

Facebook Page ID field, 234

Facebook tab, 246

features, effect on results of, 323

feedback, negative/positive, 227

Feedback button, 26

file cabinets, 65

file transfer activity, 153–154

file-naming patterns, 151–152

files, flat, 86

filter activity, 154

Filter button (Journey Builder), 278

Filter tab (Audience Builder), 124

filters, applying, 134

Filters tab, 97–98

finding

content in Content Builder, 96–98

JavaScript snippets, 143

flat files, 86

Flow Control section (Journey Builder), 293, 295–299

folders

creating, 98–99

moving, 99

organizing content in, 98–99

Folders option (Content tab), 96

footer, 44

Forward to a Friend section (Email Studio), 183

from names, testing, 186

fulfilling

customer journey with Marketing Cloud, 20–21

objectives, 73–74

full users, in Social Studio, 212

full_name field, 235

G

general messages, 200–201

geographic data, 66, 67

getting started, with Social Studio, 213–214

Gmail, 172

Goal Attainment column (Journey Builder), 278

Goals (journey canvas), 283–284

Google

about, 231

audience refresh, 242

as a supported network, 240

Google+, 213

Google Ads, 245

GroupConnect app, 189, 202

groups, as a tool, 176

growing audiences, 226–227

H

header, 44

help

asking for, 325–326

Marketing Cloud, 27

Hide Tips option (User menu), 26

History menu option, 278–280

P

parentheses, 127

Password Policies section (Security Settings page), 43

patterns, file-naming, 151–152

pausing email sends, 185

Performance tab (Social Studio), 219, 221–222

performing QA tests, 175–176

permissions
opt-in, 203
role, 39–40

Personalization Builder app
about, 30, 131
accessing, 144
tools, 144

personalized message, 10

personalized URLs (PURLs), 245

personas, creating, 16

pie chart icon, 278

Pinterest, 213

Playbooks box (MobileConnect), 195–196

point-of-sale system, 64

Populations view (Data Designer menu), 117

positive feedback, 227

post-purchase customer journey, 314

posts, creating in Social Studio, 220–221

predictive intelligence, 143–144

preference attributes
setting up, 83–84
in subscriber/list model, 77

preference center, 244–245

preheader, best practices for, 169–170

preheader text, 169

preheaders, testing, 186

preparing
automation, 21
channels, 21
data-based insights, 20
emails to send, 174–178
for mobile marketing, 190
publish labels in Social Studio, 214
to use Marketing Cloud, 21

prerequisites
for Contact Builder, 270
for data extension, 270
setting up for Advertising Studio, 238

preview text, 169

previewing emails, 174–175

primary key, 78–81

product/service offerings, testing, 16

Professional edition (Advertising Studio)
about, 230, 237–239
accessing, 238
ad network account ownership, 239–240
creating audiences, 241–242
refreshing audiences, 242
supported social and ad networks, 240–241

profile attributes
setting up, 82–83
in subscriber/list model, 76

Profile Center, 77

proximity feature, 208

publish labels, preparing in Social Studio, 214

Publish module (Social Studio), 218–223

Publish tab (Audience Builder), 125

publishing content, 255–257

purchasing
supplemental data, 71–72
support, 318

PURLs (personalized URLs), 245

Q

QA tests, performing, 175–176

quality assurance (QA), 175–176

queries, creating, 268

question mark icon, 141

R

random split, 268, 295, 297–298

real-time, operating in, 16–17

real-time metrics, 300–301

Recent Email Sending Summary report, 138–139

recent purchases, data on, 67

Recent Send Summary report, 133–134

records, evaluating, 289–290

Redo button (journey canvas), 282

re-engagement campaigns, 19

re-engagement customer journey, 315–316

Refresh button, 127, 128

refresh group activity, 155–156

refreshing

  audiences, 242

  lookalike audiences, 237

registering social accounts in Social Studio, 214

relational data model

  about, 76, 78–81

  compared with subscriber/list model, 81–82

  setting up, 85–86

relationships, 120

Remember icon, 2

rendering, best practices for, 170–171

reordering attributes, 125

Repeat field, 288–289

Replace option (Content Builder), 105

reports. *See also* standard reporting

  creating from scratch, 134–136

  Journey Builder, 301

  modifying, 133–134

  running, 136–137

  saving, 135

reputations, establishing, 48

researching on social media, 225

resources (Litmus), 173–174

Responsive Email Support in Gmail is Coming (website), 173

reusable code snippets, creating, 109

reusable content blocks, creating, 107–109

reviewer, 111

reward, customer journey as a, 17

roles

  assigning, 39

  creating, 41

  editing, 41

  in Enterprise 2.0, 37–39

  overriding permissions, 39–40

rules and expectations, setting, 203

Run Once button (Automation Studio), 149

running reports, 136–137

S

Sales & Service Cloud section (Journey Builder), 293

Salesforce data, as an entry source, 267

Salesforce Help & Training option (User menu), 26

Salesforce Marketing Cloud. *See also specific topics*

  accessing, 21

  administration, 33–48

  data models, 76–86

  email marketing in, 164–167

  fulfilling customer journey with, 20–21

  getting data into, 86–89

  getting help, 27

  logo, 25–26

  managing users, 34–37

  navigating, 23–31

  preparing to use, 21

  uploading content outside, 100–101

Salesforce Marketing Cloud icon, 24

Save button (journey canvas), 285

saving reports, 135

Scalable, Fluid or Responsive: Understanding Mobile Email Approaches (website), 173

Schedule/Publish button, 255

scheduling events in Calendar tool, 52–53

screen (Campaigns tool), 55–56

screen-sharing technology, 239

SDK (Software Development Kit), 200

search bar, 98

security, for Marketing Cloud, 41–44

Security Settings page, 41–44

Segments tab (Audience Builder), 125

selecting

  audiences, 176–178

  data extension fields, 283

  templates, 248–249

  tools for customer journeys, 270

About Trendline

Now in its seventh year as one of the world's premier email-marketing agencies, Trendline's founders and team members have decades of combined experience using Salesforce Marketing Cloud (SFMC) to create and manage incredibly complex email programs for some of the biggest brands around.

With the agency's deep expertise both in the then-current iteration of SFMC, as well as a thorough understanding of (and input on) new features available in rapidly approaching updates, Trendline's Chester Bullock (VP of Solutions Consulting) and Mark Pollard (Senior Platform Architect) are uniquely positioned to provide expert insight on helping marketers get most from SFMC.

This book is the result of a joint (and sustained) effort among SFMC's product developers, marketing managers, Chester, Mark, and the whole team at Trendline.

About the Authors

Chester Bullock holds a degree in Aviation Business Administration from Embry-Riddle Aeronautical University. In his role as Trendline's Vice President of Solutions Consulting, he leverages his eight years of experience with the ExactTarget/Salesforce Marketing Cloud platform to bring a technical perspective to the art of marketing.

A recognized Salesforce MVP, Chester has sent millions of emails to audiences of popular brands and has presented solutions to practical problems at several high-profile conferences. Prior to Trendline, he held consulting roles with Ticketmaster, Merkle, and AAA. He lives in Colorado with his amazing, supportive wife and has three marvelous daughters who patiently listen to him talk about marketing.

Mark Pollard is a Senior Platform Architect at Trendline Interactive and has worked in a variety of roles related to digital marketing since the turn of the century. Mark has worked with several email service providers and has been using ExactTarget/Salesforce Marketing Cloud for over eight years. In 2016, Mark was among the first group of marketers to earn a certification as a Salesforce Marketing Cloud Consultant.

Mark currently works with several well-known brands, helping to solve the technical challenges that come with operating enterprise-level digital marketing programs.

Mark resides in New Jersey with his wife and sons.

Dedications

To my wife and family. Michelle has been supportive of any crazy idea I've put in front of her, such as writing a book. Natalie, Taylor, and Megan help me keep things in perspective. All four inspire me to do my best. I am forever grateful to all of them. And, to the SolCon team at Trendline — Mark, Amy, Elise, Mollie, and Bryan — thank you for everything you do.

— Chester Bullock

To my wife, Rachel. Without her love, encouragement, and support, I doubt I would've found myself in a place where writing this book was a possibility. To Joseph and Adam, you amaze me every day. To colleagues present and past, thank you for the inspiration and encouragement.

— Mark Pollard

Authors' Acknowledgments

Special thanks to Amy Fandrei and Susan Pink, our editors at Wiley. They did a superb job at helping us stay on track and motivated to get this book into your hands. Amanda Cross was critical in our ability to get our thoughts and experiences into a working guide on how to use this marketing platform. Justine Jordan at Litmus deserves a big shout out for her insights on rendering and related topics. We've been fans of her work at ExactTarget and Litmus for some time.

Due to the rapidly changing nature of software, it was essential to get input from longtime product shepherds at Salesforce, including Brian Brames, Dawn DeVirgilio, Eric Hannon, Kara Schoeler, and Joanna Milliken, all of whom provided invaluable resources and expertise. And to Scott Thomas, thank you. We couldn't have done this without you.

No book about SFMC would be complete without special thanks to a few people who have had a tremendous effect on our careers over the last several years. Joel Book — you've been retired for only a short time, but your legacy will go on forever. You are an inspiration to everyone who has wanted to drive success via a marketing platform.

Scott McCorkle — a lot of what we cover in this book came out of your mind. Your vision, combined with your willingness to hear us out in that conference room at Lake Mary so many years ago, made us customers for life. To the legions of "Forever Orange" people who have put up with us on support calls, at Connections, or during sales pitches: Thank you. Keep Orange alive.

Lastly, our greatest thanks to the family we have at Trendline. Morgan Stewart and Andrew Kordek have assembled one of the most talented — yet selfless — teams of people we have ever been a part of. It's truly an honor to work alongside each and every one of you.

Publisher's Acknowledgments

Executive Editor: Amy Fandrei

Project Editor: Susan Pink

Copy Editor: Susan Pink

Proofreader: Debbye Butler

Editorial Assistant: Owen Kaelble

Sr. Editorial Assistant: Cherie Case

Production Editor: G. Vasanth Koilraj

Cover Image: © marigold_88/iStockphoto